7

the two of me

the two of me

ANDREW
JOHNS

WITH NEIL CADIGAN

HarperCollins*Publishers*

HarperCollins*Publishers*

First published in Australia in 2007
by HarperCollins*Publishers* Australia Pty Limited
ABN 36 009 913 517
www.harpercollins.com.au

HarperCollins*Publishers*
25 Ryde Road, Pymble, Sydney, NSW 2073, Australia
31 View Road, Glenfield, Auckland 10, New Zealand
77–85 Fulham Palace Road, London, W6 8JB, United Kingdom
2 Bloor Street East, 20th floor, Toronto, Ontario M4W 1A8, Canada
10 East 53rd Street, New York NY 10022, USA

National Library of Australia Cataloguing-in-Publication data:

Johns, Andrew, 1974– .
   The two of me.
   Includes index.
   ISBN: 978 0 7322 8653 8 (hbk.).
   1. Johns, Andrew, 1974– . 2. Rugby League football –
   Australia – Biography. 3. Rugby League football players –
   Australia – Biography. I. Cadigan, Neil. II. Title.
796.3338

Cover photography: Mark Mawson
Unless otherwise credited, photographs in picture sections are
from the collection of Andrew Johns
Cover design by Matt Stanton
Typeset in 11.5/18 Sabon by Kirby Jones
Printed and bound in Australia by Griffin Press

79gsm Bulky Paperback used by HarperCollins*Publishers*, is a natural, recyclable product
made from wood grown in a combination of sustainable plantation and regrowth forests.
It also contains up to a 20% portion of recycled fibre. The manufacturing processes conform
to the environmental regulations in Tasmania, the place of manufacture.

5 4 3 2 1   07 08 09 10

To my two grandmothers
June Bowden and Margaret Johns.
I wish you could both still be alive to
experience this great journey.

CONTENTS

FOREWORD
By Phil Gould

I've been seriously tempted to write my own book about this bloke. I have this desire for people to meet and understand the real man behind the many faces of Andrew Johns. His true story simply must be told and I'm so glad he has opened himself up to you in this book.

I once heard a saying that, if applied to Andrew, would go something like this: 'Some people play professional sport to enrich their life. Others play professional sport to define their life.'

If ever a player defined his life by the way he played football, it is Andrew Johns. His leadership influenced the behaviour of others. He possessed an unshakeable trust in his own ability and honestly believed he could make anything happen on a football field. Of course, the more times he did it, the more he believed he could do it again, and again, and again.

More than a game, rugby league was a science to him.

From a very young age, Johns was not content to simply kick a football and allow it to land with unpredictable bounce. He wanted to know why it bounced the way it did, and he challenged himself to make it bounce the same way every time. He was a real student of football and footballers. His ability to extract the very best out of the players around him made him the ultimate team man. His ability to target and exploit the weaknesses in opposing teams made him the most feared attacking weapon in the game.

His skills excited us. His competitive nature inspired us.

Johns was one of the most gifted players ever to pull on a boot. Yet despite a personal skill set that players would die for, Andrew Johns, for the most part, chose to play this game in a tough and most uncompromising manner.

His brutal honesty in self appraisal was sometimes staggering. His loyalty to his club and his team-mates was unquestioned. You would go to war with this man.

From the humble beginnings of working-class Australia comes a man who, through sheer determination and talent, rose to be the greatest rugby league player of his generation; and arguably the greatest of all time.

However, success comes with its own problems. I got the feeling Johns sometimes struggled with the notoriety and publicity that follows a sporting superstar.

His personality could change from one meeting to the next. He was often caught in this conflict of either living up to what he thought other people expected of him, or living down the image of the true celebrity he had become.

Sometimes you had to raise your voice to get the real Andrew Johns to emerge. During the last couple of years of his playing career, I got the distinct feeling the only places where Andrew felt truly comfortable were out on the football field, surfing the ocean waves, or immersing himself in the anonymity of the race track.

My suspicions were confirmed with Andrew's recent public admissions regarding his battle with bipolar disorder, depression and his recreational drug use. I'm sure he'll elaborate on these issues in the following pages, but it appears quite obvious to me that Andrew did not always enjoy being famous.

His stunning confessions on the Channel Nine *Footy Show* of his 12 years of drug use and the lie he had been living was one of the most honest and soul-baring interviews I've ever heard in my life. I said at the time he was very brave to confront his issues in such a public forum. But that's typical of Andrew. The bigger the game, the bigger the challenge, the more he rises to the occasion.

I truly hope he finds peace and relief in revealing his inner demons to the world.

I do know that interview and this book will help others who find themselves in similar situations. In fact, maybe that is why Andrew is on this Earth. Maybe the high profile he has earned as being the greatest rugby league player of all time was simply a vehicle for him to make a difference in his post-football life as the face of drug reform amongst our youth.

The spotlight he has shone on mental illness and the attention he has drawn to the incidence of recreational drug use in our society must surely provide incentive for Andrew to become a campaigner for public awareness on these important issues. I hope so.

I hope Andrew devotes the rest of his life to helping others deal with these problems. Time will tell. What I do know for certain, though, is that my life has already been enriched in so many ways through having known the great Andrew Johns.

PREFACE
By Neil Cadigan

Andrew Johns and I were sitting on the front porch of my house. It was mid-February 2007, our first meeting to map out a plan for this autobiography. The conversation was only a few moments old when he squeezed out something like: 'I don't want this book to be a fluffy tribute to my career. It has to be the real story about my life, no lies. Mate, I've led a crazy existence. Did you know I'm bipolar? And I've nearly destroyed my life on alcohol and sometimes drugs?'

Wow! There went the strategy of tip-toeing around the 'colourful' aspects of his life — which had created so many rumours — until I had his confidence.

That ice-breaking come-clean by the world's most celebrated rugby league player of his era set the tone for our assignment — the real warts and all story of Andrew Johns, a man I got to know better and admire more the further this process went. And it showed how he was ready to confront his demons and confess to the world the guilt he felt because he was not the hero he'd been made out to be. On the way home that evening, he called fiancée Cathrine Mahoney and announced with relief, 'I told Caddo everything ... yes, everything,' as if to signify the monster within him had been released.

That was the start of the end of Andrew Johns' painful journey that ran parallel with — but hidden from — the glorious sporting career and the wonderful moments he treasures. He felt he'd lived a charade for too long and this was the soul-cleanser he needed to get out of his system, and finally felt able to. And it was painful at times; I could see that in his eyes as he spoke. On other occasions, we laughed at his funny tales and he had me captivated at the insight into his great football talent and mind and the great depth to his introspection.

This book is about much more than what one newspaper described as 'the dark divide between Andrew Johns, footy star, and his secret world of drugs, alcohol and depression'. It is mostly about a great footballer reflecting on his career and the game itself, which in itself is a fascinating story. That has to be stressed because it has been lost somewhat in the pre-publication publicity.

Little were we to know that two major events would overtake us before this book reached the printer: one in April 2007 when he was forced into premature retirement, and the other in August when he was arrested for possession of an ecstasy tablet at a London underground railway station. Thus, this is not the preface I originally put together. A stupid decision by Andrew during an end-of-career jaunt, which was supposed to act as a get-away-from-it-all excursion between his life as a footballer and life as an ex-footballer, saw to that.

Some of his story that was to be revealed in this book exclusively, thoughtfully and in its complete context had its cover blown, to use a pun. In an emotional interview with his coaching mentor Phil Gould on Channel Nine's *The Footy Show* on 30 August, Joey felt he had to come clean on his illicit taking of social drugs over a decade and the fact that he suffered from depression. He couldn't tell a half-baked story knowing all would be revealed when this book hit the shelves two months later.

It was devastating to lose the opportunity we had so carefully moulded in telling in its entirety what we knew would be one of the most controversial stories Australian sport had known — but it had to be revealed then, considering the circumstances. He then had to sweat for two months before this complete chronicle could be revealed.

Andrew will explain that episode, why he shocked rugby league fans in that Channel Nine interview and what effect it had on him, later in the book. But what must be clarified at the start is that, contrary to what was accused by some, he did not blurt out a confession that night because he had been 'caught' red-handed in London; squirming out a token confession only because he had been cornered like some crazed criminal.

He felt he had to come clean so as not to contradict the confessions he had made months earlier for the following pages. He was very conscious of the shame such an admission would bring him and was acutely aware of the impact it would have on the sport of rugby league, which had given him so much in life. With the expected media reaction to his revelations so predictable, we'd spoken at length about how important it was to choose the right words in this book. The only changes we've made to the original text are where we felt we needed to clarify or explain things a bit more, given all the media coverage of recent events.

That was the second perceived crisis that Andrew was confronted with during the months this book was in the making, almost totally superseding the first — his sudden retirement. Yet both instances provided him with relief that the burden that those aspects of his life had placed on him had been lifted.

Let me take you back a little, to where this preface originally began. To Good Friday, 6 April 2007, when we met to do some tapings for the book.

'Mate, you wouldn't believe the day I've had,' Andrew told me. He then went on to explain the previous 24 hours that had just upended his life: an innocent collision with team-mate Adam Woolnough at the previous evening's training session that sent pins and needles down his right leg; a visit to Dr Neil Halpin, then a trip to Sydney to see spinal specialist Professor John Yeo, whose initial diagnosis left Andrew facing what, deep inside, he knew was almost inevitable — a sudden end to his career. Four days later, after results of an MRI scan showed a bulging disc putting pressure on his spine, Professor Yeo was to become his referee of fate and officially called 'time'.

On that Friday, 'Joey' seemed surprisingly calm about the threatened halt to his 14-season rugby league career. He seemed stunned yet somewhat relieved; relieved that he may no longer have to push his gradually eroding body through more battles, or to push himself through the endless public and media scrutiny; but stunned that all he had known for most of his adult life, the one thing he felt comfortable doing and the one thing he had mastered better than perhaps anyone in the game's history, was to be so dramatically taken away when he least expected it.

Come the time for a media conference the following Tuesday to announce he'd played his last match, Andrew was as emotional as anyone had seen him (until the interview with Gould five months later). The finality had hit home in the preceding hours, which included confronting his team-mates whom he felt he had abandoned so early in the season.

The subsequent barrage of newspaper print, Channel Nine interviews and radio talkback opinion was so prolific it bordered on the bizarre. In the next two days the *Newcastle Herald* devoted 15 pages to his career and its ending and later published a 32-page magazine about his career, while Sydney's *Daily Telegraph* provided six pages on the Wednesday and was still prolonging its sales boon with an eight-page lift-out section devoted purely to a 'Joey tribute' on the Friday. Channel Nine's *The Footy Show*, which had as panellists his brother Matthew and his grand-final winning skipper of 1997, Paul Harragon, was converted to a special Andrew Johns tribute episode, with the studio audience standing twice for prolonged ovations before the man of honour could utter a word.

Joey became an innocent victim of a debate about whether he should be instantly inducted as the eighth of the game's official 'Immortals' (best post-war players) alongside Reg Gasnier, Bob Fulton, Clive Churchill, John Raper, Graeme Langlands, Arthur Beetson and Wally Lewis. Interstate debate raged over suggestions he was the best the game had ever seen, ahead of Queensland's God-like figure Lewis.

All he wanted to do to 'celebrate' the end of his playing days was to take his seven-year-old son Samuel on a small vacation while school holidays were in their last week and then to fly away to somewhere secluded with Cathrine to spend some time being himself and taking in how he had so suddenly hit the junction of his life's journey.

That had to be delayed for the Knights' next home game after his retirement announcement, on Sunday 22 April, when the Newcastle International Sports Centre Trust christened the two-year-old grandstand at the Knights' home, EnergyAustralia Stadium, the Andrew Johns Stand. Thousands turned up to formally farewell their hero, many of them sobbing uncontrollably, including his father Gary, at the realisation that such a glorious era had ended. Team-mates from his two premiership teams, of 1997 and 2001, plus '97 coach Malcolm Reilly, stood as a guard of honour. To those who were applauding Andrew Johns he was one of them; a coalminer's son who stayed in Newcastle and the Hunter to chase, and achieve, his rugby league dreams. And that's what was so dear to the residents of Australia's most parochial town.

In his speech Andrew choked as he talked about the privilege of being able to chase his dreams from his home-town area; the debt he owed his team-mates and how treasured their friendship was; how he could not have achieved what he had without his family, including his brother Matthew, who stood on the field as part of the Channel Nine commentary team, his eyes watering. Specifically, he told of his awe of the Knights fans when they kept filling the stadium during the 2005 season when their injury-hit team lost 13 games straight. 'There was no greater honour than to run out in front of this crowd and, late in my career, to run out as captain of this club and go out and do my best.'

The fact that his retirement came within months of those of cricket giants Shane Warne, Glenn McGrath and Brian Lara, and swimming champion Ian Thorpe, who all held similar standings in their chosen sports, was greatly ironic, and appropriate. Joey is the only player to have won three Dally M medals (the Australian competition's most valuable/best and fairest player) and ran second on three other occasions (although disqualified in 2001 after being suspended); he captained his country and his state and twice won the Golden Boot as the world's best player; he played in two grand finals, winning one single-handedly in the 80th minute (1997), and being judged best on the field in the other (2001).

But in the scores of articles and tributes, what were greatly overlooked were the contradictions of Andrew Johns the rugby league hero and public property, some of which have now been revealed. The drug revelation saw him castigated and ostracised; he had shattered the perceptions of those who saw him as a sporting demi-god and a hero and role model for every aspiring young footballer. People were quick to make assumptions and jump to conclusions without knowing the full story of his very fragile life. That story can now be told.

While Andrew Johns was the envy of thousands, he was rarely the envy of his own consciousness. He indeed was a flawed genius, a complex human being. That is why the following pages are so compelling.

As you read this book, Andrew will still be confronting his footballing after-life. Impressing those who were so concerned about his well-being after football had been taken away from him, he appeared so at ease with himself until his life so sadly and dramatically changed overnight on the last day of a jaunt in Europe, which was designed to provide a chance to travel and ponder a new life before he embraced career opportunities and a new family life with Cathrine.

The jolt will, I and others pray, prove the ultimate nudge he needed to straighten out his private life and to ensure he has success in his post-football career; somewhat like that of his brother Matthew, who was equally consumed by his passion for rugby league. With the most wonderful family, plus Cathrine and Samuel, as his greatest incentive, he has to take full responsibility for that himself — he can no longer hide from that fact. But he can do so with the love and support of the many who have rallied around him and whose strength he needs.

This book explains the make-up of a champion, albeit a flawed and somewhat fragile one. I don't think any Australian sports person has been as revealing, self-effacing and honest in an autobiography. It will shock some people, or it may explain the complete circumstances for those who have already been shocked by recent revelations. The many, many hours of assisting Joey in telling his story have engendered in me a greater admiration for, and a far greater understanding of, the Andrew Johns phenomenon.

CHAPTER I

THE REAL ME

Let's get to the heart of my story from the first page, because I want this book to be a very frank insight into the life of a person who might well be a hero of thousands of footy fans, but really is a living contradiction. The 'Joey' Johns you saw on the football field is not the real Andrew Johns I know.

When I set out to do this book, I was not interested in a conservative 'that's my wonderful life' autobiography, simply back-tracking the football achievements that I have been so fortunate to have enjoyed. I knew I had to be open and reveal all — well, just about all — about my life and my personality. I could not have done that five years ago when the idea of writing a book was first thrown up. There were too many things in my life I couldn't deal with.

To be brutally honest — I hated Joey Johns. I hated the superstar-type figure I was perceived to be and I hated as much the person I really was. Now, and I'm only talking about since the second half of 2006, I am finally comfortable with who I am as a person.

Now I am not complaining one bit about the many things that being a good rugby league player has given me. I am very, very privileged to have had such a career and to have enjoyed its rewards. It still seems extremely surreal to me that such an ordinary bloke from Cessnock could achieve what I have, with all my imperfections that I will soon describe to you. I know that without rugby league I would still be living in Cessnock, plying a living as some sort of tradesman — and enjoying it, I might add — or, far worse, having become a local no-hoper.

The 'other' side of Andrew Johns I had planned to reveal here was that I suffer from bipolar disorder — but unfortunately that came out prematurely in the wash-up from my stupid act of being arrested for possession of an ecstasy tablet in London in late August 2007. Although it wasn't diagnosed until much later, I have suffered the condition — also known as manic depression — since my early to mid-teens. Basically I suffer manic highs which can make me feel almost indestructibly confident and possessed with boundless energy on the football field, as well as sparking erratic, unforgivable behaviour off it, behaviour that I am ashamed of; then terrible lows which have seen me shut myself in my house for days, paranoid about the outside world and with a deep hatred of myself; or turning up to rugby league matches in the foulest of dark moods. At their worst, these occurrences would be almost weekly during a football season.

For many years I refused to confront the problem, to the extent that I turned my back on those who obviously knew I had the medical condition and tried to help me. At other times I have been a very good actor, covering up my true feelings and refusing to face my insecurities.

I suffered from manic depression my entire senior football career, although I didn't know that for most of that time. This won't be any great disclosure for my team-mates, coaches or people who have been close enough to witness my erratic behaviour and massive mood swings over 14 seasons. But now they have a public confession and an explanation and medical label for it. For the fans who would have had no idea, I know this is a bit of a shock.

I'm naturally worried about the stigma this admission will bring me now that it is out. I am not comfortable with divulging this at all but I know I have to. To be honest, once I made the decision to let it out in this book for everyone to see, recording my inner thoughts over the past few months has been a good kind of therapy for me. I've carried the guilt for years that the perception of my life has been such a lie.

The motivation behind exposing this part of me is twofold: firstly, to explain to people — including those in Newcastle who have seen me at my crazy worst at some nightspot — why the hell I tick like I do; and, secondly, that if my story helps just one or even a dozen young people identify that they have a similar problem and can get help, it might save them enduring the torture that I have gone through in my life. That would be worthwhile to me.

I wasn't able to talk about my bipolar condition to even my parents or my brother Matthew or sister Kate all these years. They know now, of course, but it was just too hard a subject to discuss face to face. I can only guess how tough it must have been for my parents to handle my erratic highs and lows when I was growing up; well, I *can* guess through what I've been told only fairly recently.

I go into my depression in a chapter solely on the subject and the Knights' consulting doctor and good friend, Dr Neil Halpin, has given his side of my story for this book, which I am very grateful for.

The cat was unfortunately let out of the bag in regard to my drug taking too, when I decided I couldn't carry the shame and deceit any longer after the horrible experience in London, and came clean on *The Footy Show*. I had planned to confess about the bipolar and my problem with alcohol and use of drugs exclusively in this book so I could reveal them in the right context, as part of the full story of my life, but my stupid action in London blew all that.

Let me make it perfectly clear that admissions in this book have nothing to do with that event. In fact, we'd already finished writing the book and it was in the final stages of editing, although I've gone into detail about that dreaded episode in my life, and its effect, in the final pages, plus brought up to date a few other issues which were aired during the *Footy Show* interview and in the days afterwards.

There are some sides of my life that unfold in these pages which, unfortunately, are going to shatter some illusions about me for those who have admired my achievements in rugby league and placed me up there with other far more deserving sporting heroes. I am worried about the reaction I will get; I am very worried about any negative publicity it might give the game of rugby league which has provided me with so much — in material things, in friendships and in unforgettable memories. That is something that I know I have to deal with, but the fact is I couldn't offer my memoirs as another version of the lie I feel I have lived.

Alcohol has been my undoing on too many occasions. I am mad when I'm on the drink. And I've been blessed with how tolerant the people of Newcastle have been when they've seen an absolutely obnoxious Joey Johns going crazy in a pub or nightspot, making a fool of myself. I still cringe at the thought of being someone I'm not, somewhere I don't even remember being at, and having little recollection of it later. I can't describe the shame and the guilt that has brought me.

I've now admitted to also having taken social drugs. I'm not using it as the only excuse, but that has been a product of my manic highs, when I get out on the grog and lose control and don't care for a second about consequences while I ride this powerful, all-consuming tidal wave; in a way it's about trying to escape from the real me. I am ashamed of that too. I am more determined than ever now to make it just another part of my life that is past tense.

I know I am seen as a role model for kids. I understand how so many of them idolise successful footballers just as I idolised my football heroes when I was young, whether from my home town of Cessnock or the State of Origin players I saw on television. I worry about the danger of shattering young aspiring players' perceptions of me. I just hope my message is clear: that while I am so happy and proud of the joy I have helped bring to so many people through my football exploits (with the massive help of my team-mates), particularly Novocastrians, how equally regretful I am that I have sometimes negatively affected the lives of people around me.

I hope my story is taken in the right context and that my regrets are a motivation for others who might be thrust into the limelight — and into such an artificial life — to not retrace my steps and live on a razor's edge; to instead be wiser and in more control of their lives.

I also hope that when media take extracts of this book, and sensationalise only small components of it, that they balance it with my thoughts, my regrets on the emotional harm I may have done and understand the inner battle I have had with myself all these years while trying to deal with my short-fallings.

Now that's off my chest, I'm happy to say that most of the following pages are about the overpowering valuable memories and wonderful things rugby league has given me — and the fantastic and funny times I have had being a footballer. To have been able to stay in first grade for so long; to hold the Knights' record for most appearances; to be the highest points-scorer in the competition's history; to have played for and captained Australia; to have had the incredible buzz of playing State of Origin; to have won some big awards; to have met so many famous people. Honestly, those sort of things were beyond my wildest expectations. I don't undervalue the privileges I have had in life but I know I'll better appreciate those things and reflect on them more deeply the longer I get into retirement.

I hope this book also gives an interesting insight into the world of professional rugby league and how someone like me was able to be successful. I am so lucky to have in my life a wonderful family, and to have had such great team-mates, and mates outside of the game, a caring understanding soulmate in my partner Cathrine Mahoney, and to have been given so many special opportunities.

This book is about my journey, warts and all. It is the medium I have chosen to cleanse my soul to some extent, to reveal Andrew Johns and Joey Johns in my own words.

CHAPTER 2

ANDREW JOHNS V JOEY JOHNS

As I tell my story, you have to understand that there are two distinct sides of me; well, make it three, if I am to be perfectly accurate.

A lot of people see Joey Johns (the footballer, the larrikin or the party boy) and think that is who I am. That's the public persona, but that's only part of me. Few people get to know the other part, Andrew Johns when he is not a footballer or public figure.

I have learned to look at Joey Johns the footballer as being almost a separate identity; like a role an actor would play in a television serial. That's the best perspective I can offer. You hear about actors being stopped in the street and people talking to them as if their characters are real people.

That's how I see Joey Johns; the figure people see on TV screens or at the stadiums. When I get away from the public limelight, I try to divorce myself from that side of my character. I feel I don't deserve the positive recognition Joey Johns gets, and I cringe at the negative profile I have quite deservedly earned at times by being a 'dickhead' on the field, blowing up at team-mates or match officials. My only way of dealing with this is to treat the famous footballer as an alter ego.

Andrew Johns is a bloke born into a humble, working-class life in Cessnock who craves anonymity. He reads at least a book a week, loves to get out on his board in the surf or go to museums, he enjoys cooking a nice dinner and the company of family, close mates or the love of his life in Cathrine Mahoney. He does not like at all being treated special and, in fact, knows he definitely is not.

It took me a long time to be able to remove myself from all the hype around Joey Johns and go back to being Andrew Johns. Andrew Johns knows how hypocritical it is that Joey is put on a pedestal he does not deserve.

If I sit back and think too much about some of the stupid things Joey Johns has done, it nearly puts me into a panic attack; I get real self-conscious about it and so embarrassed, so I try to divorce myself from that figure.

I also really try not to think about my achievements and how well I could play on the football field. When I was younger I used to get caught up with all that and I didn't handle it. It took me years to be able to retract from the footballer and live a life as another person; Cathrine has really helped me with that. I see myself as the most average person in the world, as vulnerable as anyone. When I did get caught up in all the bullshit and believe the hype, I carried on like an idiot, so I have to avoid that high.

Don't get me wrong, I would not trivialise one bit how rewarding and successful my footy career was, but I do get embarrassed at the accolades that come with it. I hear all the time how good I was and really don't know how to take it; I prefer not to hear it. I feel most uneasy at functions when a big deal is made of me.

I've lived in a fake world when you look at it — everything is done for me. I only have to make a few calls to different people and everything is organised. Many of the things I get are free. Only recently have I had to learn basic life skills others take for granted. I have been in the media so constantly it makes my head spin, and while I'm sure many people have the impression that 'gee, this bloke loves being in the papers', I hate it. And I certainly don't chase the attention. I try not to read most of it, but usually it gets back to me.

I very quickly went from being a young hopeful footballer to being put on a pedestal. Bang! Straight into this false life. I didn't know how to handle it when I was first introduced to it; and I've never been able to quite handle it since. I have trouble being the centre of attention and sometimes people interpret my discomfort as being rude or ignorant, particularly if I am in one of my low moods. I certainly don't mean that.

I'd watch myself on the field sometimes and think, 'Pull your head in, you're going berserk,' but that's just what the adrenalin does to me during the massive high I get on. There are things that I'd do off the field too and I'd think, 'Gee, people must think you're such a wanker.'

I was lucky my team-mates accepted my blow-ups as part of my nature, but I know it wasn't fair on them. I would apologise afterwards and they'd just say, 'That's OK, mate, we know what you're like.' Like most things in my life, I slowly learned how to tone them down. When I was out there competing and trying to win, I'd expect others to be at my level of competitiveness, but I learned to understand some weren't.

One thing about Joey Johns I do like is the way he worked bloody hard to be the best footballer he could be. Footballers have a varying degree of natural talent but you will find the best ones always work tirelessly on developing those skills and trying to be better every year. I am proud that I did that. I am proud that I was able to perform consistently over a lot of years, and come back from injury and attain a certain level again. I sometimes marvelled at my own mental capacity to overcome setbacks.

Cathrine always says that when we get away on holidays, I instantly turn into a different person; into Andrew Johns. I can physically feel the tension release from my body and a peace come over me the minute I go somewhere where I know I won't be recognised and I don't have to try to be anyone but Andrew Johns. She loves the fact I become totally relaxed and even tells me how I keep eye contact with people and can keep a prolonged conversation with them; not being able to do that is usually my worst habit, which I'm sure people have noticed when I am on television.

Every year Cathrine and I go away on a surfing trip: I'm fortunate to have gone on surfing holidays over the years to the Maldives, Samoa, the Philippines, Lord Howe Island, Indonesia and Hawaii, and other places I have enjoyed visiting include quite a few parts of Europe and the Margaret River area in Western Australia. I would love to live in WA; it's like another country to me because rugby league doesn't rate there so 99 per cent of people have no idea who I am.

Surfing is my great outlet; I feel like the worry of the world dissolves in the water once I get out on a wave. That's when I feel like Andrew Johns — no special favours, just me and the sea and a few mates or some like-minded surfers who understand I need time and space for myself. Surfing has been a very positive part of my life.

I also love going to museums and reading books (Cathrine opened my eyes to that sort of thing and enticed me to start reading a broader range of books too), which have widened my interests. I read a book on Jackson Pollock, the great American painter, which fascinated me and that's why we went to the Guggenheim museum in Bilbao, Spain. I love going to the art galleries and make a point of seeing the Archibald Prize entrants every year. If the Knights played in Auckland I'd grab our club doctor Peter McGeogh and go to a museum; when we played in Canberra in 2006 I went and saw Jackson Pollock's *Blue Poles*. When Matt Hoy — a great mate and one of Australia's best surfers of the '90s — gets me a new surfboard I get him to do the Pollock splatterings on: I love it. I have got no idea about the finer side of art but I just love getting in there and thinking about how they had an empty canvas and created something that is just phenomenal. I've even tried to do some painting myself but the results are embarrassing.

Sometimes when I'm walking around museums the curator might recognise me and seem pretty startled and ask what I'm doing there. They seem blown away when I tell them I'm genuinely interested and often I've been taken behind closed doors and shown some of the more private collections. One time when I was in camp in Brisbane with the Australian side, our doctor Hugh Hazard and I went to a gallery and the curator took us back and showed us this special glossy album of Mohammad Ali's life; it was amazing. I love taking my son Samuel to museums too, he is absolutely crazy about dinosaurs. He knows every dinosaur there is, what they ate, where they lived.

But reading is my favourite pastime other than hitting a few waves; for the past eight years I would have read a book most weeks. I'll read anything. Like everyone, I love a good biography which I find easy to read, but also novels. The Les Norton books by Robert G. Barrett got me kicked off, they're a great light read. I got a mention in his last one, something like: 'I picked up the *Newcastle Herald* and the headline was "Andrew Johns cuts himself shaving".' I like books by Australian writers Tim Winton and Wayne Grogan and the biographies; those I've read include Joe Namath, the American quarterback; *Scar Tissue* is another, by Anthony Kiedis, the Red Hot Chili Peppers front man. I love reading about the rock stars for some reason. I've also read Bon Scott's *Highway to Hell*, Keith Moon's *Moon the Loon*, Janis Joplin's. John

Belushi's was a cracker, as was Jim Morrison's *No One Here Gets Out Alive*. It's a bit ironic that they're all tragic figures; Cathrine laughs at that. And so many died at age 27 — Jim Morrison, Janis Joplin, James Dean, Kurt Cobain and the comic actor Chris Farley.

One of the most fascinating books I've read is called *Shantaram* by an Australian called Gregory David Roberts, who broke out of prison and ended up going to India, getting involved with the mafia, then becoming a freedom fighter; it just blew my mind. When my father was ill with peritonitis I took the book into hospital to help him occupy himself. Typically he said bluntly, 'I don't read books,' and I said, 'Mate, read this one, it will change your life.' Next thing he'd get visitors or Mum would be there and he'd say, 'Look, I'm sorry if I seem rude but I just can't put this book down.' The boys at the Knights often bring books to training and swap them and I tried to make a few blokes read it. I bought *Shantaram* for Todd Lowrie for his 21st birthday and every week at training I'd say, 'Have you read it yet?' and he hadn't got around to it. Once he started, he said, 'Oh my God, what a book.' It is soon going to be made into a movie, so watch out for it. The most amazing thing is that it's based on a true story.

I never read much at school — I was such a little punk I didn't think it was cool. And I was always that hyped up and on the go I didn't think I had time to read, but now it relaxes me so much. I hardly watch television, other than the footy or the races. Sometimes I'll have dinner and go to bed and read for three hours — that would be the perfect night when

Cathrine is not here — or I'll sit and read in the day-bed in the living room. If someone said to me 10 years ago that is what I'd be doing now, I would have laughed them out of the room, but it comes with maturity.

I get great enjoyment from cooking too, something I had to learn to do when I started living by myself. I enjoy the challenge of learning to cook different things; it's all trial and error and Mum gets plenty of evening phone calls from me asking for advice. My culinary repertoire ranges from good old baked dinners to stir fries, pasta dinners and Mexican; sometimes I get the boys over and cook for them and I really enjoy it.

I also love going to the movies, not that I go as much as I'd like to. I particularly like the arthouse type films. I now appreciate the colours and shades in the movies and how they are shot. I'll sit there and Cathrine will point it out to me. I wonder, 'How do they see that?' I appreciate actors' ability to learn lines and deliver a powerful performance; it's the same with musicians. I don't know how people like Daniel Johns can sit down with a guitar and write 50 songs, then pick the best which he'll record; it is just phenomenal. It has made me appreciate that most people have some special talent inside them but they just have to find it, then use it positively. The sin is if you don't use it. I'm so glad I found the way to use my football ability when I was pretty wayward in my life.

But one thing I have definitely found hard to handle is the degree of fame that goes with being a high-profile footballer; the expectation of how I should act being a 'role model' and doing the right thing. Going out there and playing to a standard expected of me was a piece of cake, that didn't worry me at all. And if anything, the bigger the pressure and the higher the stakes, the better I felt. I don't know if it is the bipolar or not but it put me on a massive high; I felt like I could not be stopped. I was indestructible — I could take on the world and win.

CHAPTER 3

GROWING UP IN CESSNOCK

I had a great upbringing in Cessnock, a tough coal-mining town on the edge of the rolling Hunter hills covered by vineyards, which is now a more trendy stopover for tourists than it was when I was a kid. But to be perfectly honest, until I was in my mid-teens all I aspired to do was to work down the mines and play first grade football for Cessnock, like my father did. It was a reasonable expectation in our town. I had no great dream to get out and see the world or achieve anything any grander than that ... and if it wasn't for rugby league, I reckon I might not have done anything exciting at all with my life.

Dad was a miner, as was his father, his grandfather and his great-grandfather, who emigrated from Wales in the 1860s or

1870s, I believe. Most of the people we mixed with growing up, either through sport, school or my dad's work, had jobs somehow associated with the local mines. I thought I'd end up with a similar job — until the day my father took me for an unofficial orientation trip down the Newstan Colliery near Fassifern where he worked. He had taken my older brother Matthew there in his last year of school to give him an insight into work underground and there was a 'fall-in' while he was down there. No one was in danger because of the safety precautions and everyone was prepared for it, but it showed Matt just what the dangers were. Three years later it was my turn. I'll never forget it — we hopped into the carriage that went pretty steeply three kilometres down and the confined space and darkness just freaked me out. I screamed to Dad to let me out and tried to wrestle free but he had to hold me down and just said it was too late, I had to go all the way to the pit floor. It was a worthwhile experience in that it showed I wasn't cut out to follow the long, long Johns family path underground.

As it turned out, I didn't show much ambition for any sort of vocation other than playing rugby league, which I regret in some ways. A lot of my mates left school at the end of Year 12 and took on trades such as electricians or mechanics or plumbers, and maybe I should have done that too. I was clever enough at school when I pushed myself, which was rarely after I hit high school, and feel I could have gone to university. But then again that would have taken away from my football focus and I might not have ended up as fortunate as I have in the sport.

My parents, Gary and Gayle, still live in the same house we grew up in — just a few hundred metres from Cessnock's main street, Vincent Street. They'll have to drag them out of there, I reckon. They've been in that house since 1972, but that's not surprising when you look at the Johns family history. Dad's father, Cecil James Johns, was born in Cessnock Street, Heddon Greta (a town not far from Cessnock) and died in the same house, and his father William was born in Lambton in Newcastle but spent all his life in nearby Kurri Kurri. William served in World War I and was wounded in action, a victim of gassing while fighting in France in 1916, and was discharged and collected a war pension for the rest of his life. I'm told he received the British War Medal, a Victory Medal and a Star Medal for his bravery.

Dad was a promising lock with the Kurri rugby league side when he married Mum. They were looking to buy their first house and Dad was playing for match payments only at Maitland, when Cessnock offered him $500 a season. That was a fair deposit on a house, so he took it. They reckon you could count on the one hand how many players had crossed the line from Maitland to Cessnock or went the other way over the many decades before then, so it caused an enormous stir. The rivalry between the two towns, particularly on the sports field, is still bloody intense. As I was growing up, if you mentioned Kurri you'd spit on the ground and say, 'That's Kurri, with a K not a C.' Even Dad's parents were dirty at first that he was going out with a Cessnock girl — which Mum was — but they obviously warmed to her and it was all accepted.

The Newcastle competition was extremely strong back then, with the top quality of local players topped up with a lot of former internationals like Johnny Raper, Peter Dimond, Garry Sullivan and George Ambrum captain-coaching or playing through the different clubs and plenty of players who were good enough to go to the Sydney competition. Dad was recommended to St George by a local scout, but a couple of weeks before they were due to come up to watch him play he dislocated his knee and was out for quite a while, so that was that.

The old man retired at 28 after wrecking his Achilles tendon. Apparently a few of his opponents weren't sorry to see him go; often someone has come up to me and relayed the story about how the old man copped him a high one or smashed him with a ferocious tackle and rearranged his nose, and they've still got the scars. My Knights team-mate Steve Simpson's father Gary played with my father in the Cessnock team. He got the nickname of 'Psycho' Simpson. Dad reckons it goes back to the time he was doing chin-ups at the goalposts at training and the crossbar came crashing down from his weight and hit him on the head. He had to get rushed off to hospital with a nasty gash and they had to insert 20 stitches, but Simmo turned up the next day and played.

Dad went into coaching after that, first in the lower grades, before he got the call to go to the Cessnock leagues club one day, two weeks before the 1980 season began. Former Parramatta grand final coach and New South Wales and Australian coach Terry Fearnley had come up a few months earlier to be secretary-manager of the club and coach the first grade, but his family didn't come with him and he suddenly decided to head back to Sydney. Dad had won three competitions in four years with the second grade and then went OK as a first grade coach, taking Cessnock to the 1981 grand final and 1982 preliminary final, beaten by the 'millionaires' Western Suburbs both times.

We had footballers coming around to our place all the time, like Barry 'Panda' Andrews who had a year in Cessnock after a good career with Cronulla and Easts, and Terry Regan, who we signed from Bathurst. Terry was a NSW Country player of the year, who then went to play for Easts and Canberra. Let's just say Panda and Reago were no choirboys off the field. I reckon the only time my mum ever thought of trading the old man in was the year Panda was at Cessnock. Panda would always be carting the old man out for a drink, getting him in a poor state and Mum would be fuming, only for Panda to lob next day with flowers or a box of chocolates to sweeten her up. Reago tells people these days he's the bloke Matty has modelled his Reg Reagan alter ego on, and yeah, I think there's part truth in that. I think there is a fair bit of Gary Johns and his other mates in Reg too.

Matty and I idolised the local players who had come from Sydney or were good enough to play in Sydney. When Newtown, Balmain, then Parramatta came to Cessnock for pre-season trials, that's all we would talk about all summer. I can still remember seeing Brett Kenny, Peter Sterling, Mick Cronin and those Parra players; they were like absolute gods. Mick Schofield ended up going down to play for Balmain, so we watched his career closely. His father, Don Schofield, who played for Australia and had a lot to do with the Cessnock minor league, used to take us down to Leichhardt Oval in the early '80s sometimes to watch the Tigers play. It was just mind-blowing for us as kids, to go down and see a game live, then get in the sheds afterwards. He was a great bloke, old Donny, and did a lot for rugby league in our town.

We went to a State of Origin match in Sydney for the first time when our under-13 rep side was taken down on a mini-bus in 1987. It was pouring rain but there was a record Origin crowd at the time of over 42,000 at the Sydney Cricket Ground. I remember Greg Dowling scoring a great try for Queensland — not the famous one when it came off the crossbar (that was in 1984) — and Peter Sterling being man of the match in a losing team. But what I most remember about the night was that we came home in the bus, got in at all hours in the morning, and the next day I heard that we'd left one of the players, Nathan Oliver, back in Sydney. He ended up getting a police-relay escort home, as they tried to catch up with the mini-bus. I think his dad was a solicitor, so the coach and manager would have been shitting themselves, I reckon.

I was ball boy for about four years for Dad's teams, until I reached 12 and it wasn't cool any more. I was on duty the night in 1986 when Mick Cronin did that shocking eye injury that put him out for most of his last season, before coming back and winning the grand final in his last game. Matt was ball boy for a few years before me; we used to love it. I used to go over there at 12 o'clock and do third grade, reserve grade and first grade, just spend the whole day there.

It wasn't hard to pick our home, it was the timber house with the holes in the garage wall. We were always kicking footballs or hitting cricket balls into the garage; as soon as we got home from school it would be footy in winter and cricket in summer. We had a trampoline in the back yard and in those days they had *Sports Action* with Rex Mossop as host on Channel Seven every Sunday morning, with the Commonwealth Bank 'Pass the Ball' segment, where players had to try to pass through the 'bullseye' and a big elephant cry was played if they got it through for 10 points. Matty and I used to turn the trampoline on its side and spend hours and hours passing the ball against it.

Other times we'd play footy behind the town hall with Chris and Michael Dever, who were our best mates, and a heap of kids and we'd play all day. I was generally the youngest so every game I'd end up in tears after one of Matty's big bully mates would jump on me or sit on me. When Dad was coaching they'd always have a barbeque behind the town hall or when Tyrrell's Wines sponsored the club (Dad and Murray Tyrrell were good mates), the families would go out along Broke Road to his winery and all the kids would just be constantly playing footy against each other. They were wonderful times and have left me with such great memories.

Athol Peden owned the Aberdare Hotel in Cessnock, although everyone knew it as Peden's Pub, and his son Billy (later to become a Knights team-mate) became a good mate of Matt's in their late teens. It was Dad's local and Matt and I used to get a packet of chicken chips and pink lemonade and play footy out the back while Dad had a quiet ale.

Gary and Gayle Johns were teenage sweethearts who married on 6 February 1971 when they were both 19. Matthew is the oldest of the three children in our family, born on 27 July 1971. I came along on 19 May 1974. Can you believe the old man wanted to give me a good traditional Welsh name of Tighe! Thank God my mum had her way and told him she was not going to have a son with a name that phonetically was pronounced 'Tige' and she put her foot down and christened me Andrew Gary (mind you, I'm not real fussed on Andrew either). But the old man wasn't happy with that so he apparently said, 'Well, I'm going to call him Joe.' So, as I grew up in Cessnock, everyone called me 'Joe', including Dad and Matty, and they still do. From that grew the football nickname of 'Joey', although 'Nugget' is just as commonly used by the Knights players.

Kate was added to the Johns household seven years after me, on 1 February 1981. The big gap between Kate and me was caused by years of heartache for Mum and Dad. Mum had a difficult pregnancy and was in hospital for 17 weeks before she had a girl — they named her Christine — who died at birth. She then had three miscarriages before Kate was safely delivered. Kate is the private member of the Johns family. Mum and Dad's faces are quite well known now as they hardly missed a game Matt or I played and have been interviewed occasionally over the years, whereas Kate is happy to stay right out of the limelight.

I'm really proud of the woman she has become. She's got a young family now, with a son Fletcher born in 2002 and a baby girl Emerson June who came along in March 2007. Kate moved up to Nelson Bay for a while but is back in Cessnock, not far from Mum and Dad. Kate is so laid-back she almost sleeps on her feet with her eyes open, but it's something Matt and I envy. She never went to any of my games once she grew up, not even a grand final or Origin clash or Test match, which was fine; she really isn't into footy at all.

Mum is a Mudgee girl who came to Cessnock when she was in primary school after her parents bought a pub. Apparently they were looking at the pub at Byron Bay that John 'Strop' Cornell owned until recently, in the main street right on the beach, but decided a hard-drinking mining town was a better option. Unfortunately, Mum's parents split up and her father, Kenneth Charles Bowden, who passed away just over 10 years ago, headed to Queensland where he did well as a developer on the Gold Coast, which meant since we were kids I'd hear from him without fail every bloody time Queensland beat us in State of Origin.

Mum's mother, June Bowden, played A grade tennis and then there is Mum's grandfather Samuel Unwin who was an outstanding country jockey who rode something like 2000 winners and had a book written on him, called *Only Winners Can Laugh*. Mum herself was also sports-minded — she played competition squash and netball for years, plus social tennis.

I was very close to both my grandmothers. Margaret Johns, Dad's mother, is a bit of a legend in Kurri for all the work she did for the junior and minor rugby leagues there; she was a life member and they named an oval after her. She was a pennants golfer too and her two sisters, Nellie and Mollie, were apparently captain and vice-captain of the Australian women's cricket team (they called it 'cricko' in those days). Mollie (Worthington) also worked for years as a netball official and the courts in Kurri Kurri are named after her.

Unfortunately, Grandma Johns died when I was about 14. I used to go down and stay at her place at Kurri all the time, especially if I was going through a rough time in my teens and wanted to get out of the house. She loved footy and didn't miss many of our games, or Kate's netball. In fact, there wouldn't be a match where one of our grandmas was not there cheering us on.

Grandma Bowden was just an amazing lady; she had the time of day for anyone and a heart the size of Phar Lap. She was only tiny, so we used to call her 'little grandma' and when I went to live in Newcastle in my first house at New Lambton, she came and lived with me, as well as my housemates Billy Peden and Andrew Tangata-toa, and looked after us. I used to have friends popping in at all hours and she would get up and cook meals and cook breakfasts for whoever woke up there and never once complained. She was like a second mother to Matthew, Kate and me — she was always around the house or we'd stay at her place. She passed away from motor neurone disease in June 2002 and it was really tough to see her go like that; her brain was there but physically her body just shut down.

Dad worked just about all his adult life in the mines, starting at Aberdare North, then went to Liddell Colliery. He then spent 23 years at Newstan Colliery where he also became the union secretary. Mum worked for 20 years behind the bar at the Cessnock Leagues Club; they're both now retired. They'd come down for dinner at mine or Matt's place in Newcastle and we'd say, 'Stay the night, don't drive up there now' — it's about a 45-minute drive — but they'd always say,

'No, we better go home.' Matthew reckons they have to head back there before the gates close because they don't let anyone in after 10pm.

Our second home was the family caravan at Fingal Bay, just near Shoal Bay. We would be there every weekend in summer and always for school holidays. Some of the best memories of my childhood are from those days at 'The Bay'. We had an old 16-footer aluminium van with a canvas awning until it got blown over in a massive storm in 1990, so our folks bought a new one just a few sites away, which was a 20-footer with an aluminium awning. Old Gazza and Gayle can still be seen there pretty regularly these days — that's when the old man isn't down the Shoal Bay Country Club Hotel with his mates from all these years, having a bet and a beer. When we were younger we used to tag along with him and hang around the jetty at Shoal Bay, jumping in the water and playing on the sand, and we used to watch the local fishermen bring these massive sharks in that they'd caught.

There were a lot of kids in our street in the caravan park and we were all like one big extended family. There were the Feenans and the Youngs especially, plus the Browns and Thoroughgoods; Mum and Dad are still great friends with them today and they've all still got their vans up there. It's funny how we've grown up now and occasionally we take our kids up and you sit there and just smile at how it has all evolved. I love getting up there with my son Samuel, but we have been too busy the past few years to do that too often. When we do we always make sure we get out on Dad's boat and go over to Tea Gardens or go somewhere quiet and for a swim around the bays; it is beautiful. I love going in the pub with him and having a bet and a few beers — they're good times.

I learned to surf at Fingal Bay and it has been my second love after rugby league ever since. I was probably nine or 10 when I got my first surfboard — one of my dad's mates, Wayne Baggs, came back from Hawaii with it. I've still got the surfboard at home, a Dick Brewer single-fin. I'd get out on it all day long and absolutely loved it; even in winter time, if I wasn't playing footy I'd catch the bus to Maitland, then the train to Newcastle — which took sometimes two hours — and I'd surf all day at Nobbys Beach or Newcastle's main beach, then get back home at night.

The waves seemed pretty good at Fingal Bay when I was young, although I grew to realise they were always small and pretty average. Sometimes all the kids would head down to the beach and walk for a kilometre or two looking for a good wave, then go back to the caravan for something to eat, and go back out again and again. Matty was never much of a surfer — he was never much good at anything, to be honest (this book is my big chance for 'Barge Arse' to get a few get-squares in) — but he was a try-hard on a board.

So, as I record my upbringing, I can only say I loved it. I suppose Cessnock was a bit of a tough area, not particularly affluent and very blue-collar, with so many of the fathers being miners or tradesmen. It really toughened you up as a personality because if you showed any weakness at all you used to get picked on by other kids. There used to be a hell of a lot of fights but you always had to carry yourself as if you weren't scared or hurting. Not that I got into much trouble — I was too scared of what the old man would do.

We used to live on our BMX bikes. I remember on weekends we'd get up, have breakfast, and the rule was we had to be home by five o'clock. Looking back now, you shudder to think about letting your eight or nine year old go out all day like that, but in those days there were no worries, particularly in a country town. We'd ride all over Cessnock, in the open cuts, going over jumps and stuff, finding tracks, riding through all the creeks, going to mates' places; it was easy to amuse ourselves. We were outdoors the whole time, there was always something going on. But I tell you, Cessnock is the hottest place in the world to be in summer, and the coldest in winter.

We had a modest three-bedroom house, typical of the miners' cottages in the town, and Matty and I used to sleep in a double bunk in the same room. We only had two television channels — the ABC on Channel 5 and NBN on Channel 3, which was a Channel Nine affiliate. You needed a big powerful aerial with a booster to get the Sydney stations in those days and we never bothered. So the only club football we saw was the ABC Saturday match of the day. When the games were on Channel Seven and then Channel Ten in the '80s we used to go to different people's houses to watch it, right up until I was about 16. Thank God State of Origin was on Channel Nine.

We had a separate garage and a flat front yard and one of our favourite pastimes was to peek out the windows on the front verandah on a Friday night and watch all the drunks stagger home from one of the six or seven pubs in Vincent

Street. Some would end up having a kip on our front yard or the verandah itself, thinking Gary and Gayle wouldn't mind.

To have a brother who is truly my best mate has been one of the greatest things in my life — although Matthew has always been a bit odd, as I explain in the chapter on my dear brother. Matty was small and timid. When we used to fight I'd always get over the top of him, even though he was three years older than me (Mum will verify these stories). As a footballer, Matty was just an average player but he was so determined and I have so much admiration for him for the time and dedication he put into his game in his late teens.

When he was playing for Cessnock, his under-16s weren't even in the A division competition. Matt played five-eighth but although he was never the best player in the team he kept plugging away and training so hard by himself. He never made a Newcastle Knights junior rep team but he eventually built up his strength and skills and got his crack at the Knights when he was 19.

I was only 15 when Matt left home to live with mates in Newcastle, and at that age you don't want a 15-year-old younger brother hanging around, so after knocking around all our lives and having mutual friends until then, we drifted apart a bit until I made grade with the Knights.

Ever since he was young, Matty had to cope with people saying I was a better player, which would have been hard for him, but he was never jealous and just always encouraged me. Once he went to grade and he worked so tirelessly on improving himself, he kicked ahead of me as a footballer for a while.

But he was always a wimp. We went to St Patrick's Catholic primary school in Cessnock, about 600 metres from our home. To get to school we had to ride through the TAFE grounds and there used to be one tree that was full of magpies, so in their springtime breeding season it was either run the gauntlet past this tree and through the TAFE grounds or go the long way around, which would take 15 minutes. Matthew, being the big coward he is, would never want to go near the TAFE college after going through the grounds a couple of times with me riding beside him and bawling his eyes out as the magpies would be swooping on him.

People who have seen his reaction to snakes on *The Footy Show* know how much he hates them, but let me tell you why. Matt must have been about 15 or 16 when we went up to Forster with the families we used to hang around with at Fingal Bay — the Feenans and Youngs and others — all in a mini-bus. On the way home, near Bulahdelah, Matty was complaining to Dad that we had to pull over and let him go to the toilet. Dad pulled up on the side of the road and it was pretty narrow so we had a line of traffic behind us having to carefully go around the bus. Now we thought my good brother was heading into the bush to do a 'number one' and, as he started to disappear into the scrub, one of the boys yelled out to look out for the snakes, that they were everywhere in there. Matty did an abrupt U-turn back to the side of the road, dropped his duds and was laying this massive 'cable', a 'number two', which left us in stitches of laughter. Right behind us was a bus full of nuns, looking straight at Matthew out their windows. Matthew was horrified and ever since he nearly faints at the mention of 'snake'.

After St Pat's we went to St Peter's up to Year 10, then Marist Brothers in Maitland, which is called All Saints College now. I was an above average student all through primary school and into about Years 7 and 8 in high school, but by Year 10 I was probably more focused on football, plus the hormones had started to kick in and the mind started wandering a bit. I went on to Year 12 mainly to try to make the Australian Schoolboys team and didn't have much of a go at schoolwork; I very rarely studied, which I now regret. I didn't think it was cool to read and study and learn. It wasn't until I finished school that I found that I loved reading books.

I remember in Year 9 or 10 we had a careers advisor called Mr Mate and we had to sit down and tell him what we wanted to do after we left school. I told him I wanted to play football, and he looked at me and said: 'You've got no chance.' He was a great old teacher, Mr Mate; he was only trying to steer me in the right direction and influence me into pursuing something more stable and worthwhile in his eyes, but it has always stuck with me.

I played any sport that was available in Cessnock — swimming, water polo, athletics, and I did some boxing at the police boys club. I fancied myself as a cricketer and was good enough to play representative cricket for Cessnock. I remember once going down to the Central Coast when I was about 12, and scoring 50-odd, which was a big deal. For a while I probably loved cricket more than I did footy. I played it religiously in summer — in the domestic competition on Saturday mornings against the other schools and then in the rep team on the Sundays where we'd play against other teams as far away as Singleton or Gosford.

I have a great memory too of going to the Sydney Cricket Ground once for an Australia v West Indies one-day international in the late 1980s, with the Fingal Bay crowd. I literally did not sleep the night before I was so excited about going. Viv Richards was on fire that night; it was an awesome experience.

The other thing about my childhood is that if I had grown up in a soccer family I could have so easily ended up chasing my dreams with a round ball, because I loved the game, and I still love watching it on television, especially the English Premier League. I played soccer before I got into league — like at age two and a half. Mum took Matthew down to register for soccer and they were short on kids so I played, and was still wearing nappies for my first few matches. I played until I was 13 before soccer and league clashed on the same day.

A close mate from high school, Richard Johnson, left at 16 for England where he made a great career out of soccer. He played for Watford for 11 years and also for the Socceroos. He then came back to Australia to play for the Newcastle Jets and is still playing for Wellington Phoenix in the Hyundai A-League. Richard was just one of those natural sportsmen. In Year 10 I talked him into playing one season of league and he won the player of the year award, playing lock. He was fearless and didn't really understand what the game was about, but used to just smash kids in defence and charge like a runaway bull in attack.

I was fairly nuggety when I was young, but by the time I was 10 or so I had become tiny for my age and pretty thin. Matt and I played for St Pat's, our school team, in the Cessnock league against four or five other teams. My first game was in Matthew's team when I was four and he was seven; I can't remember it but apparently they put me on the field and Matthew passed me the ball. I passed it straight back to him, but he was offside and we were penalised. Matt said something like, 'You passed it forward, you're not allowed to do that,' and I said, 'Well, I didn't ask you to pass me the ball anyway.'

It wasn't until I was about 12 or 13 that we progressed to the coalfields competition where we would play against Kurri and teams from East Maitland, Raymond Terrace, Beresfield and these places. In the Cessnock competition we were never beaten and I used to win all the awards. When we progressed to the coalfields competition we used to come second or third. I was a bit small, and too timid by then and I no longer won any player of the year awards.

When I was 15 I started to get sore in the knees, or just below the knees, after I'd been running around for a while and, after quite a few months of putting up with it, it got to the stage where I would be in agony after playing a game of football. Doctors weren't able to diagnose what was wrong, until one said he thought it was Osgood-Schlatter disease and sent me to a specialist who happened to be Neil Halpin, who would become such a big part of my life years later. Osgood-Schlatter disease is fairly common in active kids during adolescence and is caused by a growth spurt putting pressure on the bone below the knee. I had a pretty bad case apparently; all I could do was waddle around and couldn't run anywhere near top pace, and I would be in excruciating pain after I'd been on my legs for a few hours. Neil put each leg in plaster for six weeks at a time to immobilise them.

After I recovered from that, I started doing a little bit of weight training and got a lot stronger, and with that strength I gained a lot more confidence and my football improved tenfold.

Stuart Collins was the stand-out player in my age group. He was a big front-rower who captained most Newcastle teams I played with in the juniors and he was earmarked for big things. He was really skilful but just never developed once he got past his teens.

I was selected in Newcastle's Harold Matthews team (then under-15s) but I was probably lucky to be picked because at that stage I hadn't really matured physically; it wasn't until I got bigger and then played S. G. Ball (under-17s) that I started to really develop as a footballer. I remember people in Cessnock saying, when I was playing Harold Matthews, that I'd never make it because I was just too small.

In Year 12 I was chosen to play in the NSW Combined Catholic Colleges Schoolboys team that went away to Darwin for the '91 Australian Schoolboys Championships, with the Australian Schoolboys side to tour England being picked from that tournament. The major reason I went through to Year 12 was to try to make the Australian Schoolboys tour but I was just awful in Darwin and missed out, so I was really dejected. I knew I'd let a chance slip by.

I remember Damian Chapman, who played in our NSW CCC team, was the gun schoolboy player at the time and he got the halfback position; he went on to play a bit of first grade with St George. Michael Buettner was the five-eighth and captain in the Aussie Schoolboys, and he played first grade with Parramatta the next year. He was huge back then, much more physically developed than I was. I wasn't physically ready to play that standard, but I really filled out the following year, becoming taller and a lot stronger.

Stuey Collins made that Australian Schoolboys tour along with a heap of blokes who went on to play regular first grade, like Sid Domic, who played with Hull in England until recently, Jack Elsegood, although he was known by his real name of Barry back then, Ken Nagas, Clinton O'Brien, Jamie Olejnik, Sean Ryan, Josh Stuart and Danny Williams.

Now, because I was so preoccupied with footy, there are two things that didn't play a big role in my early life — girlfriends or 'real' jobs. I think my first girlfriend was a girl called Nicole Bartlett, with whom I shared my first kiss, but like most of my girlfriends since, she eventually brushed me. I had one serious girlfriend before I left high school; she lived in Maitland and her name was Belinda McTiernan. Her dad played rugby league for Maitland; he was a winger and a really fast runner.

Jobs? Ha. I never had a part-time job like a paper run or stacking shelves at Woolies, so it wasn't until I had left school and been taken on by the Knights that I entered the workforce — and that's not a good story, I am afraid to say. The Knights got me a job as an apprentice plumber in 1992 when they first put me on their books … I lasted just two days. I am scared of heights and I had to get on a roof to do some guttering, and when I looked down at the ground I felt crook in the guts. Anyway, the boss told me it was lunchtime and as the 'boy' I was assigned to go and get his tucker, and some for myself while I was at it. He told me to get him a pie and a large chocolate milk, so away I went — and I never came back. I can't remember his name. Sorry, he was a really nice bloke and it was a weak act on my behalf, but my heart just wasn't in it and I tried to use my fear of heights as an excuse. My father was ropable, and so were people at the Knights; the senior sports writer on the *Newcastle Herald*, Stewart Roach, even touched me up in the paper. Yeah, I copped a big backlash for that.

After that I did a few labouring jobs, including a couple of weeks out at Cypress Lakes golf course, then worked for about six months at Mr Sports sports store at Maitland in 1994–95. Adam Muir also worked there and the owners were brothers from Cessnock, great blokes. I then helped Matty in the Knights development office occasionally when he was there for a couple of years. So up to the time the game turned full-time pro in 1995, that was the sum total of my working life.

So there you have it, a very normal life growing up — except for one thing. There was a downside of being a teenager for me — what I now realise was my emerging depression. There were times when I would lock myself in my room for days on end and I wouldn't let anyone in. I would sit there and have music blaring and just stare at the roof. Understanding it now, I can see that I was probably just riding those highs and lows and that would just come and go.

Only in recent years did I find out that Mum rang different places like Lifeline to see if they could do something to help.

She just didn't understand what it was — very few people did. I remember being so down for no reason, or things creeping up on me from school, or something might be said about me that would just stick with me and I'd churn on it over and over. I'll never forget finding, in Year 8, that a boy I went to school with hung himself; I used to think about that a lot. I wasn't even friends with him — I played footy against him but he wasn't really a mate of mine — yet I remember thinking about it all the time: what made him do it ... and could that happen to me.

It was awful when I felt so low and couldn't explain it, and it's still hard for me to speak about it or think too hard about it now. My parents were obviously very worried and tried to talk to me about it, but I'd just shut them — and everyone else — out until I felt 'normal' again. I really can't remember any specifics about what was said or how we addressed it as a family; maybe my mind has shut it out over the years. I hope my story will awaken some teenagers or their parents about just how vulnerable and fragile any of us can become, and when you see a young person not coping with life, to think deeply about what it might be.

Generally, I had a wonderful childhood with a loving family, great mates and family friends, but something inside me wasn't right. And it took a long while before I could understand it, let alone come close to overcoming it.

CHAPTER 4

A SHARP KICK IN
THE PANTS

Peter Sharp, now coaching Hull in England, was the first football coach to have a large influence on me — when I was a member of the Newcastle Jersey Flegg (then under-18s) side in 1992. He was my first real footy mentor and is still a great mate. When I was struggling with things in later years and felt I needed someone to talk to, I'd still call 'Sharpy' even though he was in England. I don't know how old he was when he coached us in Jersey Flegg — I'd say late 30s — but I felt like I could speak to him at my level; I trusted him and I could see that he really, really wanted to help me out. At the time in my life when I was a little bit troubled, I was sort of isolated from people around me and my first instinct was to push people away, but Sharpy understood my make-up and was never afraid to tell me how it really was, and even then accepted the rough diamond in my personality. And I found that out good and proper that year in what I now look back on as a pretty funny incident.

We usually trained on a Thursday afternoon and because I was still living in Cessnock, I used to stay at a team-mate's house most of the time. This particular week we all arranged to get together to have dinner that night as we were due to train again on the Easter Friday, the next morning. We had a few beers and we all ended up in town, about 18 or 19 of us. I tried my luck with a certain lady and, well, let's just say succeeded and stayed over at her house.

I'd planned to get up early, go back to my mate's place where I was supposed to be staying, pick up my training gear and get off to training which started at nine. But I slept through the alarm and when I woke up I only had 20 minutes to get there. When I arrived the boys were doing their warm-ups and I had to walk in with my going-out gear still on: jeans, best collared shirt and going-out shoes. Anyway, Sharpy made me train the whole session in that gear, and made me continually breathe on him to see if he could smell alcohol, which he couldn't, thank God. I told him a 'porky' and said I'd been to the movies and slept through the alarm. Little did I know that a few other players were late and had turned up looking very seedy.

We went to Sydney the next day to play Balmain at Leichhardt Oval and Sharpy gave me a big dressing down, told me we'd better win or else after pulling a stunt like that at training. I think we were winning by 24 at half-time, but in the first five minutes I'd suffered the worst corked thigh you could imagine and could hardly run; I was limping through the whole game. I pleaded with Sharpy to bring me off at half-time — we had the game well and truly won — but he refused and decided to teach me a lesson. I stayed out there the whole match (we won 30–2) on one leg, then got an even bigger 'raz' after the game.

We had a very good Flegg side and it was a really enjoyable year — although I was disappointed at first I'd been put back to the junior reps after being called up to train with the Knights after playing S. G. Ball in 1991. It was like a dream come true to be called up by the Knights; all of a sudden I could see that I might end up being a first grader and I was so pumped about it. But I didn't 'put in' at training, I probably thought success would come easily from there. I got a good kick up the arse when I was put back to Flegg. It hurt at the time but it also taught me a valuable lesson and I now look at it as a blessing in disguise.

I can still remember the under-21s coach Robbie Tew calling me over and telling me I should go back and work on my game and my attitude, that it just wasn't good enough. He had called over Matthew a week or so before that and said something like, 'I don't know how to handle your brother — he's got all this ability but I fear it's going to go to waste. He just doesn't know when the good times have to finish and the hard work starts. There are all these other guys busting their guts to impress, but I just can't get through to him that he has to be a lot more fair dinkum.'

Matty had been called up to grade in 1990 and was playing regular reserve grade in that '92 season, with Steve 'Joey'

Fulmer playing halfback inside him (he was the Knights' first grade halfback in their initial season in '88). Matthew was a bloke that just busted his gut and worked that hard on his game because he knew he wasn't as naturally talented as a lot of players. He couldn't believe my slack attitude and how rebellious I was. I spat the dummy and for the first week at training didn't really put in before Sharpy pulled me into gear and, with his help, I turned it around. I really knuckled down … well, except for that one incident I just talked about.

I can readily admit now it was probably the best thing in my footy development to get put back to Flegg. I wasn't under as much pressure and it wasn't as intense football as under-21s would have been at the time. I just wasn't ready to play grade football, physically or mentally.

We had a really tight team in Flegg and had a great coach in Sharpy. We generally played Saturdays and after the game just about everyone from the side would go out together. We lost one game all season (we used to play eight games plus a semi-final and final) and won the final against Western Suburbs, which that year was played as a curtain-raiser to the third State of Origin clash at the Sydney Football Stadium; what a buzz to play in front of a massive crowd. We won 26–16, five tries to three, with our centre Gary Sainsbury picking up three tries. I didn't score a point but played OK, I thought.

An interesting thing, considering that I'm now fortunate enough to hold the record as the top points-scorer in NRL/ARL history, is that I wasn't goal-kicker that year. I always kicked as a youngster and started the season as kicker, but I got 'the yips' for some reason and missed a couple in front and then got pretty much put on notice by Sharpy. He told me to practise, practise, practise, which I did, but I was no better next game. So for the rest of the year our five-eighth Jamie Thorpe was our goal-kicker. He was an unbelievably naturally talented kid from Condobolin, but unfortunately was never going to be big enough to make it in senior football. Even though I wore the number seven jersey, Jamie played halfback and I played five-eighth all that year so I didn't play much first receiver.

It's strange that so few of that winning Flegg side kicked on to play a lot of first grade. Stuart Collins was our captain; he'd played Australian Schoolboys and also for New South Wales under-19s the next year, but was only ever selected for a handful of first grade games. So too were Scott Conley and Troy Fletcher, who both went on to play in the Knights' 1997 first grade premiership side. 'Fletch' was a bustling winger back then but became a back-rower in first grade.

That was the year I first realised I might be good enough to make a career as a professional footballer. The fact that the Knights had identified my talent and asked me to train with them before the 1992 season gave me a massive shot of confidence. But I didn't know the 'how' of being a professional footballer, and Sharpy was the first to help the penny drop there. Until then I didn't really 'put in' enough, I just tended to sit back and really didn't understand that to get to the top you had to push yourself. I didn't make any sacrifices at all that off-season, I knew nothing about doing extra training or following the right diet, I was eating terribly. Sometimes I'd wake up in the morning and for breakfast I'd have a can of Coke and a Kit Kat and Matty would just shake his head at me. I was still living at home and then I met a girl, Brittany Owens; I moved out and lived with her family. I knuckled down after the Flegg competition finished and felt, 'Hey, you're now part of the Knights system, they've shown you what they expect after dropping you back to Jersey Flegg, now make the most of it this time.'

That 1992 season was the Knights' best to that stage; they made the semis in all three grades, as well as winning Jersey Flegg for the second year in a row and the Harold Matthews Cup. The place was buzzing. I remember playing under-21s (President's Cup) and we'd have the presentations after the matches and we always seemed to have won all three grades — it was just great to be part of this massive momentum the club was gaining. The development structure David Waite had put in place — he was development manager and reserve grade coach before being promoted to first grade coach — was really paying dividends.

The under-21s won our last eight games to get to the semi-finals but we were beaten by South Sydney. I kicked the ball in-goal at a crucial stage and a Souths forward — I still remember the bloke's name, Brent Hill — picked the ball up and ran 100 metres to score. I see Brent at the races now and then, and he is always quick to remind me what happened that day.

In those last few weeks of the 1992 season I would play under-21s, then sit on the bench in reserve grade, where Matty was playing, and had a few more runs at hooker than at halfback. Reserve grade made the preliminary final that year before being knocked out by Balmain and first grade were knocked out 3–2 by St George the second week of the finals.

I started the 1993 season in reserves as halfback with Matt at five-eighth and we really struck up a good combination. The first grade side was struggling (they had only six wins from the first 16 games), I was playing really well and I thought I should have been given a shot in first grade. First grade coach David Waite held me back at the time though, which I couldn't believe, but looking back now I know I wasn't ready. Matt had had five runs off the bench in firsts in 1992, then he was promoted to five-eighth in round six of '93 after the 1992 Norwich Rising Star (rookie of the year in the entire competition) Matthew Rodwell was dropped after Waitey had moved him to five-eighth for one game. Our signing from Norths, Jason Martin, was halfback and wasn't setting the world alight either and I thought I could handle being the first grade number seven; I just needed a chance.

Matty made his run-on debut at five-eighth against Gold Coast at Seagulls Stadium, with Jason Martin at halfback. Ironically, it was also the day I tasted first grade for the first time after playing a full game in reserve grade. In those days, you could use two fresh reserves and two players who had played in the lower grades. It was bucketing down with rain and our fullback Robbie O'Davis was hurt and came off at half-time. I had to go out and play fullback and the Seagulls, coached by Wally Lewis, had a cyclone at their backs in the second half. I'd never played fullback before and it was an experience, to say the least. We got dusted 22–6 and couldn't score a try. It was the Knights' third loss in a row, so it wasn't a particularly auspicious occasion for the Johns brothers. Matt picked up a knee injury late in the game and missed one week, then we were in reserve grade the following weekend against St George at Kogarah. Matt says he always remembers that game because it was a pretty hot Dragons team with Phil Blake, Jeff Hardy, Gorden Tallis and Andrew Walker in it, and I picked up a line-dropout from Blake and stepped through the line and scored. He reckons that was the day the Johns brothers started to get a name outside just the local Newcastle scene. Warren Ryan and Allan McMahon, who was Newcastle's original coach and was going to Illawarra the next year, were at the ground and apparently mentioned our names to a few people. In fact, we had approaches from the Western Reds — based in Perth — shortly after that but we never really pursued the interest.

Soon after, Matt started wearing the number six jersey permanently, with captain Michael Hagan, my future coach, moving to the centres for the rest of his last season with the club. I had two more runs off the bench in firsts, in round 10 against Parramatta and round 13 against Balmain, but didn't get more than 10 minutes each time.

We had a pretty smart reserve grade side under Robert Finch, who was an excellent coach; I really enjoyed being coached by him. Early in that '93 season Matty and I really started to fire together. Our fullback was Robbie Ross, who played Australian Schoolboys the year before, and he used to stick to us like glue on the field — it was a brilliant combination. Matty and I used to feed off each other and try to outdo each other on the field, just waiting for our chance to be recognised as first graders. Robbie used to work in the club's development department with Matt and they would talk football and work on things together. It was fantastic.

Then when Matt went up to first grade permanently halfway through the year, our New Zealand international Tony Kemp was dropped to reserves and played five-eighth. To his credit, he didn't spit the dummy and really helped us out with his experience, and we made it to the grand final against a very strong North Sydney side. How are these for some big names for reserve grade: their backline was Paul Conlon, Paul Smith (who'd played in Penrith's 1990 and '91 grand finals), Matt Toshack, Les Kiss, Jeff Doyle and Mark Soden — and they had Adrian Toole, Alan Wilson, Tony Hearn and Peter Jackson in their pack. That's two ex-internationals in Kiss and Jackson and Origin players in Wilson and Hearn.

Mind you, when you look at the names now, we had a pretty awesome side too, with myself, Robbie Ross and Rodney Howe, who all went on to play for Australia; Tony Kemp, who played a lot of Tests for New Zealand; then Darren Treacy (on the wing), David Smith, Tony Herman, Wayne Richards and Tim Maddison, who all played a lot of first grade, plus Paul Marquet who won two first grade grand finals. We went down to Norths 5–4 in the grand final, a try apiece, with a Peter Jackson field goal winning them the game.

Matthew used to pretty much run the show when he was in reserves, and when he went to first grade I had to take over calling the shots. I was pretty hesitant to start with, but towards the end of the year really got a lot of confidence from it. Again, I look back now and think I was lucky I had that great structure around me and that David Waite held me back, because I didn't understand the game well enough.

As it turned out, that reserve grade grand final at the Sydney Football Stadium was the last lower grade game I played. Luck turned my way at the start of the next season with Matt Rodwell getting hurt in the trials and giving me a chance ... I was ready to make the most of it. I knew I was a first grader by then; I just had to prove I was mature enough and fit enough to match it with other blokes who were in the same boat. There were plenty of Andrew Johnses around at the time — young blokes who thought they were good enough — but not all of them made it.

CHAPTER 5

JOEY THE FIRST GRADER

The first time I wore the Newcastle Knights number seven jersey in first grade, against South Sydney in the first round of 1994, is recognised as a fairly incredible debut in which I was lucky enough to score a record 23 points from two tries, seven goals and a field goal — in a 43–16 win at the Sydney Football Stadium. I remember being interviewed by a heap of journalists after the game and thinking, 'You've arrived, mate.'

I don't remember a lot of the specifics of that match, but most of the lead-up to the game and coming back to earth with a thud just one week later are still vivid in my memory.

David Waite decided to room me in Sydney the night before the game with a wise old owl in Tony Butterfield, our veteran front-rower, and I was absolutely horrified ... not with pre-match nerves, but because 'Buttsy' walked around the hotel room with no clothes on the whole time. As anyone who has seen Butts in his birthday suit can testify, he's no oil painting in the flesh. Still, I remember being so relaxed the day of the game; I knew the team was going to play well, that I was going to play well. Matthew and I went for a walk from Rydges at North Sydney where we used to stay, to underneath the Harbour Bridge. We had a competition to see who could kick the ball and hit the bottom of the bridge above us. Neither of us could kick it high enough but we mucked around there for a while just like two kids in our Cessnock back yard, before we realised it was time to go back and get out to the ground. It just all clicked that day; the team played really well against a Rabbitohs side that was coming off a big victory against the premiers Brisbane in the Tooheys Challenge pre-season final. I think I got man of the match, but our forwards laid a fantastic foundation for me.

The following week was just chaos with so much written in the papers about my debut. I remember being at work, at Mr Sports at Maitland, and all week the phone never stopped ringing and it would be journalists asking questions. Crews came up from Sydney to film me at work; my head was spinning and then I'd get to training and the cameras would be on me again. I also had to go to Sydney during the week for a function for the Norwich Rising Star Award, which interrupted my training. By the time I got to the game on Sunday I dead-set didn't know how I was going to be able to play.

We were up against Wests, coached by Warren Ryan, and it was a big occasion for me, the first time I would run onto Marathon Stadium in front of a home crowd as a first grader. It ended up being a nightmare. Paul Langmack and Jason Alchin sledged me the whole game, cheap-shotting me and trying to rattle me. And it worked; I was just awful. The Magpies led 16–2 just after half-time, but we clawed back to 18-all and I had a chance to win the game with a field goal attempt from in front but it missed by a mile, then Jim Serdaris kicked a left-footer for them to give them a one-point win.

I felt so flat during the match and I really came back to earth in a hurry. I learned a valuable lesson that you shouldn't believe your own publicity. After the game we all went to the Cricketers Arms, the pub we used to go to, and I felt responsible for the loss. I just wanted to go home and get away from it all.

The following week we went to Canberra and were smashed 34–8. I was defending opposite Bradley Clyde and Mal Meninga and all they were doing was attacking Matty coming off their line, and every time they'd go forward they'd do a two-pass shift to send 'Clydey' straight at me. I think we went in at 8-all at half-time but in the second half they just steamrolled us.

We lost four in a row after that opening win against Souths and I thought, 'That must have been a lucky day — this playing first grade consistently is a lot tougher than I thought.' Our season turned around in round eight when we went to North Sydney to play the Bears, who were undefeated after seven games and were searching for a club record ninth straight victory (including their last game of 1993). Mark Sargent scored a great try near the end to give us a 24–20 win and we won six of eight from there, including our first-ever win over Brisbane, which took us to fifth place. Then the next week we played Souths at home and I threw three intercept passes and we lost 28–14. I was devastated and our season went all downhill from there.

Getting whipped 52–16 by Canberra at home and Brett Mullins scoring three 100-metre tries from fullback (and four for the game) sticks in my mind to this day. That's when I learned what a top-class forward pack was all about. They had Quentin Pongia and Johnny Lomax, who literally destroyed our pack that day; they were just hitting blokes that hard. If people ask me what is the best team I played against, it was Canberra that Friday night; they were unstoppable, they were frightening … and Laurie Daley didn't even play. They had Noa Nadruku on the wing, Mal Meninga and Ruben Wiki in the centres, Jason Croker and Ricky Stuart in the halves and a pack of Pongia, Lomax, Steve Walters, Brett Hetherington, David Furner and Bradley Clyde. They went on to win the grand final that season 36–12 against Canterbury.

I look back now and laugh at how I really didn't understand the game at all in 1994. I was lucky I had a great forward pack in front of me — 'The Chief' (Paul Harragon), 'Sarge' (Mark Sargent), 'MG' (Mark Glanville) and Butts, plus Matthew there calling a lot of the shots. Matty and I had worked hard since we were young on our passing, to hit the spot from 20 to 30 metres away, but that's all my game was — kicking and passing the ball to Matty and occasionally running myself. I didn't understand reading numbers, I didn't understand pushing my team to the middle of the field and attacking the right numbers. I was also lucky that with the structure David Waite had put in place, that was all done for me.

And the knowledge his assistant Alan Bell passed on to me helped give me the best possible grounding. Waitey was a great educator with an incredible understanding of the game, but was at times painfully pedantic; yet a great first coach for me at the time. We didn't play much 'ad lib' football, a lot of our game was structured; we played a deep second phase ball — as they used to call it — and just tried to keep errors to a minimum and dominate in the forwards. 'Belly' had a great mind for the game and was an unsung hero of the Newcastle Knights. He used to make videos up for me on different ball plays by halfbacks like Allan Langer, Greg Alexander, Ricky Stuart and Kevin Walters and great ball-players like Gavin Miller and Darryl Brohman (who I didn't even realise played first grade), and it helped me enormously. Actually I've still got the tapes at home. We'd sit through them and write down what they did with the ball, why they did it, what was going through their heads, why they'd do this that way. I'm sure that is why my game was a mixture of all those guys; I'd like to think I had the passing and kicking game of Ricky and the short running game of Alf; I sort of watched the way they played and put it into my game.

A lot of people were saying I wasn't quick enough, but once I started doing power weights the next season I really did get some burst over 10 to 20 metres and that was a bit deceptive to my opponents. I was 84 kilograms in 1993 but went to over 90 kilograms within a couple of years.

I roomed with Tony Butterfield most of that year; he probably saw me as a wild young bloke and he really helped me out. At the time we lived not far apart and knocked around a lot together; he was like a mentor to me, really taught me how to prepare for a game. He was one of the blokes that typified what the Knights were about. He wasn't the most skilful of players but he could really tackle, was really tough, and each time he played, he played to his best.

I felt really intimidated by the senior players in the team like Chief and Sarge, even though they were great towards me when I was a rookie. I was watching them play rep footy two years earlier and I couldn't even look at them at first; they were heroes of mine and suddenly I was in the same team as them. Once I was on the field I was alright, but telling them where to run and where to get to at training made me feel really uneasy. As did things like getting my food at the buffet in a motel and turning around and there was only one seat left — next to Chief and Sarge. Those things can be really intimidating for a young player.

But I tell you one thing, if anyone went to 'cheap-shot' me on the field or target me, Chief, Sarge and Butts really looked after me. I'd get sledged regularly or hit a bit late or high and the big forwards would run at me a lot, but often one of our big buggers would come from nowhere and shorten them up.

The game wasn't as fast as it is now but it was more physical. I don't know whether it was because I was young, but some of the collisions that used to take place seemed a lot more intimidating than in later years. But the skill level was nowhere near what it is now; in those days your half and five-eighth could throw a 15–20-metre spiral pass, but your front-rowers were lucky to pass the ball. Nowadays everyone can pass a ball left and right and everyone can torpedo bomb, and most can step. The defence was as well structured as it is today, but the attack wasn't and players weren't as fit. The skill base went through the roof during the course of my career; it is just evolving all the time.

I was like a kid in a candy store that first season of first grade — I just couldn't get enough of footy. Matthew and I were always down the park when we weren't training with the Knights, kicking a ball around, throwing it to each other; we constantly had a ball in our hands. I was really dedicated, and Matty was such a great influence. I came second in the Norwich Rising Star Award to Norths' Matt Seers, which I was proud of, and I thought I'd certainly cemented a first grade position. It was ironic that Matthew had come second in the award the year before, behind Manly winger Jack Elsegood.

Equally ironic when you look back now is that the 1992 Rising Star was Matthew Rodwell, who was sort of responsible for me getting a call-up for round one when he did his knee badly in the last trial. He then left mid-season to be a foundation player with the Western Reds for the 1995 season. I'd received what was a pretty big offer from the Reds in 1993 myself — I think it was about $60,000 a season for three years, and I hadn't played first grade at that stage. But there was no way I was going to leave Newcastle, or the chance to play first grade with Matthew. Instead they signed Rodwell. I was on $30,000 a year at that time, which the club told me was the most they would ever pay a reserve grader.

The 1994 season was a dramatic one for the Knights: we were running fifth after 15 rounds then lost our last seven games and David Waite got the sack amid all sorts of drama within the club. Most of it went above my head. I was just happy to finally be a regular first grader, although I was blown away by the politics and how quickly it all happened and how Waitey was shafted. There was talk Robert Finch was going to get the job, which I would have been happy with; then out of left field Malcolm Reilly was announced. Now his arrival was a culture shock, that's for sure. No one knew much about him, other than he had played for Manly and was a Great Britain legend. My dad told me what a tough sort of player he was, and then the word filtered through about what a hard task master he was, and how, if blokes weren't putting in, he'd physically grab them and give them a shake and maybe a clip over the ear. I was terrified.

I'll never forget Malcolm's first training session. The club had also employed a new fitness coach, Ashley Jones, and he and Malcolm decided to train us at Broadmeadow racecourse and we were doing 1600-metre time trials in the lush long grass. The slowest would start off and it would accumulate down to Robbie O'Davis, who was the fittest bloke in the club and the backmarker. The plan was that by the end of 1600 metres we'd all finish close together. We had to do five of those, and Malcolm was screaming at blokes, plenty of whom were physically ill and blown away by how hard it was. Next day, we all got a note from Malcolm sent to us in the internal mail saying that he'd come all this way to coach men, not 'wooses' and he expected higher performance and higher intensity at training. I remember thinking, 'This guy is a tyrant.' That off-season we just got flogged but it showed for the better — we won our first nine games in 1995.

As it turned out, Malcolm was a thorough gentleman and the players just wanted to play for him. He brought out some set moves and when he first explained one of them I remember looking at Matthew, thinking, 'What is this bloke talking about — this is the weirdest move and it will never work.' He had Matthew and I running parallel across field, doing this move called 'para-one' and he said, 'I'll tell you, lads, it will work.' We did it at training and it was no good, then we tried it in a trial match and Adam Muir went straight through three times in a row — we'd do a cut-out and he'd hit the inside. During that season we'd score off it just about every time.

Malcolm was just phenomenal with the mental side of the game and I don't think I've had a better leader of men as a coach; he would do anything for you and you would do anything to win for him. And he was a fit and determined bastard. When we were doing a series of push-ups, say about 50 or 60, he'd match the backs one for one, then do it again with the forwards five minutes later.

I'll never forget the day he did a beep test, all loaded up on the anti-inflammatory tablets from the night before for his croaky old knees. Another time, we were at a recovery session and we were having a competition to see who could go the furthest under water. We were all getting 25 to 30 metres and

Malcolm called us a 'bunch of sheilas'. He was dressed in his suit as usual and we're ribbing him, saying, 'Well, why aren't you in there, you old Pommie?' So Matt gave him his Speedos and Malcolm dived in and went 50 metres under water. When his head bobbed up it was as red as a beetroot, but that just showed his determination.

One day, we were at training doing a boxing session. One of our front-rowers, Steve Crowe, is a real parochial Australian and he was always giving it to Mal about being English. This day he challenged Malcolm to get into the ring for a spar. He did and they were both bleeding in the end it got so intense; no one could believe how hard they went.

The local TV station, NBN, had cameras there and taped it, so Matty made it into a documentary. He had Malcolm shadow sparring and practising and doing a fake press conference about the upcoming bout and we put it on the bus on the way to a game. It was sensational.

We just hit the ground running in that 1995 season. All the boys felt better for the tougher training and loved playing under Malcolm; we had the best start to a season in the club's history and the whole place was buzzing. Little did I know my life was about to race into a crazy tailspin.

CHAPTER 6

THRUST INTO THE LIMELIGHT

It was the night of 1 April 1995. And a sequence of events began that night that was surreal for a young halfback who hadn't yet turned 21 and knew little about anything other than playing a fairly simple style of rugby league. What unfolded in the next chapter of my life typifies the good and bad of my football and my character.

Matty and I were rooming together at Parramatta Travelodge, trying to get a good night's sleep before the game against Balmain at Parramatta Stadium the next day. The phone rang in our room at about 10.30: it was a player manager who said, 'Get in a taxi now and come into the city, you have to sign up with Super League.' He told how News Limited were going crazy signing the best players in the game and the ARL was going to all but fall over.

Matthew and I didn't have managers at that time — few players did — so we were pretty shocked that this bloke, and I won't say who he is because he's still a practising manager, was pretending to be looking after our interests.

I said, 'Who has already signed?' and he said, 'Stuart, Daley, Clyde, Meninga, Langer, Ettingshausen; all the superstars.' So I put Matty on the phone and we just looked at each other and the manager said, 'Get in a cab now, otherwise you're going to miss the boat.' We got off the phone and thought we'd better ring our football manager Robert Finch in his room. He came straight down, and I don't know if he'd heard anything about the Super League raids or not, but he said, 'You've got a game tomorrow — if there is going to be a Super League they are going to want you two, so don't worry, you'll be looked after.'

Next thing, the manager was back on the phone. I wanted to tell him to piss off and Matty was freaking out as he was saying, 'You're going to miss out.' We told Finchy again and he went down and got reception to divert all calls for players to his room. I don't know who else got calls, but we went for a walk the next morning and all the boys were talking about was this Super League raid, which was in all the newspapers. Matt and I decided we'd sort it out after the game; we beat Balmain 46–12, but unfortunately Matty damaged the medial ligament in his knee after just five minutes and was out for a couple of weeks. From that night it went crazy — we were getting phone calls from both sides and we didn't know which way we were going. One minute we were going to go to Super League, and the next minute we were going to the ARL.

The next day Paul Harragon went down to Sydney and signed up with the Australian Rugby League and then Matt and I had the heat put on us by both sides. We were at training one day and Super League were on the phone promising us something like $500,000 a year for the next seven years and my stomach turned into a knot — I felt sick. I said to Matty, 'Look, we've just got to sign. This is crazy — we'll be set for life.' Matt was real close to Adam Muir so we spoke to him about what sort of money was being thrown at us and he was set to go to Super League too. We were all on peanuts compared to what was being offered.

Chief had signed with ARL so he was keeping us informed about what was going on, and the minute we got home from training — on the Tuesday I think it was — we heard from different people from the ARL and the heavies who'd been called in to help them; including broadcaster Alan Jones, who was an ARL supporter, then Ken Cowley and John Ribot on the Super League side.

That night, we all decided to meet at the ground and Phil Gould came up to talk to us on behalf of the ARL. 'Gus', the master orator, gave one of his great inspirational talks. Matty and I were sitting together and the whole time it felt like he was staring at us; like he was talking to us directly. He was talking about the tradition of the game and this sort of stuff and it was impressive, whereas Super League had fallen down earlier in the day when they sent up a couple of representatives from News Limited, Malcolm Noad and John Atanaskovic, their solicitor. I remember calling Atanaskovic 'John the Mexican' and we were all taking the piss out of him.

Then they pulled out this overhead projector that didn't work, which prolonged things; we had just trained so we were busting to get home. I still reckon if they'd sent up, say, Mal Meninga, who'd retired the year before as Australian captain, or Allan Langer or one of the other senior players who had signed on, we would have jumped ship.

Gus spoke to us for about 20 minutes and our CEO Brad Mellen was up the back of the room, listening in and occasionally showing his head. Gus would question him about the club's intentions or responsibilities and make him look like a fool when Brad didn't know what to say (it turned out he was pro-Super League all along). Then Matthew and I went into one of the sponsor's boxes with Gus to 'talk turkey'. Now he tells the story as if he didn't think I was listening, but I was — as I've mentioned, I've just got this bad habit of not looking people in the eye. I was looking up at the roof, looking outside, everywhere but back at him. Then he wrote on a bit of paper what they were going to give us — I think it was $255,000 up front and $350,000 a year, and we signed that night. I was on $30,000 with the Knights and the ARL would make up the difference of $320,000, so it wouldn't come out of the Knights' funds.

I remember to this day Phil Gould saying to me before we left the room, 'I've coached a lot of young guys with so much potential and they sign big-money contracts and can't live up to it — they get caught up with it all.' I eye-balled him and said, 'You wait … you just wait to see us go.' He still reminds me of that. It was Gus' way of challenging me, but it hit a nerve, that's for sure.

We walked back into the main room, with Matt and I so relieved we'd made a decision and were staying with the ARL, when one of the club officials said from behind me (I still don't know who it was): 'You just fucked the club.' I'm sure I speak for all the players in saying we were looking for some leadership, rather than being left to our own devices to handle the unbelievable pressure both sides were putting us under. We had no idea what was happening in the big picture: we didn't know the Knights were nearly bankrupt and that the heavy hitters at the club thought by going to Super League it would secure the club's future and see the stadium developed. We received no leadership and no decent communication from the Knights management. I would have just gone with what the hierarchy asked me to if the money was about the same; well, as long as Matthew did too. I was probably inclined just to follow what he did. We were just kids really — we weren't equipped to confront all that was happening.

The funniest thing I remember about Super League's visit to Newcastle was when we went into individual meetings to talk money. Seeing as Matty and I didn't have managers, we elected Tony Butterfield to do our negotiating. Butts walked into a room with us to meet Noad and Atanaskovic and said, 'Right (referring to Matty and me), you've got Elvis Presley and Elton John here,' as if to pump up our importance. One of the News guys replied real deadpan: 'Yeah, but they haven't had a top 10 hit yet!'

The night after signing our ARL contracts, we were out smoking cigars and I tasted champagne for the first time (which I thought was awful, by the way). But luckily all the money didn't change my attitude on the training paddock nor on the field. After that crazy week, we just got home with a victory over Penrith and I think I got the man of the match award.

Even after we'd signed with the ARL a few of us agreed to have a chat with Super League, as they were claiming the ARL contracts were not valid because they were signed under duress and that we wouldn't have a competition left to play in, anyway. We told Super League we'd signed with the ARL and that was that, but, and I still don't know why, we went down to the Crowne Plaza at Terrigal on the Central Coast to hear them out. Lachlan Murdoch turned up with John Ribot and some others. I remember thinking, 'Why is Murdoch talking with an American accent?' I didn't know he grew up in the States. I also remember vividly how nervous I was. They had this bowl of Kool Mints and I must have eaten about 30 of them. I was chewing away and Lachlan said to another bloke, 'And the guy there, I think we can just pay him in Kool Mints.' I was totally embarrassed.

It was the first time I understood body language; people were doing this and that with their hands over their heads, talking really confidently, and I was thinking, 'Geez, this is powerful stuff.' The money they were offering just got higher and higher — it was astronomical money for a bloke who'd had about 20-something games in first grade. I look back now and I think that Super League were trying to do some great things for the game, but they just went about it the wrong way. It was a crazy time, the next 30 months: the game suffered not just from the fans' point of view, but the football really went downhill for a while too. For me, it opened the way to get fast tracked into rep footy; I played for NSW Country, State of Origin, then went on to the World Cup, all within a few months, so I was happy with my decision, but it was great when it all came back together again in 1998.

I can't remember how long it took but a cheque arrived in the mail for all this money. Matty and I still didn't have managers so Tony Butterfield got us in contact with an accountant and financial adviser. At one stage I had $50,000 sitting in my savings account and, instead of going to the races with $50 in my wallet, I'd go with $500; instead of going out for a night with my mates with $60, I'd go out with $600 and have a ball. Instead of eating out once a week, I was eating out for lunch, dinner and breakfast.

I blew 50 the first year; blokes were cashing their cheques straight away and spending it, some blokes were going out buying Mercedes-Benzes. At least that was one thing I didn't waste my money on — I kept my beat-up old Nissan Pulsar, I paid off the old weatherboard house I'd bought in Lambton and just left the $50,000 in my account and said, 'That's my party money.' Matthew was in a serious relationship with Trish then so he wasn't as frivolous as me.

Only four weeks after all hell had broken loose with Super League, I was picked to make my representative debut for Country — alongside Knights team-mates Ashley Gordon, Adam Muir, Darren Treacy and Paul Harragon, who was captain. Matt would have been selected but he was still out injured with the knee injury he'd suffered against the Tigers. It was a terrible game played in driving rain at Wollongong and we went down 16–8. But I was picked to play for New South

Wales ahead of the City halfback Jason Taylor, although I knew I was nowhere near ready to play at that level; my head was still spinning from the sudden surge into prominence.

It was great for Matt and I to make our debuts for New South Wales together, at half and five-eighth with Brad Fittler playing lock, but there wasn't much else to fondly remember the night for. It was the infamous game that NSW were beaten 2–0 against all the odds by a supposed 'no-name' Queensland side coached by Paul Vautin. I was knocked cold early when Trevor Gillmeister hit me with a beauty; I didn't do much at all after that.

We went to Melbourne to play the second game at the MCG and I didn't do much better. There had been talk all week about there being a 'stink' put on by the Maroons and we were on guard, thinking their call of 'Queenslander' was the prompt that they were going to bung it on. In the first scrum our hooker Jimmy Serdaris hit Wayne Bartrim, then everyone squared off with an opponent. I conveniently worked my way to the fringe and, as was the pre-match contingency for such an occasion, paired off with the Queensland halfback Adrian Lam. The quota of successfully landed punches was minimal — we had plenty of air swings, but I reckon I landed a couple of good upper-cuts on 'Lammy'. The brawl headlined all the TV news bulletins and when it was shown on the plane on the way back to Sydney the next day, I screamed: 'Watch this, boys, watch the big shot I put on Lammy' ... but it wasn't shown. They took the piss out of me all the way home from then on. By the way, we lost the game 20–12 and we were stunned. Everyone had been saying we were the biggest favourites for years. The talk when we first went into camp was what a good side it was, that we'd smash these blokes in the first two games and then we'd go to Queensland and they'd have to pick their Super League players and we'd beat them too — that was the talk from the people within the camp (not the players).

Personally, I was unbelievably intimidated by the presence of blokes like 'Freddy' (Brad Fittler), who was like a god, and to be playing with Chief, Terry Hill and Brad Mackay. I was dropped for the third match and the selectors brought in Geoff Toovey, who was Manly captain and playing well. I was disappointed naturally, but I was just happy I'd had a chance to play Origin; I didn't think I'd play for New South Wales again because Ricky Stuart would be back in the mix and I'd never get a start for NSW or Australia ahead of him.

The Knights ended up making the finals, finishing fifth, and got close to making our first grand final, but went down 12–4 to Manly in the preliminary final, with 'Toovs' having a blinder for Manly. The Sea Eagles went on to flog Canterbury 17–4 in the grand final. Thanks to our great run that season, and the fact that selectors refused to pick players who had signed for Super League, I somehow made Australia's team for the Centenary World Cup, which was celebrating 100 years since rugby league began in England as the 'Northern Union'.

Trouble was I damaged the AC joint in my shoulder against Manly in July and carried it into every game from then. I had to get a heap of painkillers before each match to get through the season; I especially remember it was like clockwork that around midnight every night after a game the pain would hit me and the agony would just start throbbing in my shoulder and up my neck. But there was no way that was going to stop me from the chance to play for Australia overseas.

However, it seems I was already getting a reputation as a party boy off the field, because Australian coach Bob Fulton, who is great mates with Malcolm Reilly from their playing days with Manly, rang Malcolm and asked if I could handle being away with the team for six weeks. Malcolm sort of said to me, 'Would you handle that, would you misbehave? Are you mature enough to go away.' I told him I'd be fine.

I went away as second string halfback behind Geoff Toovey. Toovs aggravated a neck injury in our opening game against England, which we lost 20–16 at Wembley (Matt played off the bench but I just watched on). Three days later, I made my debut in the green and gold against South Africa and we flogged them 86–6. I was lucky enough to get a couple of tries and 11 goals for 30 points, which was a record international debut and equalled Michael O'Connor's world record for points in a match. 'Bozo' (Bob Fulton) then came up with the idea of playing me at hooker and Toovs at halfback in the scrums to protect his neck, but I would be first receiver in attack and Toovs at dummy half. We played that way against Fiji (we won 66–0) and in the semi-final against New Zealand, which we won 30–20 in extra-time to go into the final.

The semi-final was a classic match, with Matthew Ridge missing a conversion attempt from wide out at 20-all just before full-time, after we'd let a 20–6 lead slip. Matty came on in extra-time and had a major hand in a try that got us the lead, then Brad Fittler, who was just phenomenal on that tour, scored a brilliant individual try to put us into the final. Freddy got us home in that match — he just stood up when we needed someone to lead us. Thank God for that because I kicked only three goals from seven or eight attempts and nearly cost us the game. I'll never forget Freddy's try in extra-time; he went inside Steve Kearney, went bang with a big left foot step, got on the outside of him and went past Ridge and scored under the posts. I thought, 'Now that is a try.'

Going into the final Bozo made me do two extra practice sessions with my goal-kicking and called in the goal-kicking guru, David Aldred — who teaches the British Lions rugby kicking freak Jonny Wilkinson — to give me some one-on-one tuition. I did two sessions with Dave and I was kicking them really badly. Then Matty came out and tried to talk me through it, and I sat with Dave Aldred and he talked about my technique and timing, but my confidence was just shot. I was thinking, 'This is the biggest game of your life, the Centenary World Cup final at Wembley, and you can't kick for the life of you.'

The day of the final, against England, we arrived three hours before kickoff and there were already 20–30,000 people there. So Matty and I went onto the field as I was desperate to have a kick before the game. I was standing in the middle of Wembley and kicking the ball from the front of the posts, from 20 metres out, and missing. The whole crowd was jigging me. Matty suggested I head to the sideline and try from there, so I did, but I was missing them by 10 metres. All of a sudden they were testing the sound system and the song 'Stuck in the Middle' by Stealers Wheel, from the movie *Reservoir*

Dogs, started playing. I'm there singing about clowns and jokers and being stuck in the middle, which seemed so appropriate at that particular time.

Next thing, Matt and I start dancing and bopping away and giggling to ourselves and he says, 'Go on, kick one.' I put it down and hit it ... and belted it straight between the posts. Matt looked at me and said, 'Do that again.' We were dancing and hamming it up — and the crowd were all singing the song and laughing. I put it down and, *whack*, hit it sweet as a nut and 'black dotted' it. The song was still going so I had one more kick from the touchline and black dotted it again.

Matt said, 'Mate, just keep that song in your head when you line them up in the match, you've got the rhythm,' and I was like, 'Yeah, yeah, I've got my rhythm back.' We were laughing and high-fiving and giggling and the crowd were jeering us and probably thinking, 'Who are these weird Aussies?'

So we went out for the biggest match of our lives and Rod Wishart scored a try in the first five minutes after he got to a grubber I put into the in-goal. There were over 66,000 people there and I got my first kick from the touchline, right where I was landing them earlier. I went back to line it up, I looked to our bench and there was Matty standing up doing this stupid jig, just like we were before the game.

The old Wembley (it was torn down in the late '90s and replaced with a new stadium) had a dog track around the playing field, which made it really difficult for kickers when you were on the sideline. I went back two steps, then there was a drop of half a foot, which meant you had to climb a ditch as you moved in to kick the ball — which normally would have done my head in. Anyway, all I had in my head was the song and I'm singing to myself about clowns and jokers and, *bang*, I nailed it. If you watch the video of the game as I jog back for the kickoff, I'm pissing myself laughing and Matty is up out of his seat still dancing around. It was such a cool moment in that most people had no idea what we were on about. As soon as we got back from the tour, I went and bought the *Reservoir Dogs* soundtrack.

I kicked four from four that day and we won 16–8. The only downside of the final was that Matty was on the bench and didn't get on, which he was really upset about.

I couldn't believe it but, at a time when I was only in the Australian team by default and would have been a million miles away from a Test jersey if the Super League players weren't banned, I won the man of the match award in the final, the most valuable player of the series and top points-scorer with 62. But I still felt out of place. I was intimidated by the people around me and where I was in the game just then. Because I watched the game so much when I was in my teens, I just thought blokes like Brad Fittler were on another planet; even though he's the best, laid-back bloke you could meet. He was the Australian captain and a superstar and I thought I was in the same team as him on false pretences. I was terrified of Bob Fulton especially; because he was an Immortal and called a spade a shovel, though I get on great with him now.

The whole of my first tour overseas was just such a buzz: I roomed with Terry Hill who was great; Matthew was there with me, and I played all but the first game. And playing hooker on that tour gave me a whole new insight into the game. Until then I was getting by on natural talent and benefiting from having good team-mates around me, but I'd also had my best off-season before that 1995 season and played a lot of extra football, so I thought of myself as being really fit. I was young and the game wasn't nearly as quick as it is now, so I never really had to confront fatigue on the field. But when I played hooker in defence and had to pack into the scrums, I realised how much tougher the game was for the forwards. There were times when I couldn't get to the ruck; I physically couldn't run to get to dummy half. Right through 1995 I'd pushed the Knights forwards really hard, but it wasn't until those last two games in the World Cup, against the Kiwis and Poms, that I understood the fatigue factor and how you have to pace yourself in the forwards. It made me respect their role a lot more.

I also remember packing into scrums against New Zealand and their prop Quentin Pongia would call me 'boy' every bloody time. In one scrum he was just glaring at me and the look in his eyes was really ferocious. He had a heap of blood coming from a cut on his face and he was saying, 'I'm going to get you, boy.' I was terrified of Pongia; he used to scare the hell out of me. Early on I was worried that someone would head-butt me in the scrums but it only happened once — and it was an accident — when Hitro Okesene got me; I thought my head was going to split open.

I understood the hooking role better the following year when I played hooker for New South Wales in State of Origin. That was a step up in pace and intensity. A lot of people probably don't realise that I played hooker in the next two Origin series — in 1996, we had Laurie Daley back and he played centres with Brad Fittler and Geoff Toovey in the halves, so I felt lucky to have made the team at all; then in 1997, even with the Super League players out again, Freddy and Toovs were preferred in the halves and John Simon even played halfback one game. It would take me two or three days to physically get over a game when I played hooker; I was making 40–50 tackles, but then in attack I had to play first receiver and organise the play.

Yeah, 1995 and 1996 were very steep learning curves for me ... as much off the field as on it.

CHAPTER 7

GOING OFF THE RAILS

When I came back from the World Cup tour in early November 1995 I became a different person. Matthew said something like, 'You lost your innocence on that tour,' and maybe he was right. I became too big for my boots; I was getting around town like some sort of big shot. I was single, getting paid massive amounts of money compared to what I was on a year earlier; I was out on the town most nights of the week, taking girls home all the time and living a playboy's life.

I was getting a whole lot more attention, from the public and the media, as I took on a much higher profile and I had no idea how to handle it. The Knights players were heroes in town, with the unpopular Super League team Hunter Mariners having started up, and that only added to the public adulation. I was OK when it came to football — well, for the

ABOVE: Very early days with our pet cat, which I can't even remember. Looks like Matthew has had too much sugar. RIGHT: I was extremely close to Grandma Johns and used to stay with my grandparents at Kurri Kurr a lot during my teenage years. She loved rugby league — I wish she'd been alive to see me play my whole career.

BELOW: Matt and me at the local pool.

ABOVE: Grandma Bowden was like a second mother to us. She later lived with me in Newcastle in '95 and '96 ... some interesting times. That's my sister Kate, Matt and me with her when we were kids. BELOW: Matthew was always ahead of fashion trends. Looking at some of these photos, is it any wonder he never had a girlfriend until age 18?

RIGHT: With childhood
hero Sterlo at Cessnock
after a Parramatta
trial match.

BELOW LEFT: Where it all started, playing for the Knights'
under 15s in 1989. As you can see I didn't grow till my late teens.
BELOW RIGHT: Debut game at Gold Coast, looking a touch
bottom heavy.

ABOVE: MJ laughs as I dribble over the hotel floor — Origin debut year for both of us, 1995.

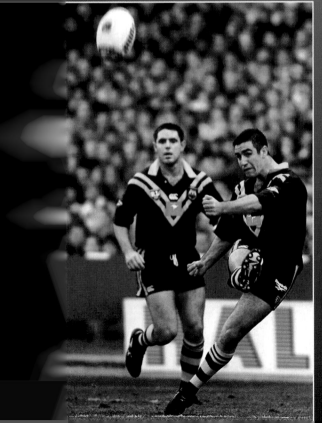

LEFT: Kicking a great goal at Wembley in the '95 World Cup final with that song 'Stuck In The Middle' in my head.

RIGHT: I always liked blending in but I don't suit being ginger (Brookvale Oval, 1996).

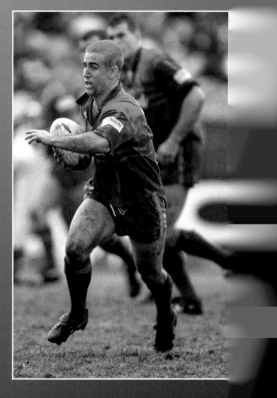

BELOW: Wearing the number nine jersey for the Blues in 1996 (with my Newcastle team-mate Adam Muir in support). Playing hooker made me appreciate how tough the workload is for forwards.

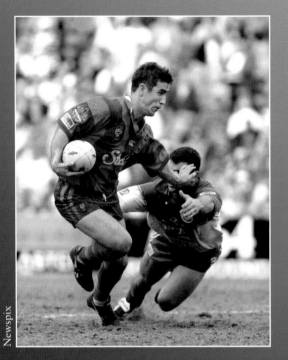

Newspix

LEFT: One of the biggest on-field punts of my career, and I'm so glad I came up a winner here. A left-hand fend on Danny Moore starts the blind-side run that set up Darren Albert's try in the last 10 seconds of the 1997 grand final against Manly.

Newspix

LEFT: A few seconds later the celebrations of the century began after Alby touched down

RIGHT: 'Get home, get some sleep and lose some weight!' The 1997 grand final celebrations.

RIGHT: My first Dally M Medal (and the Provan-Summons Medal), 1998: it's the best individual accolade a player can receive and I was lucky to have won two more. Unfortunately I don't know where they are (long story).

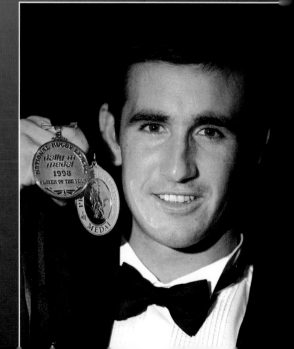

Newspix

ABOVE: Great photo. My and MJ's greatest supporter — our dad.

first half of the season anyway — but deep down, I'd become full of myself.

A few times Matty and I came to blows after training — that's how bad my behaviour became. Then came the widely publicised 'blue' between us late in the year. We had a Knights Christmas party to celebrate the end of training before the break, and I turned up hungover from the big night before and got on the grog all day again. I was walking along Darby Street with a few of the boys when I saw Matty, Adam Muir, Steve Crowe and their partners having dinner in a restaurant and I started shouting obscenities at Matthew through the window, telling him what an arsehole he was. I can't remember much because I was so drunk, but we went to a pub down the road and within minutes Matty came in absolutely fuming. The next thing he was punching the buggery out of me, which was much deserved. The boys put me in a taxi and sent me home; my shirt was covered in blood and half ripped off me as I slept off another kick in the arse. Typically, I was sheepish for a few days and put the tail between the legs. I realised I was wrong and we sorted it out.

The first round of the 1996 season was marred by the Super League clubs forfeiting after losing the court case to start their own competition that year; so we had a forfeit against Cronulla. The next week we beat the Western Reds in Perth, then lost our first match in round three against St George at Kogarah when Paul Harragon and I had a bit of a stand-up fight on the field. It was probably the first time anyone had snapped at Chief because he was so respected and such a 'give it everything' player; but that day I said things I shouldn't have and we blew up at each other in front of the team. He came off the bench early in the year and Matty was captain and this day we were just getting smashed when Chief started unloading on the team. He said to me, 'If you start having a go, we'd be better off,' and I said, 'We'd go a lot better if you had a go,' with a few expletives and other opinions thrown in. He eyeballed me back and I thought he was going to belt me. Chief grabbed me after the game and said, 'Don't show disrespect to me like that again,' and clipped me around the ear. I'd settled down and thought, 'Fair enough.'

A few days later I was rushed to hospital with acute appendicitis and had to get my appendix removed, so I missed the next two games. I took painkillers so I could be rushed back for the game against Wests, played Country Origin the week after and was picked as hooker for New South Wales a week after that.

With all the Super League players back we struck up a great combination in that Blues team and won the series 3–0. I felt I was a genuine rep player after that, but when I came back to club level it felt like a real letdown. After earlier winning six straight the Knights were really struggling and I was starting to feel really stale. We won only two games (plus a draw) in the last 10 rounds and crashed from equal second to miss the top eight.

That was when I started getting the real highs and lows in my moods; my head was all over the shop, I couldn't think rationally and I went right off the rails. My life really was a roller coaster and I was pretending there was nothing wrong with me, that I just needed a bit of space and to get away from all the pressure that had built on me. What I really needed, with hindsight on my side now, was some help, but I was inclined to turn people away and try to keep it all to myself.

I couldn't handle all the extra attention when I was out in town so I'd just get blind drunk, and got led into taking ecstasy for the first time, wrongly believing I was escaping to another world where I'd feel anonymous and people wouldn't be staring at me ... but, of course, it would just be making things 10 times worse. When I was a teenager some mates would smoke marijuana, which was pretty common in those days, but I'd never touch it, so this was a dramatic change in my behaviour and is an indicator of how unhappy I was.

That was the period I also dyed my hair red and played the worst game of my career against Manly at Brookvale Oval. I dead-set don't know what I was thinking, but that is a day in my career now which is unfortunately the most enduring testament to just how much my life had so quickly got itself out of order.

It was a disaster. I think my girlfriend Renae, who was doing a hairdressing course, talked me into dyeing my hair for a bit of a laugh and Matthew was going to do it too, but wimped out. Anyway, I couldn't give a shit about anything at that time, so away I went. It was the Thursday night when I had the hair dyed and we left Newcastle on the Friday afternoon to go to our Sydney base, the Rydges hotel at North Sydney, the night before a game as usual. My team-mates must have thought, 'What the hell is going on?' and I wouldn't have inspired them too much that I had my head right for a game against the competition favourites, in which we were also chasing the club's first-ever win at Brookvale. When I woke up Saturday morning (we played that afternoon) I must have realised how stupid I'd been, and I was frantically walking around North Sydney trying to find a hairdresser that could get the colour out, but I couldn't find any. I shaved my hair thinking that would get rid of the colour, but that didn't help either.

We were terrible at Brookie, behind 20–0 at half-time and were dropping the ball and missing so many tackles; and I was our worst player. Nothing was said by anyone in the team but they didn't have to — their stares were enough. When I got back to Newcastle that night I had my hair changed back to its normal colour. Before the game Malcolm Reilly knew something was not right with me and asked if I was OK, but I just shook him off. I think the red hair was the last straw. Malcolm was so frustrated with my behaviour he went to my dad and said he didn't know what to do with me.

Looking back now, that red-hair episode was like a cry for help. I knew I was out of control but couldn't stop myself. That period was probably the first time in our lives Matthew didn't know what to say or do to help me. He just shook his head as I started to behave more erratically. I wasn't talking to my team-mates, I wasn't talking to Malcolm. I'd blow up at training for no reason and even try to sabotage the sessions at times by throwing loose passes on purpose: I was just a total prick.

I know at the time that I was really depressed; I don't know if that was because I was coming down off the binging on alcohol (and sometimes drugs), but I wasn't worth anything to anyone and that showed in the way I was playing. I was just totally sick of football, and bored after coming down from such an incredible ride in 1995. I was binging on alcohol, drugs, food — anything; I was so up and down and my weight would balloon, then plummet, as I ate excessively then starved myself.

Peter Sharp was coaching reserve grade and he grabbed me a few times and said, 'Mate, we are hearing all these bad things about you off the field — what the hell is going on?' but I couldn't connect even with Sharpy. A few people in the game in Sydney even grabbed me and said, 'We're hearing stories about you when you're out.' We were in the middle of the Super League war and if stories got out about one of the ARL's internationals playing up, it would have been a nightmare for the game. But I had no concept of that, or anything really, other than the need to somehow escape all the attention and pressure my increased profile as a footballer had created.

Malcolm tried to set up meetings at my house to get to the root of the problem but I wouldn't answer the door; or we'd be supposed to meet at the club's offices and I wouldn't turn up. I was just doing irrational things — I'd go missing for three or four days and he'd track me down.

If I had to go to a function I'd sit in the corner, paranoid that people would be talking about me and I'd be thinking, 'Did I see that person last week when I was out or am I dreaming that?' It was an awful time. What should have been the greatest time of my life — earning good money being a full-time footballer, playing for NSW and Australia — was, in fact, one of the lowest, in terms of how I was living my life and the effect it was having on me.

That's the period, in 1996–97, when club medical officer Neil Halpin grabbed me a few times and tried to talk to me. He'd say things like, 'I don't think you are well within yourself … I'm hearing stories … you are looking through people … you've lost the colour in your eyes … you're not yourself, is something wrong?' I'd just tell him to 'fuck off and mind your own business'. That was also the time when all the paranoia in my mind started; I began to get paranoid about what people knew about what I was doing, terrified the newspapers would find out what I was up to the night before a game. It was an awful time in my life, brought on by myself.

The Knights had to beat Cronulla away in the last round to make the finals. We were smashed 22–0 and our season was abruptly ended. Then I went crazy off the field for a while and couldn't care about anything in my life. Someone borrowed my car, a V8 ute provided by a club sponsor, Kelly Holden, and wrote it off when it hit a parked car 100 metres from my house. It just sat there for a week all banged up — I couldn't be bothered doing anything about it.

I was burnt out from playing a lot of high-intensity football, I was carrying a big head and it just all got to me. I don't think Malcolm Reilly knew how to handle it; Mum and Dad didn't know what to do — they were just a bit stand-offish; Matt tried to get through to me but couldn't; Paul Harragon sort of tried to talk to me a bit. I just pushed everyone away.

Finally, one of my mates, local surf photographer Peter 'Bosko' Boscovich, said to me, 'Mate, you've got to get away,' so he grabbed me and I went away to the Philippines surfing for a couple of weeks while the finals were being played. It was there that I cleared my head and realised I'd been carrying on like an absolute dick and that I'd let everyone down and had to pull my head in. Bosko told me some home truths while we were away. I also looked around me and I realised how little the Filipino people had, yet how happy they were, and realised how fortunate I was.

Not long after I got back, I was picked in the Australian team and had to go to Port Moresby for a Test against Papua New Guinea a week after the 1996 grand final. Malcolm was absolutely fed up with me by this stage and shocked me by turning up at Sydney Airport when I was there to link up with the Kangaroos. He just gave it to me with both barrels, told me what he thought of me and what everyone else thought of me; how I was ruining my life. He had me in tears. It was another big wake-up call. I realised just how shocked I and everyone else was about my behaviour and how poorly everyone thought of me.

I hardly ever left my room in Port Moresby and I started to reflect even more on how bad I had been; I was so ashamed of it. Mind you, no one went out of their rooms much in Port Moresby — the place is anarchy. I was having a sleep in·my room one day and woke up and one of the two security guards assigned to our floor was lying beside me with his pump action shotgun between us. He was eating all the stuff in my mini-bar and flicking the remote control trying to get the movies on the TV.

When I got back from PNG Renae moved in with me, which really helped, and she became a steadying influence for a while. By the time the 1997 pre-season came around I had woken up to myself a fair bit and just ripped into training. I was so keen to make amends.

Then I tore my ankle ligaments in the last trial match which meant I'd miss the first 15 rounds of the season and see my life spiral downwards again.

CHAPTER 8

THE BLACK DOG

This is the hardest chapter of the book to write — about my battle with manic depression. The stigma of having a mental imbalance is terrible and I used to feel ashamed of it. I have just never felt at ease with people knowing about it, but those close to me, especially Cathrine, have encouraged me to come clean on it. I am becoming more comfortable about it now, I admit, and doing this book has helped. But talking into a tape recorder and coming clean with my confessions is one thing; being splashed all over the newspapers and the news bulletins after this book is released will be a different thing altogether. But I know I have to live with that.

It helps that so many people, and quite a few famous people, are admitting to suffering from manic depression. In my case I was worried people would say, 'What's he got to be depressed about? He's wealthy, he's a hero — how can he be

97

feeling sorry for himself?' That's fair enough. I don't feel sorry for myself. I feel more sorry, if anything, for the effect my condition has had on others; the harm I may have caused them through my erratic behaviour over the years. I accept the harm I have caused myself and can only learn from that. I can't erase the past but I look at the future far more positively than I did a few years ago.

I've lived on a razor's edge and I'm lucky I've had rugby league to focus on and obsess with. I sometimes feel lucky to still be alive, so many times have I put myself in a position where I could have done real harm to myself, either when I was drunk on a manic high or when I ever got to the stage that I was on such a downer I couldn't cope any more.

Did I ever consider suicide? Yes, occasionally. More so in my teenage years from when I was 13 or 14; but also at times in recent years, when I got really down and bunkered myself inside my house. But there was something inside me that would say, 'Stop, you can't do that to your family, it's a weak way out to torture your whole family and friends.' To think that 15 per cent of people who suffer bipolar disorder take their own lives is pretty frightening.

A bipolar disorder often manifests itself in early to mid teens. And that was the case with me. It must have been terrible for Mum and Dad, they would have been thinking, 'What is wrong with this boy of ours?' I have never opened up to them about it, even after I finally sought help and learned to understand it better. I have tried to hide it from virtually everyone. My family now understand more about my depression — from what Dr Neil Halpin has told them and talks they've had with Cathrine — but we had never discussed it directly until recently, because they knew how sensitive I was about it; until I came out with the public confession. It was the same with Matthew. He knew about my condition and would sometimes say, 'You travelling alright — you OK?' but we would talk around it more than get to the heart of it. He's said he's felt guilty about not delving more into how I felt, but he shouldn't. I was good at acting and pretending it wasn't so bad, and I was happy to shut him out and keep it to myself; I regret just as much that I didn't open up to him. That is why these pages are like therapy for me, and an ice-breaker for those I love and those I have come across in my career who have been trying to put together the complex puzzle of Joey Johns. But I could only do it in this form; without having to look them in the eye and try to explain it face to face.

For those who don't understand what a bipolar disorder is, www.blackdoginstitute.org.au, run by Black Dog Institute in Sydney, will give you an insight. 'Black dog' is a term sometimes used to describe clinical depression and is a term associated with Winston Churchill, the British prime minister who suffered badly from a bipolar disorder. Later in the book, Neil Halpin contributes his views on how he has seen it affect my life.

But first I'd better give a layman's description of the condition: basically, it is a chemical imbalance in the brain which causes extreme moods which can last for days. The high, called 'mania', is where in my case I have extraordinary energy, a feeling of being invincible and have no sense of consequence and have impaired judgement. Then there is the low mood — depression — where you feel so miserable, worthless, unmotivated and irritable for no apparent reason and worry about every little thing.

I was in denial for years that something physiologically was wrong with me and I just shut out people who dared to tell me something was psychologically astray. When you are brought up in a town like Cessnock, you can't admit to weakness.

That was until I felt my life was on such a dangerous downhill spiral after my split from my wife Renae in 2002; and I let Neil in. He has given amazing support and I am so blessed he stuck with me. I have been taking medication for it since late 2003, but only in the last year or so have I learned to — and been prepared to — work hard enough to control the condition. Before that I was happy to ride with the euphoric highs, despite consistently dodging so many bullets that could have exposed my wayward lifestyle and created the controversial headlines. I have grown up and now fight hard not to put myself in that position — but I know I'm not going to be strong enough to fight the urge every single time.

The mania is like a coil unwinding in my stomach and it is very, very difficult to stop. I can get an uncontrollable boost of energy and hyperactivity; it might happen going into a football game and I would feel absolutely indestructible, be on an unbelievable high in confidence and go out and play the best game of my life. After the game I would feel so exhilarated and energised I didn't want to stop. I'd drink with the boys and the alcohol would just amplify the phase — or 'episode' as it is medically termed — into a sort of frenzy. As too many people in Newcastle can testify, I go crazy. I get so fuelled with adrenalin, I can go on a three-day bender without sleep. It's honestly like one of those Eveready battery adverts on TV — while others konk out I'm still going strong and couldn't care about anything in the world other than having a real big time.

I would be uncontrollable when I was manic, on one of those real agitated highs. I'd take my clothes off, get up on the bar and go mental; I would just do completely irrational things. I would be the drunkest person in the place, and I am a terrible drunk. If there were drugs available, I'd take them. I got myself in situations where I could have been hit over the head with a bottle in pubs because I was obnoxious and out of control. I've woken up in gardens and other obscure places and not known how I got there.

My mates used to baby-sit me; taking shifts so someone would be with me and look after me when I'd 'go', when a monster was unleashed. Probably 50 per cent of Newcastle knew what I could get like when I was out and about, but I was in a state where I didn't know what I was doing. Bouncers around Newcastle would bundle me into a cab and say, 'Go home, Joey.' It's a very vulnerable, stupid place to be.

I would go for a couple of days, then crash hard into the dark side of the condition; for the next two or three days I wouldn't talk to people and I'd have such a sinister outlook on life. I would bury myself in my house in the darkest mood, paranoid about what was outside; worried to the stage I was physically ill about what I might have done the two nights before and whether it was going to be in the newspapers. I'd pace up and down the house, thinking people were outside looking at me; everyone I passed in the street was talking about me; the boys at training were whispering behind my back. It was a crazy, uncontrollable cycle.

The phone would scare the shit out of me and I wouldn't answer it. I'd freak out to the point of nearly having a panic attack. I'd look at the number and see it was my manager John Fordham and I'd hold my breath, thinking, 'What's up, what's happened?' and go 'whoa' and breathe a sigh of relief if all was OK. I could be at someone else's place and the phone would ring and I'd tense up, thinking, 'What have I done?' Or I'd be driving and I'd see a police car and watch it, thinking they were going to follow me. It was dead-set paranoia.

I'd start having panic attacks and think, 'Where have I been for the past two days?' if I didn't know. I would think real hard about it to the extent that I couldn't distinguish whether what I remembered was real or whether I'd dreamt it. And it always seemed to be about people I went to school with, for some reason. I'd think, 'I must have dreamt I was with people from school when I was out of control, or was I actually out with them last night?' It got to the stage I'd be vomiting, I was so worried.

The Sunday papers worried the hell out of me. I'd wake up with a knot in my stomach, then I'd have to go down to the newsagent and get a paper. As soon as I got in the car I'd read the gossip columns and say to myself, 'You've dodged a bullet again.' If the drug testers came to training and didn't pick me, I'd say, 'You've dodged another bullet.' Living a lie like that is no good for your self-esteem.

The Knights must have received emails or phone calls on so many Mondays about what I'd done. Then again, they'd get reports on these unbelievable things I never did do, like being rushed to hospital with syringes hanging out of my arms. They've dealt with things over the years and swept them under the carpet because of who I was as a footballer, which makes my behaviour even more intolerable, because if I was a fringe player I would have been sacked years ago.

I'd get fined endlessly by the club and they'd generally get Neil Halpin to talk to me; I'd promise I'd behave myself and there wouldn't be another incident for a while. But it would never last. In the end, it all came down to alcohol. I don't know what comes first — the hyped-up mania that triggers the need for alcohol, or the other way around — but all the trouble I have been in is alcohol related. If I am honest, I didn't want enough to control myself.

At its worst, this was the pattern of my life almost weekly. Yep, it is unbelievable to think about it. People would see me killing 'em on the field and have no idea what my life was really like. I used to be off the planet every weekend after a game; it was a crazy cycle.

I was so lucky not to have done something crazy that made front page news. The media and the people of Newcastle have really looked after me. Then again, had there been a Ben Cousins affair or something like that, maybe it would have been the spark for me to do something about myself. I'm very lucky that the Newcastle public have overlooked my terrible behaviour and been so tolerant. If I wasn't their favourite footballer I'm sure I would have been bashed — figuratively in the media and literally — meaning physically by someone who just couldn't take any more of my shocking behaviour.

I hid the depression from so many people. I kept everything in for so long as I struggled with so many things in my life. I just wouldn't trust people; I was wary of strangers. I would struggle in a group when I was younger anyway, so when all this fame came and I was the centre of so much attention and conversation, I wouldn't know how to talk to people. People would take it as arrogance or ignorance, not knowing what I was going through. I am basically a very shy person; well, Andrew Johns is, but when people see a hyped-up, out-for-fun Joey Johns, they'd think I was the opposite.

I read this quote recently, something like, 'If you say you're shy, why stand in the light?' That is what I was doing. I'd say that I didn't want all the fame and attention, but then I'd click and go on this manic phase and be the centre of attention everywhere, contradicting myself all the time.

My team-mates got used to my highs and lows; in fact, they would make fun of it, obviously not knowing that I suffered a serious medical condition. Football adds to the mania; I could sense that feeling going into a game. I just had so much confidence, I felt super-human. People who suffer from the condition say that it's a feeling like 'nothing is going to stop me tonight'.

The boys at the Knights would have names for it; they'd say things like, 'Look at the cyclone brewing over there,' or 'The cyclone is out tonight, uh-oh, there's going to be trouble.' Matt Parsons nicknamed me 'Cyclone' or 'Cyces'. But when I was down they'd say, 'Look at the low pressure system circling around A. Johns, and have a joke. I'd say, 'Good one, piss off,' and go out of the dressing room and they'd know to leave me alone until kickoff. I would just stare into space, not talk to anyone or look at anyone, then go out and sometimes even try to hurt myself by coming out of the line and trying to smash blokes. There was just a reckless abandon and no fear. Some of my best performances came when I turned up feeling absolutely dirty on the world and really brooding before the game. Things triggered it for no apparent reason. I could wake up feeling down. I'd always play the same music when I was down, real depressing music like Everlast, and I'd listen to it before a match. When I was up I'd have the up-tempo music blaring.

I confided in Michael Hagan that I was bipolar when he was coaching at Newcastle, and he was just an unbelievable support. 'Hages' copped plenty of flak for the leeway he gave me, allowing me to take off for a few days at a time during the season, but he knew I needed it and that it would be best for the team. I'm sure, though, that plenty of senior players would have been filthy that I was getting preferential treatment and seemed above the team.

There were times when Hages used to say to me, 'Go away, I want you to go surfing for two days and come back with your head right,' which would be magic. I'd go up to Forster with Renae when we were together, or with Matt Hoy, and just spend hours in the surf, and I'd come back a different person. Hages could see the signs: I'd be at training and someone would drop a ball and I'd bite his head off, or on the field in a game I'd fly into the boys. It's something I think I toned down towards the end; there were earlier times when I'd fly into blokes with the slightest provocation. It was not a good look and I know the other players didn't appreciate it.

On tour with the Australian team, my aggressive highs and reclusive lows were terrible. I remember one time Chris Anderson sat me down for a coffee and talked me through it, just saying, 'Mate, you have to curtail it.' But the boys would really look after me on tour. There were always Newcastle blokes there — Ben Kennedy, in particular, would know how to help me. A lot of blokes go loopy on tour; you get really homesick and go crazy sometimes.

During the 2000 World Cup tour, I was at my manic worst, just out of control. But others were struggling too — it was a long tour. I remember BK was extremely homesick, so down and missing home and his family. It can be hard to be away for so long, and for me that tour was really tough, because this was just after Samuel was born.

It has recently come out about Gorden Tallis' concerns about the behaviour of some players on that tour — especially mine — and that he approached the Australian Rugby League authorities about it. I confess to having a few big nights on the booze and taking ecstasy some nights, but never leading up to a match and never when it could have affected how I played. I found out 'Gordie' wasn't happy about it, although he said nothing directly to me during the tour, and reported it to the ARL after we got home. At the time I was dirty as hell, but I look back now with a wiser head, as a more mature person — not as self-centred and selfish as I was then — and I realise he was only trying to help me, as well as protect the game, which was a pretty brave stand. I let him down.

One of the Australian physios in 2005, Tony Ayoub, took me aside when I came back from Warrington for the Tri Nations games against New Zealand when he was treating my crook knee. He must have guessed I was bipolar. He said, 'You're just so high and low.' I screamed, 'I'm right, I'm good,' then four hours later I came in and said, 'I'm fucked, I'll never play again.' Tony said, 'See, you're up and down all the time. Are you OK?'

It's a little strange how people in the media would have seen my highs and lows and heard about my incredibly erratic behaviour, but no one ever really put the hard question to me and hit the nail on the head about my depression. No one would ever ask too deeply about my personality or anything but football. I remember Channel Nine's Tim Sheridan asking me once whether I got depressed. My whole body felt like a lightning bolt had hit it. I was thinking, 'Shit, how much does he know?' Then Roy Masters did an excellent article in the *Sydney Morning Herald* in March 2005 and it was the closest anyone has got to publicly describing how I really am. He had obviously spoken to someone and knew I was bipolar. Roy wrote: 'Andrew Johns ... shares a capacity to brood, to endure dark days, to experience what Churchill called "the black dog".'

I was probably at my craziest with my lifestyle in the late 1990s, from about 1996 to 1999. I settled down for a while after Renae and I got serious and when she became pregnant with Samuel and we got married. I look back on articles now where I said I'd grown up and tamed my wild ways — but I was kidding myself.

I carry a lot of guilt; the biggest regret being how I ruined our marriage. Renae deserved more than I gave her but I can never put that right, and that hurts. Mother Teresa couldn't have lived with the Joey Johns of then. To think I almost sent Renae around the bend with my erratic, crazy behaviour and almost lost contact with my son. The big wake-up call was when Renae left — that hit hard. We were together five years, were married for 18 months and had a son, and it was purely my fault that the relationship ended. We get on well now, which is great.

When Renae walked away in August 2002, unable to cope with my moods and crazy lifestyle, I was the Newcastle and New South Wales captain and had just captained Australia for the first time in the record 64–10 victory over Great Britain. But off the field, my life was a mess. I was just hitting the drink and sometimes 'other stuff' that hard; that was why Renae left in the first place.

I'd like to mention that during that time, when my life was in dire straits, a wonderful lady named Helen O'Donoghue came into my life. I didn't know how to pay the bills, or look after what other people find daily organisational things, when Matt Hoy's step-father recommended Helen to help me. She paid my bills, cleaned the house, cooked meals and sometimes sat me down and gave me a lecture if I'd been misbehaving. She is a single mother with two young daughters, Ruby and Lucy, and over time we've become great friends. I can't thank her enough for the guidance and help she gave me then, and did until 2005 when Cathrine came up to live with me.

Eventually I started to realise that I had to stop being so selfish and sort myself out, because I could see I could end up dead — I could really see myself going down that road. I was at a stage where I knew something drastic might happen; that I might put myself into a situation where I was going to fall off a building or get run over, or my downs might get so drastic that it would be too much for me and I might think about taking my life.

By this stage I was a major burden on Neil Halpin; I owe him so much for helping me get through it. There were times I'd be 'wigging out' at four or five in the morning; I'd scream down the phone and he'd talk me down, saying, 'Is Renae there?' or in later years, 'Is Cathrine there — how is she dealing with it?' and often he'd come straight round. Or I might be screaming and 'going off' unnecessarily and Hages would ring him; or I'd just be in a really bad low or off my tree and it would get back to him and he'd call in and say, 'Mate, this can be managed. You shouldn't live your life like this.'

He'd come to my home and I'd be pacing the house for hours, thinking people were staring at me through the windows. He'd give me something to settle me down and talk me around. I'd start to make sense and be OK — until next time. He'd just happen to call in to my place every few days just to monitor how I was feeling. He has been a great friend to me, Neil.

Sleeping-wise I'd have one night on, and one night off. If I wasn't active during the day I knew I wasn't going to sleep that night, and I'd get into a state where it was two o'clock and I'd be looking at the clock. I could also go three days on a bender and not sleep, then just crash and sleep for a day and a half.   •

In September 2002 I met Cathrine Mahoney when she had to do the PR for the DVD that Sony released on my career, called *Joey Johns: The Story So Far*. Straight away I was attracted to her spirit and honest personality; I felt so comfortable around her. I'd always struggled to talk with people and keep eye contact, but I had no trouble with that with Cathrine. After we started a relationship months later Cathrine helped me to confront my manic depression, and I'm glad I met her when I was older, 28, and a bit wiser. I just felt as though I was coming out of the haze and could become a person I could like.

Finally the penny had dropped. It had got to the stage where I didn't want to live my life that way any more. I knew I needed expert help. Neil put me in contact with experts and bit by bit I started to understand my condition.

Neil referred me to a few specialists in Newcastle, then to Professor Gordon Parker, executive director of Black Dog Institute in Sydney, who was a great help. He put in place what they call a 'get well plan', which consists of putting energy into positive things and making them your routine — for me it is reading, walking and surfing — rather than the destructive things. I take medication for the chemical imbalance, which keeps me on an even keel. Originally I was scared to take it because I thought I played great when I was up, and generally I enjoyed being high and lived with being low. But the medication keeps me on a moderate level; it cuts out the jaggedness. I'm not the life of the party or lying in bed for two days not wanting to get out. Neil even thought placating my highs would affect my football because my energy levels might have gone down, but it actually improved my performances.

For a while they tried me on Ritalin to stop hyperactivity, but I would be like a zombie: I'd train then come home and just veg out on the lounge and watch television. I didn't want to live my life like that. I enjoy having so much energy, being up at 6am and surfing, then going to training, surfing again, and at eight o'clock winding down.

Professor Parker wanted me to find a mentor who I could work with, and mentioned John Konrads, the former Olympic swimmer, who is bipolar. I did ring him once and left a message, and Professor Parker spoke to him about me, but I never followed through — although I hope to one day. That's something I should do.

I don't know if it is my upbringing in Cessnock, a man's sort of thing where you don't reveal something is wrong with you — you don't show you need help, you have to look strong. But, as the experts have said to me, if people have asthma they need a puffer, or if they have diabetes they need insulin; people with manic depression need treatment too.

I've learned how to manage my life and control myself, although I have to face the fact there might still be times when I might lose the plot in the future, but it won't be very often. I understand myself more now. I've grown up a lot, had such different life experiences, settled down, and I'm more comfortable with the person I am. I look back at the young

Andrew Johns as a different person now that I'm not as erratic and not drinking as much. I'm not 'coming down' all the time and being short with people; I can get away and relax a lot easier and I consciously try to manage my moods when I feel the spring uncoiling inside me. Surfing is a massive outlet for me, and when Cathrine can see I'm starting to feel manic, she says go surfing and I might be out there for half an hour or two or three hours, and when I come in I'm right.

Reading is also a great relaxant for me; or sometimes, when I can feel the triggers coming on, I will put on my iPod, put my head down and walk for an hour and a half. I've only been able to do that from about late in 2006. Before that, I didn't want to control the highs — I used to love getting out of control.

I'd really learned how to overcome that urge, and that's why I'm so disappointed with the London episode. I had been coming to grips with my condition so well, but being out of routine while I was away and eventually being without medication was enough for me to lose control. It is such a big regret.

Cathrine has been the best thing for me in coming to grips with who I am, and how I have to manage my life. She left a wonderful job at Sony and some wonderful friends to move in with me at Newcastle in 2004. It was just great, and I really became a better person with her being around. But I spun out of control in 2006 and almost lost her too.

We were first engaged in 2006 after we went to Lord Howe Island for a brief holiday in June. Then in September I pretty much went missing for a month as soon as the season finished. I was always out on the town and uncontrollable again; I became a different person, cold and insensitive to others. My 'turns' had become less frequent in the previous year or two and I still don't know what set me off.

Cath found it very hard to deal with and had to walk away. She told me to get my head together and sort myself out or she wouldn't be there. She went back to Sydney, then headed off overseas to clear her head; she didn't need my erratic existence in her life any more. She said she'd always love me if I sorted myself out, but I had to do it not just for five minutes but for good.

That was the real turning point in my life; I realised what I'd lost, and then I had half the people in town — and her friends I'd got to know — telling me how much I was going to regret losing her (not that I needed telling).

We had a few months apart, even though we spoke on the phone regularly, and finally we started seeing each other again when Cath saw that I was genuine in sorting my life out. We got engaged again in late March 2007 and we're rock solid. I don't want to contemplate life without her but I know that whatever future we have is up to me.

I'll still have a beer now and then and I'll never be a choirboy — I just have to control myself. When my life is good, I am so clear headed, I am happy with the person I am. I've learned to like Andrew Johns — today's version — after hating myself for so long. I hated the way I was living and I hated how I was up on this pedestal that I felt I didn't deserve, because I knew the sort of person I really was.

I am ready for the challenge of living with being bipolar for the rest of my life. My biggest challenge is facing life without the structure that comes with training and playing on a weekly basis, having to work hard on fitness and my game and the discipline of being in team sport. Cath's concern is what I'll be like without football and all the activity I've previously had to fill my days with. But I am not near as worried as she is; I'm enjoying life after footy, and the absence of weekly football games I had to get myself up for to help me stay in the 'moderate zone'.

I am quite structured now. I have to keep myself busy, otherwise I get distracted. If I don't fill my days up with constructive stuff I feel myself creeping towards the dark side. I have to do it because, one, I want to do it; and two, I want Samuel, Cathrine and my family to be proud of me and we want to start a family too. How could I bring another child into the world if I was an unpredictable mess?

I just hope others who suffer from depression can read this and say, 'Hey, that's me too … I can do something about this if Andrew Johns has.' If it helps a couple of kids who are bouncing off walls, then it will have been worthwhile. If it leads to a few people wanting to take the piss out of me, well that's their problem.

I used to think I was the only one who suffered from depression and thought it was such a negative. In the last couple of years I've accepted it and understand that my mind ticks differently to others, but I have this endless energy and creativity that I can funnel into something positive.

A lot of creative people, artists and musicians, very successful and high-profile people, suffer from bipolar disorder. I don't want to become an active advocate about the disease and go out lecturing on it; that's not me. But by telling my story here, as hard as it is, that's enough to show that anyone in this world is fallible, no matter how strong or talented you think they are.

CHAPTER 9

A PART OF HISTORY

I am honoured that I am remembered for creating the try for Darren Albert that won the Newcastle Knights the 1997 Australian Rugby League grand final. But what is not nearly as well known is that I was looking at playing reserve grade that year after completely wrecking my ankle in a pre-season trial.

After an ordinary performance on the field in 1996, and going off the rails off the field, I was so determined to start the '97 season flying. But that dream soon ended in Coffs Harbour in a pre-season match against Manly when I tore the ligaments in my right ankle and had to have an ankle reconstruction. I missed the first 10 rounds of the competition and my replacement, Leo Dynevor, played out of his skin and was a major reason why we were in a position to win our first premiership.

There was talk around town I was going to play reserve grade when I returned, which really drove me hard in getting myself fit; I busted my gut on the weights in the gym and I'd swim for hours on hours.

I didn't feel part of the team until more than halfway through the season and it was an incredibly lonely time; I felt isolated from the team for the first time. When you're not part of the main training group — in the gym while others are training on the field — they can organise to have lunch, or do something at the last minute after training finishes, and you don't get invited and you can feel really left out. When the team is celebrating victories, you feel like a hanger-on. And to make matters worse for me, even team-mates were saying I would have to come back in reserve grade because Leo Dynevor couldn't legitimately be dropped.

I was actually supposed to come back in round 10 against South Sydney but the rain was so relentless in Newcastle the game had to be called off, which was a rarity. As it turned out, it was a real blessing for me. We trained at Townson Oval on the Tuesday night before the match with the South Newcastle club, part of a scheme where we'd train with a local team once a month. The ground was as hard as concrete and because I hadn't run that much, after doing the full session my calves seized up from the hard ground and I would have pulled out of the game or, if I'd been too stubborn and played, probably would have done further damage.

The extra week would have helped the ankle and I came back off the bench against Balmain with Leo, who also kicked goals, staying at halfback. Matty came back too after tearing a quadricep muscle. Somehow I was picked for New South Wales for the first State of Origin clash 11 days later with just that one game under my belt. In the Origin game I was tackled and, in a very similar circumstance to how I did the ankle injury at Coffs Harbour, my foot became stuck in the ground, I twisted it, there was an almighty crack, and I thought I'd done my ankle again and my season was over. Fortunately, I'd only torn all the scar tissue sitting over the top of my foot, so it wasn't too bad. In essence I'd saved myself three months of physiotherapy but I couldn't goal-kick with it. I'd lost my touch — the feeling in the foot was virtually gone — and I was kicking really badly. I missed the second Origin game and the next couple of club matches but was picked for Origin III, although I couldn't back up for the club match the following weekend. Then I was chosen for Australia's game against The Rest Of The World, so at that stage I'd played more representative games (two Origin and a Test) than club games (one). Leo Dynevor had been outstanding for the Knights in just about every game he played.

I finally got back to club football in the postponed match against Souths in the rain in Newcastle, again off the bench. What stands out most about that day is that I got into the clear and was run down by Rabbitohs front-rower Matt Parsons, which is the ultimate disgrace for a halfback; made worse by the fact 'Parso' never let me forget it when he later joined the Knights.

By the time we made it to the finals in second position, I hadn't contributed a great deal and had played only nine of the 22 games. But we had such a great side with some brilliant emerging talent, we were just getting better the closer we got to the finals.

Owen Craigie had a phenomenal season. He was only 18 then, but he really thrived under the freedom Malcolm Reilly gave us on the field. 'Owie' played every game and did some freakish things with the ball. I rate him as the best naturally talented player I played with: he'd chip kick off his left foot and regather it on the full; he'd throw balls over his head and find his mark, and he had strength and a fair bit of pace. He was earmarked to be a superstar but he always had problems with his weight and attitude to training. He achieved a lot of things in the game but knows he should have achieved a lot more.

The pace and class we had out wide was incredible in '97 in Darren Albert, Matthew Gidley, Owen Craigie, Adam MacDougall, Robbie O'Davis, Brett Grogan, Mark Hughes and Jason Moodie. Every one of them, except Craigie and Grogan, went on to play State of Origin, yet we could only fit five of the eight in the side when they were all fit.

'Doogs' (MacDougall) came to Newcastle that year and we had no idea what was about to hit us; what a strange kettle of fish he was. Doogs was before his time — to him the game was all about size and power; he wanted to get as big as he could and was playing at 102 kilograms. All he used to eat was protein. We went away on a pre-season camp and he used to get these bladders of egg whites and would suck them on a tube; he'd eat upwards of 200 egg whites a week just for the protein, so he could build muscle. During our annual pre-season camp in Coffs Harbour, Doogs roomed with Evan Cochrane. Evan was dry in the mouth one night after having a few beers, so he looked in the fridge and saw this bladder, thought it was water and proceeded to skol it ... then realised it was raw egg whites!

Most of the stories you may have heard about Doogs were probably true; he was fanatical. He'd go to the movies, pull two steaks out of his pockets and start gnawing on them (you know those tales are true, Doogy, ol' mate). But it made him an absolute power player, who when he was one-on-one with a defender would beat him every time. And he was ahead of his time with the way he trained: we'd be doing endurance stuff and he'd be shaking his head refusing to do it; he'd train purely for speed and power, which is the way it is done today.

We'd all turn up for the last training session of the week and everyone would be excited and throwing the ball around; Doogs would turn up with a full tracksuit zipped all the way up with joggers on instead of boots, and wouldn't get out of a walk. We'd be passing the ball and he'd say, 'No, I'm saving myself for tomorrow.' I'd kick to the corner in training and he'd refuse to chase it: 'Tomorrow is my game, I'm not playing it today.'

And he loved taking on Wendell Sailor. We used to wind him up when we were playing the Broncos. One night we were in Brisbane telling him how the word had got through how Wendell was on a one-man mission to smash him and Doogs quipped: 'I'll tell you what, tomorrow I'm going to hit him so hard I'm going to turn him white.'

The real story about him talking to his legs? It happened in the mud in Tamworth during the pre-season. Doogie kept putting his hand up to come off and Malcolm Reilly had had enough and benched him. After he came off, Doogs was saying to his legs, 'I've put two months into you legs and you are going to let me down.' At that stage he was 'different' but he's settled down now, is married to Belinda and is now back on everyone else's level — well, almost.

1997 was without doubt Robbie O'Davis' best year for the Knights — he was just bubbling in the big games with his agility and speed. He was our player of the year, won the Clive Churchill Medal (best player in the grand final) and was outstanding for Queensland in State of Origin. He was so fit and had such good instincts he became brilliant at supporting Matty and me or an offload from the forwards.

Adam Muir was also outstanding in '97. 'Hurtsy' had played Jersey Flegg with Matthew and they developed a great combination, with Adam his 'go to' man when he wanted to ball-play. Hurtsy had great agility for a big man; he could change his lines quickly and had such big hands to catch the ball with, so every time we created good go-forward and got some quick play the balls, Matty would throw the ball across the ruck or drop off to Adam inside and the timing would be just perfect: he was almost unstoppable. Hurtsy had signed a massive contract with Norths before the season even started, I think, and he had second thoughts at times, but it was too big an offer to turn his back on.

Malcolm Reilly was great at the mental side of the game and made us tough enough and fit enough to win that competition. But we really only had two or three plays and hardly any set moves; we just used to get out there and play.

Looking back now we played incredibly laterally, sideline to sideline, which meant the centres and wingers saw plenty of ball. Albert and Craigie were on fire, Matt Gidley started to make an impression and Adam MacDougall was a real handful for the defence. We played to our strengths.

We had a move called 'M, shot, shot', where we'd go to the middle and have a shot on one side, and then just whiz the ball back the other side; opposing teams knew we were doing it but we'd get the ball there so quickly it was so hard to stop. No one attacks like that now, which is a pity. I know if I was on the edge of the ruck defending and teams went *bang bang* and shifted the ball like that it would scare the hell out of me. But to our detriment, if we played that way we could win by 40 or be beaten by 20 if we overplayed our hand.

Paul Harragon was an inspiration that year. His body was worn out from the physical barrage he'd given it and his chronic knee injuries really made him struggle at times, but the amount of hard training he did and the way he threw his body into the games was just awesome. He was also a great leader and he kept everyone tight; and in his biggest hour, the grand final, he led from the front.

In round 16 against Parramatta, I wore the number seven jersey for the first time that season, and Leo went to the bench. I remember the 28–22 loss for two reasons: one, because all Parramatta did was run from dummy half and choke us to death, leading former Test prop Steve Roach — who was then commentating for 2UE — to come into the sheds after the game and say to me, 'You might have lost the game but at least you were playing football out there.'

The second memory is that the pass I gave Mark Hughes is what I regard as the best pass of my career. I still get chills when I think about that pass. I had Adam Muir as a bonus runner just behind me and I called him to come off my hip, so as I was going to the line I had the ball shaped like I was going to play short to Adam. Then at the last moment I looked up and I could see the centre was rushing in to tackle Adam, so without looking I just went *whoosh* with the ball. At the time I thought it was only like a five-metre pass, but on the replay I realised it was a 20-metre pass — left to right — yet it was so flat, and all Boozy had to do was run five metres over the line and score, without a hand coming near him.

From that day we won five of our last six games; our only loss was against minor premiers Manly 14–12. In the last round we played Balmain at home and they had to win to get in the finals. The week before, Balmain had beaten Parramatta and Glenn Morrison was quoted in the press as saying the Tigers really got over Parramatta's forwards and were looking to do the same to the Knights pack; which was like a red rag to a bull. Our blokes ripped the article out (I think it was in *Rugby League Week*) and put it on the wall in the dressing room. We destroyed them 34–10.

What is overlooked a fair bit now, seeing as it was so long ago, is the adversity we had to overcome to win the premiership in 1997. In the first week of the finals we were down 18–0 against Parramatta and lost centre Matt Gidley who broke his leg, and fullback Robbie O'Davis who was badly concussed, and I broke my ribs late in the game. Yet we came back to beat the Eels 28–20. I tell the full story of my broken ribs and punctured lung in the next chapter.

The next week 'Robbie O' and I missed the game against Manly. Under the finals format that year whoever lost backed up the next week anyway, so the game was a bit of a 'dead rubber' and we went down 28–12. The biggest drama on the day was when Manly lock Nik Kosef threw himself like a torpedo at Matthew when he was kicking, which was a pretty dangerous thing to do against a player who was virtually defenceless. Kosef was suspended for one match.

The following week Norths and us played for a spot in the grand final, and it was 12-all for a while when Darren Albert pulled off one of the greatest try-saving tackles in finals history. Bears fullback Matt Seers was away on the right-hand side and had run 70 metres before 'Alby', who had come from the opposite side of the field, rounded him up about 10 metres short of the line. Alby will always be remembered for the try that won us a grand final, but without that tackle we wouldn't have even been in the grand final. In the end Matty kicked a field goal for a 13–12 lead right near the end, and when Norths tried a short kickoff only for us to get possession, Owen Craigie scored after one of those freakish lobbed passes from Leo Dynevor.

I watched the big ending from the bench after the complications with my broken ribs; an injury that became the biggest story leading up to the grand final — 'Andrew Johns risks death to play in grand final'.

We went into the club's first-ever grand final with history dead-set against us. Manly had beaten us the previous 11 times, dating back to 1992, and we didn't have one player who had been to a first grade grand final (in Australia) before, while Manly had a heap of blokes who were going into their third straight grand final. Manly were just about unbeatable with their incredible defence at that time: they had so much confidence around them, had a great pack; they were just a complete side. Mentally they probably had it over us; we'd get so close to beating them, then Cliffy Lyons would pull out a bit of magic or Geoff Toovey used to break our back. The great feature of our clashes back then was how Mark 'Spud' Carroll and Paul Harragon would rip into each other with no thought of their own safety. The rivalry between the two teams was the most intense I ever experienced in my career. There used to be terrible sledging going on, and in every scrum the noise of the head butts would make me cringe, and there would be brawls every game — they were just amazing contests.

I knew we could give the grand final a big shot but, to be honest, I didn't know if we could beat Manly because they were such a great side with no weaknesses. I remember the bus ride down to Sydney from Newcastle; it was so emotional seeing Chief cry as the fans lined the streets to wish us well. It made me realise what a special experience it was. When Chief called the team into his room the night before the game — no coach or officials, just the players — and went around the room and made every player explain what it meant to him to win the competition, the occasion hit home to all of us. The key moment was when it came to Marc Glanville to say his bit. 'MG' had been with the club since the first season of 1988 and was one of the players the club built its tradition on:

tough as anyone, great defender, just competed every single week. The grand final was his last game for the club before going to Leeds in England to finish his career. MG was the club's resident comedian and prankster (well, in tandem with my brother), yet when he spoke that night he ended up sobbing like a baby. I had an attitude of 'whatever' before the team meeting — I just wanted to let rip and play — but when MG talked about how hard he had worked to come back from two knee reconstructions, and how he'd battled with the club for 10 years and this was the only grand final he was going to play and how much it meant to him, it really united us. I was just blown away by it because I thought these big moments happened all the time. But here was MG knowing it was his last shot after 13 years or so (he had a couple of seasons with St George before joining the Knights).

The grand final itself is like a blur to me. I remember we were down 16–8 at half-time — the same score as two weeks before when Manly beat us — and it was just pandemonium in the dressing room. I remember shouting, 'I'll get us there — you get us right into the game and I'll win it for us.' There was just so much emotion with everyone screaming at each other.

The main things I remember are Troy Fletcher coming off the bench and doing a remarkable tackle on Steve Menzies and that seemed to lift the side; I remember Darren Albert throwing a ball over one of our players' head and it went in the in-goal and they nearly scored. So many times I thought we were gone but we kept picking ourselves up. I remember some of the physical hits Chief was putting on the Manly forwards, especially early in the game, and that things were starting to swing our way in the second half when Manly were dropping balls and looking nervous.

Robbie O'Davis scored under the posts after a great bust down the middle by Fletch to make it 16-all with five to go. I was absolutely exhausted and remember thinking, 'I've got nothing left — if we get extra-time I don't know how we'll go.' I reckon they might have got us if it went into overtime. I hadn't played much football and I was struggling to jog, let alone sprint.

Matty had missed two field goal attempts, one had hit the upright, and I think Cliff Lyons also missed two for Manly, one when they led by six. There were 20 seconds left when I had a shot at field goal but it was charged down.

OK, let's go through the last 10 seconds ...

Matty and I had watched videos that season and noticed that just about all the time when play was near the sideline and there was one marker, defenders would chase inside and there would always be a corridor left open behind the play the ball. We'd spoken previously about how easy it would be to dummy and go down the short side into the vacant corridor in the defence. I was at marker and I heard Matty calling for the ball, obviously for one last shot at field goal. I looked over from dummy half and there was John Hopoate staring at Matty, and his body language showed he was going to charge out and jump Matty and try to charge the kick down. So I said to Darren Albert, who played the ball, 'Stay alive,' and then feigned left and snuck down the short side to the right, dummied again to my old mate Mark Hughes on the right (which he is still filthy on — he reckons he would have scored and been the grand final hero if I'd passed to him), then took the tackle of Craig Innes and put Alby in for the try. I didn't know if there was a minute to go or 20 seconds, to be honest; I suppose I just backed my instinct.

From that moment, everything is an absolute blur; I can remember Matt and I hugging, but, literally, can't remember one specific thing that happened on the field after that. I can't remember the victory lap, although I've seen photos of Dad walking around with the two of us. Emotions just absolutely engulfed us. I do remember singing the victory song two or three times in the dressing room and going crazy with champagne.

I felt for Leo Dynevor not being part of the grand final because his performances that season did so much towards getting us there. He was a stand-out player for us for over half the season, and in the finals he came off the bench against Norths and started against Manly when I was out, but he didn't get a run in the grand final. It's strange that when I am at functions and they show highlights of the history of the Knights, some of the tries Leo set up — with Owen Craigie and him doing their magic that year — are out of this world.

There were a lot of other unsung heroes from that year — blokes like Brett Clements who started at hooker for a while, until a week before the grand final; Evan Cochrane, who was a tremendous club man; Scott Conley, who with Troy Fletcher played Jersey Flegg in 1991 with me (they both played most of the year as good bench players). I remember talking to my manager John Fordham after the grand final and he watched the game with Ricky Stuart who was playing Super League with Canberra. He asked Ricky, 'If you could buy any player for the next season, who would it be?' Ricky said Troy Fletcher, which shows the impact he had that season.

That historic grand final team was: Robbie O'Davis, Darren Albert, Adam MacDougall, Owen Craigie, Mark Hughes, Matthew Johns, Andrew Johns, Tony Butterfield, Bill Peden, Paul Harragon (captain), Wayne Richards, Adam Muir, Marc Glanville. Interchange: Troy Fletcher, Scott Conley, Lee Jackson, Steve Crowe.

There are two things which some people use to taint our grand-final winning achievement of 1997. One is that it was a split competition with Super League in existence for the only season. Wendell Sailor, who played for the Broncos who won Super League that year, always used to rib me and say, 'The tattoo on your back should say it was only half a comp.' I would have loved to have played the Brisbane Broncos who were the stand-out Super League team and won the first NRL grand final the following year. There was talk about a showdown between the ARL and Super League winners to declare the undisputed champions and I'll tell you all the players wanted it to happen. But it seems the officials didn't want to put any prestige on the line. You can only beat what is in front of you and I believe Manly were the dominant team from both competitions in that period.

The other point of contention is the claim that the Knights were rampantly feeding ourselves with performance-enhancing drugs that year, something our critics would allude to because Wayne Richards, Steve Crowe, Adam MacDougall and Robbie O'Davis tested positive the following season. Well, if anything was going on, I wasn't aware of it. I didn't think anyone took steroids at the time and I can categorically say I have never ever used performance-enhancing drugs. I think it's cheating and should be wiped out of the game; the penalties are too lenient. If you are caught with performance-enhancing drugs you should never be allowed to play representative football again.

I was young and naïve at the time but I was never aware of any steroid culture or anything like that. Taking drugs to improve weight or performance was never talked about amongst the team and the club never encouraged it, so if it happened it must have been the individual decisions of those players involved.

One thing I know did happen from September 1997 was that the Newcastle Knights quickly gained a massive amount of popularity and interest in the region. We always had a big profile but I think the players as individuals got really big from that point on and became easy game for nasty, unfounded rumours. We couldn't go anywhere without being recognised and someone wanting to rub shoulders with us.

The worst rumour involved Paul Harragon and his wife Pam, and Chief had to resort to revealing it — giving a response in the *Newcastle Herald* — even though it was complete bullshit. That sort of thing goes with success and a high profile, I suppose. It was the type of thing I had to put up with a lot in later years: the myth of the big rumour.

CHAPTER 10

PUNCTURED LUNG — THE UNTOLD STORY

The week leading up to the 1997 grand final was undoubtedly the most dramatic of my football career. I'd gone from having broken ribs to a punctured lung and was in hospital until Wednesday before the premiership-deciding clash with Manly.

The club and I had always stuck to the story that a broken rib had pierced a small hole in my lung when I received a knock while playing with the injury in the preliminary final against North Sydney the weekend before the grand final. The real story, I can reveal for the first time now 10 years later, is that the puncture was caused by a painkilling injection gone wrong at half-time of the final against the Bears.

I hold nothing whatsoever against our club doc Peter McGeogh, who was responsible for the injection, nor is there any suggestion whatsoever of any incompetence on his behalf. It was just one of those things that can happen in professional rugby league when you are trying to patch footballers up and get them out on the field for such crucial games — and a risk you take when you're injecting into that part of the rib area.

For years since, Peter and I would have a bit of a chuckle every time he had to 'needle' me. I'd say something like, 'That's not going anywhere near my lungs, is it?' but it was far from a laughing matter for Pete at the time. He was really traumatised with what happened, to the extent that he nearly had a bloody nervous breakdown and closed his practice for a few days after the event, because he thought he had forced me out of the grand final and blamed himself for it. Peter has been an absolutely first-class club doctor who has been with the Knights since before I started my career in 1993 and I have nothing but the highest regard for him.

Let's go back to the start of the episode.

I'd had only eight games back after completely stuffing the ankle ligaments in my right leg in the pre-season but was feeling fit and really keen as we went into the first week of the finals. We had to play Parramatta on the Sunday and we came back from 18–0 down to win 28–20. Late in the game I scored a try, but as I put the ball down Jason Smith came down with his knees, trying to stop me grounding the ball; it wasn't a deliberate act by Smithy but he cracked three of my ribs. There was no way I could play the following week against Manly in the major semi-final. It wasn't a knock-out game with the winner going straight into the grand final and the loser having to qualify the following week, so it was best for me to rest.

I had to get a heap of painkillers to take the field against Norths the week after. I got through the first half without much bother but the ribs were really sore when I cooled down at half-time, so I asked Doc McGeogh to 'top me up'. When he put the syringe in, it went in too deep and pricked my lung.

Instantly I lost my breath and became light headed and nearly passed out. I was lying on the rubbing table really distressed, having incredible trouble breathing. The team had gone out into the tunnel on the way to starting the second half and Mal Reilly was standing over me, saying, 'What is going on? Get out there!' So I hopped up and ran down the tunnel at the Sydney Football Stadium and went out to play.

When I made it to the field I could hear this gargling in my chest, *brrrrrrr, brrrrrrr*, every time I'd breathe; I just couldn't run, had no energy. So I came off and was lying there and I said to the doc, 'You haven't hit my heart, have you?' and he said, 'No, no, no, I haven't hit your heart.' I sat and watched the entire second half and was loaded up with morphine because I was in so much pain. After the game I was taken straight to Westmead Hospital and I got my chest x-rayed. I went home that night and it was really uncomfortable trying to sleep.

At the recovery session the next day it was still pretty much the same — my chest was gargling when I took any sort of deep breath. Then I received a phone call from the doc saying I'd punctured my lung; it looked like I was out of the grand final. I just couldn't believe it. The town was going crazy, with their team in the grand final for the first time and I was going to miss the biggest game of my life.

Next day I saw a specialist in Newcastle and it was agreed they'd put a tube inside me to reinflate the lung, so I went out to Lake Macquarie Private Hospital and that's what they did. The pain killed me as they put me on this machine that pretty much pumped up the lung. I was in hospital for two days hoping for a miracle.

As usual, from a tragic story there is always a piece of humour. The medical staff told me I'd have to get a massive amount of antibiotics to ward off infection and I said, 'Oh yeah, no problem.' Then the nurse mentioned the word 'suppository' and I said, 'Yeah, that's no problem.' Then she looked at me and said, 'Do you know what a suppository is?' When I said no, she showed me this tablet the size of my little finger, and I pleaded: 'I can't swallow that.' She said, 'You're not going to swallow it,' and then described how she was going to shove it up my blurter. I screamed, 'I'm not putting that up my arse,' but she was just as insistent that I had to; there was a big chance of infection if I didn't and I'd be no chance for the grand final on the Sunday.

There was no way I was letting the nurse invade my body with that bloody big thing so, in one of the lowest moments of my life, I had to get over the top of the bed, spread my arse and I got my mum to put it up there. That's what mums do, isn't it?

Anyway, I was on the tube in hospital until the Wednesday and it was still touch and go whether I would be right for the grand final. I'll never forget the pain in my chest when they removed the tube; it took three stitches to close up the wound. Peter McGeogh came to see me in hospital and he was beside himself at what had happened — white as a ghost — but I kept telling him not to worry about it, these things can happen.

I didn't train with the side until the very last training session, the day before the game. I trained OK, but as a precaution the surgeon who looked after the injury came out from the hotel on the team bus with us and sat on the bench during the grand final. There was all this bullshit in the paper during the week, with people who didn't even know the details of my case saying I could die, but that was never a chance. I loved the drama actually, it just built up the pressure and expectation which I thrived on. My parents were freaking out though, so Peter and Neil Halpin had to reassure them there was no danger and the best qualified person in the state would be close by.

The worst part of it all was having to get a painkilling injection for the broken ribs again before the match, which stressed me out a bit. They made sure they used a smaller syringe this time!

Luckily there was a happy ending; somehow I got through the match and was able to lay on the winning try. And I was fit enough to consume a reservoir of alcohol in celebrations over the following month.

CHAPTER 11

MY BROTHER MATTY

I can't believe my brother Matthew rose to play rugby league for Australia considering the player he was as a teenager. Until under-16s he was in a Cessnock team that played second division. He was always small, thin, fragile and getting hurt; and he was so timid on the field. When we'd go to presentation nights for our club I'd get a heap of trophies and Matty would come up empty handed and I'm sure that would have affected his confidence; but he was never jealous, he just went away with a single-minded determination and looked at himself, not anyone else.

He had a burning ambition to be a footballer; and once he was 16, he set his mind to making it happen. He trained so hard and while his mates were drinking grog and smoking, he never did. He got a gym set at home and nearly wore it out, he used it so often. Finally he was chosen in the Knights Jersey Flegg (under-19s) and from then he never looked back. He worked so hard on his game to get the maximum return from his talent; he'd go to the park all the time kicking the ball, practise passing, doing extra fitness training and gym work, and he would study videos relentlessly. He gradually progressed through the grades to go on to be part of the Knights' first premiership side and play State of Origin and for Australia.

Matty never had my instincts, but through his determination and dedication and studying so much on how certain players defended, he virtually manufactured himself into a very good ball player. He played for Australia at a time when there were a lot of good five-eighths around, like Brad Fittler, Cliff Lyons, Laurie Daley and Kevin Walters. I've never felt prouder of anyone than the day he was picked for Australia, because I'd seen how hard he'd worked from being a perennial struggler when he was younger.

So, football-wise, I am very proud of him, but I am equally as proud and impressed with the second part of his life as a TV personality. That 'second coming' has proven how incredibly talented and determined he is. When I watch *The Footy Show*, Reg Reagan has me in stitches.

When we were younger he'd always do things that were, well, 'out there'. When he was about 13 and I was 10 we'd be playing in the back yard and he'd say, 'Go to Mum and Dad's front room and look outside in five minutes.' Matty would appear behind the telegraph pole wearing Mum's bikini trying to hitch a ride. He was filthy, though, when Mum provided some photos of him dressed as a girl for a story written on him once.

We used to play together when we were younger but even when we got into our teens, when it must have been a pain in the arse having his little brother hanging around, it was never an issue with him. You wouldn't meet two brothers closer than Matty and me.

He's never been one to sit me down and give me advice and really preach to me, but when the need would arise he'd give me a brief heart to heart. He didn't have to give me football advice; I would just follow his lead from what he did.

When I really needed knocking into shape, he'd say something, but it was never a 30-minute lecture; he'd quickly say his piece without holding back, give me 'the stare' that told me how fair dinkum he was, and then he'd walk away. I'd either be smart enough to take notice of what he told me or, at times, I wasn't smart enough and I'd regret it. But one thing has never changed: he has always been there for me.

He used to be an incredible worrier and self-conscious, but since getting used to being on TV, he says he has extracted all embarrassment from his body and he doesn't care what people think any more, which is sensational. I wish I could do that.

But as much as he loves what he does on TV and is so good at it, he is a frustrated coach; he'd love to coach a first grade side and he'd be successful at it too. There was talk for a while — even after he left in 2000 for Wigan — that he might come back and coach the Knights. He used to do so much homework on how opposition teams defended, how to take on 'up and in' defenders and 'slide' defences. He loves rugby league, he watches all the NRL games, he has kept his toe in the water by helping Craig Bellamy at Melbourne; he communicates so well with people and would be great with players. But he would be bonkers to do it — I think he's like Peter Sterling in that way; a TV career is less stressful and just as rewarding.

Reg Reagan was created in 2000, at a press conference one day when he and Warren Ryan were clashing over how they thought the team should play. He was fed up with putting on a brave face for the media, who knew what was going on, and said, 'Listen, I've got an alter ego from now on — I'm now Reg Reagan, who is an '80s man who drinks KB and has good old values,' and launched into this different personality. It was all a cover for how down he really was as a footballer. If he wasn't deadly serious and intense about his football, he'd try to be an idiot — like times when he'd be training and take his shirt off and have one of his wife's bras on underneath.

We're alike in that we like to go out and have a few beers and let our hair down, we love footy like you wouldn't believe, and we love spending time with our kids and being a good father to them. But we are different in that Matty is far more comfortable in his media role or in a group of people, and he has the right personality to coach a team, where I don't.

We speak every day but sometimes it might only be for 10 seconds; other times we could talk for an hour. Maybe it is a sort of comfort thing just to hear each other's voice. In the 1995 World Cup Mark Carroll, said. 'I know you are brothers but you still sit next to each other on the team bus all the time — that's weird.' We just never get sick of each other's company. Christmas would always be magic because we'd get a week together, whereas we don't see a lot of each other face to face these days because he lives in Sydney, I'm in Newcastle, and we live such busy lives.

Matty is extremely protective of me too. In 2006, when I didn't accept the trophy Parramatta had organised for breaking Jason Taylor's point-scoring record, he was backstage getting ready for the *Sunday Roast* show on Channel Nine and someone was saying I should be stood down from the Knights team and should wake up to myself. Matty was backstage putting his make-up on, and when an ad break came he went on the set and absolutely tore shreds off the bloke who said it.

It's appropriate that we both convinced each other when it was time to retire. For Matty it came about midway through the 2002 season after he'd come back from England to play for Cronulla. Most of that season when I watched him play I had a knot in my stomach and I'd never felt like that before; I was worried about him. Tony Ayoub, the Australian physio who had joined coach Chris Anderson at Cronulla, took me aside and told me how concerned he was about Matty's health. Tony told me Matt had been getting knocked out a bit, his neck was crook and his speech seemed a bit slurred at times; that was pretty worrying. Then I saw him on TV get taken off in a neck brace against the Roosters after he'd gone into a tackle all wrong; he looked distressed and I really became worried about him. He'd been carrying a shoulder injury that needed surgery too.

The Knights played the Sharks at Toyota Park the following week in round 22 (and were thrashed 64–10), and

Matty didn't play because of the neck problem. I stayed at his place overnight and we decided to head into town and go to the Courthouse Hotel in the city. We were sitting there, having a few beers, and I said, 'I think you should retire.' He went all quiet and was obviously taken aback. Then he asked why and I said I was worried he was going to get hurt, I could see his timing was out and that his time had just come. He took it pretty hard because he had another year to go on his contract. He said, 'I know I'm slowing down but I love getting in and doing my tackling and ripping in with the boys.' I said, 'Mate, fair enough but I think your time is up.'

As it was he missed the next fortnight with the neck injury, then played in two of the Sharks' last four games (which included three finals) and his last game was a 30–24 win against the Dragons; he couldn't back up the next week when the Sharks lost to the Warriors in the fight for a grand final place. I was so relieved when he retired, because he already had a spot on *The Footy Show* and Reg Reagan had been born, so he had secured a career after footy.

It was only four and a half years later — when, ironically, I had a neck injury — that Matthew gave me the same advice. I'd seen when he half choked up on Channel Nine and said I should give the game away if my neck wasn't right, that I had no more to prove. He had his column in the *Daily Telegraph* on the Monday — the day before I was to get the scan results from Professor Yeo — and in it he said he was hoping I would retire, that he could see me struggling physically in matches. He hadn't told me what he was going to write in his column but I knew how he felt. He rang me next morning and said,

'You have to make sure that if it's not right [with the neck], you finish,' and that was all that was said. He had the same fear for my health that I had for his in 2002.

It's a bit eerie when you now look back on our careers: I played first grade off the bench in 1993 the same game Matty had his run on debut; we made our Origin debuts together in 1995; had our first overseas tour together that year (Matty played two Tests off the bench against the Kiwis before I made my Australia debut in the World Cup); we played in the Knights' first grand final together in 1997; then both retired before the end of our contracts because of neck injuries, when deep down we knew our time was up anyway.

Neither of us could have dreamed — when we used to throw a football at our trampoline in the back yard — that we could have achieved what we have and brought such satisfaction for our parents. It's very special even though we're just ordinary blokes. He's been a pillar of strength all the way along the line … even though he's still mad as a meat-axe.

CHAPTER 12

MY BROTHER ANDREW

by Matthew Johns

It seems strange when people point out that Andrew and I are three years apart in age — because we feel like twins really, we're so close. We always shared the same bedroom growing up and when Dad got our first VCR and we'd go out and get the horror movies like *Halloween* and *Friday The 13th*, we'd be so scared afterwards that, although we had the double bunks, we'd climb into the bottom bunk together. I suppose we have always looked to each other for a bit of comfort and support.

Everywhere I went, I seemed to take 'Joe' with me, yet I never ever looked at him like: 'I've got to drag this kid along.' It was more like: 'Come on, let's get to the park so instead of it being five on four in a game of footy, it's five versus five.' My mates were pretty hard on him too, don't worry; they'd rip into him and tackle him and pick him up and dump him and he'd end up in tears and run home; then he'd be back 10 minutes later. I remember one day at the town hall there were a lot of kids three or four years older than me and our gang sort of took theirs on at footy; they weren't much good, thankfully, but they'd rough us up. Joey was six or seven years younger than them and they'd knock him around, but he'd pick himself up and keep playing. Even then, I was very, very proud of how good and how tough he was.

I'm probably very protective of him too. One of the worst feelings I ever had was when Andrew had Osgood-Schlatter disease in his legs. He was playing under-15s for the Knights and he could barely run because of the pain. I was so nervous for him because I knew what he could do, but I knew deep down he was embarrassed, because he could only run at barely jogging pace. One day, and I'll never forget it, people were laughing, saying, 'Look how slow this kid is, get him off,' and that sort of stuff. If I had a gun I would have shot them, I reckon, I was that angry. People don't realise how bad he was with Osgood-Schlatter disease; he would be in absolute agony just running around the back yard and it took ages before it was diagnosed.

But that setback just made him more determined. You know, young halfbacks always ask me about Joey and I'll say, 'What do you think his greatest attribute is?' and they'll say his long passing or his kicking or his vision. I tell them it's the fire in his belly; that is his most special gift.

He was the same as a kid. If we were playing Trivial Pursuit and he got something wrong, he'd hurl the board and storm to his room; you'd get him out of his room and he'd miss another question and go berserk again. One Christmas I received a brand new Gray-Nicolls cricket bat and when he used it on Christmas Day I bowled him first ball. He bashed it over the drum we used as a wicket and smashed it to bits. Back then you would go 'geez, he's a bad sport', but now I realise it was just this incredible desire to win.

He was so far in excess of everybody else in his age group as a footballer; he had incredible skills, incredible footwork and just incredible 'nous' for someone so young. Joey was the sort of bloke who'd step through the whole side, then hand the ball to the worst player in the team and he'd put it down. You see a lot of boys tagged 'child prodigy' but 99 per cent of them grow up and come back to the field. Time never caught up with him — he was always a step ahead of it because of his hard work.

I know I am biased but he is the best footballer I have laid eyes on. And I'm even more proud of what he's achieved considering the demons he's had to fight along the way, which he has finally discussed in this book.

People sometimes ask me if I was ever jealous of Andrew's success. Never, I was just proud of it. My greatest dream growing up was to play first grade and I'd say to Dad, 'Do you think one day I could possibly get down there [with the Newcastle Knights] and play reserve grade?' He'd say, 'Mate, if you apply yourself you'll be able to play first grade,' and I thought, 'Oh gee, I don't know about that.' So I never really focused on Andrew. I was lucky to do what Dad said and make first grade, and when Andrew joined me, it was like the best of dreams. When we were both playing rep football, I thought I might have hit the wall; it took me a little while to get the hang of the rep stuff, where Joey took to it straight away and left me behind. I look back now and feel honoured to have played some rep footy with him and I had such a big sense of pride to sit down and watch those State of Origin games he played in when I wasn't selected or had retired.

He was his own harshest critic. I couldn't count the times he would have walked to the sheds after he thought he'd played poorly and rung me or texted me straight away and said, 'I'm embarrassed ... I can't believe how bad I went ... I've lost it.' I'm talking about 10 minutes after the siren, before they'd had their team talk!

He was really doubting himself in 2005 after coming back from the knee reconstruction. He looked awful on the field and then he got the broken jaw and went for six weeks of training at the Queensland Institute of Sport. I didn't see him for a month and when I did it was like, 'Holy shit, that's the best I've seen him look'; he looked really hard, really strong and just really fit. I thought, 'Geez, he is about to do something special here.' Then he was suddenly recalled to the New South Wales side and went *bang* and exploded in that Origin series. That was probably his greatest achievement.

Few know how close he was to going to rugby union the year before that. I had mixed views; I was excited for him to chase a new challenge — like in anything in life you can do the same thing for a long time and people start to take you for granted. I think it was going that way a little bit at Newcastle with Joey and I saw how excited he was to take on Jonny

Wilkinson or go to France to take on Frederick Michalak; it would have been a fantastic challenge for him.

It wasn't until I sat back from thinking about Joey and considered what a monumental loss it would be for rugby league that I started to realise what a mistake it would be for him to go to rugby. I know we are always pushing through young players in rugby league and he could have been replaced, but I wouldn't have liked the statement his defection would have made about rugby league or about Andrew. It's a game that has been so good for him, it has always been a part of our lives and it's the make-up of our family.

I wasn't sad when he pulled the plug three rounds into the 2007 season. Sport can be very cruel to those champions who want to drag the extra six months out of their careers when the body is just not up to it. It happened with me in 2002; my legs (and shoulder and neck) were gone, I was out there playing against younger blokes and I knew my time was up before the injuries confirmed it. With Joey, I'm not saying he couldn't have competed with those guys any more, because of his class; but he didn't have to.

The one thing between us that I resented over the years, to be honest, was when Joey told me he thought I was virtually over the hill as a player in 2002. The first I knew of his feelings was when I read it in *Rugby League Week*. Nathan Brown was doing interviews for the magazine and he asked Joey, 'What's it like playing against your brother?' I'd been knocked out three times in eight games and Joey's comments were something along the lines of 'yeah, I don't like seeing him get knocked around; I wish he'd give it away'. At the time it provided me with a bit of a lift for the rest of the season, because I thought, 'I don't want anyone's pity, especially not my younger brother's.' A few weeks later we were talking and he said to me, 'I don't want to see you get hurt any more,' and when I asked what he meant, he said, 'Your timing is out, things aren't right, I think it's time,' and I went 'yeah, right [piss off]'. Chris Anderson was coaching Cronulla and said he wanted me to play the following season, but I went away and thought, 'My brother is right, I struggled at times, it is time to just go quietly.'

I tried to return the favour five years later. I saw the signs before the 2007 season that his time was fast approaching. I did a bit of training with him in the off-season. He'd say, 'Let's take the boys for a game of touch footy down the park and do some hundreds while we're there.' Now Joey never entered a season in great physical shape but he just didn't look 'hard' in his body and I thought, 'Has he got the hunger to push on through this?' I think he was worried himself because he'd say, 'How do I look, do I look fit ... was that a hard session, did you find it hard, Matt?' and I'd say, 'Yes it was a hard session,' but I think there were some little doubts creeping into his head.

A few months later, the morning he was to get the results of the scans on his neck, I called him and said, 'Mate, if there is any doubt in your mind, if you are looking at the roof, thinking, "I don't know if I can get through this season, I don't know if I want it any more," here's your chance, regardless of what the scans say, here is your "out" if you want to go.' He just said, 'No, mate, I'm sweet, I want to play on.'

I'm glad a specialist took the decision out of his hands. He had nothing to prove to anyone, least of all himself. He'd done it all by then — better than anyone else during his 13-year career.

And Joey has achieved what he has despite the many off-field personal battles he's had to fight. There were times at Knights training when we couldn't understand why Joey wanted to throw the ball at our ankles deliberately and why he would sabotage a training session; we just thought he was being a monumental pain. There were times when I just didn't understand him. I had no idea that he was fighting his mental demons. How much do we know about mental health now? Well, it was a whole lot less 10 years ago, but he was able to get through it and become a football genius. No matter how he was feeling or what pressures he had on him, he could switch on and play so consistently well. That again goes back to that inner determination not to let his team or himself down.

Only after his troubles in London recently were we finally drawn to discussing his bipolar disorder more deeply. I came to understand the enormity of the demons he has faced for so long. I was very proud of the way he made his frank admissions about his life in the *Footy Show* interview. On that night he set himself free of the shame and guilt which had hung over him for 10 years.

I can recall many things which I should have seen as, if not a cry for help, at least a signal that I should have looked deeper into his moods. But I didn't.

When I heard the phone ring at 3.30am on Monday 27 August 2007, I held my breath. It was my mate Brian Carney calling from Ireland; he told me he'd received a call and had some bad news about Andrew. I feared he was calling to say my brother had died. 'Mate, he's been arrested in London for carrying a tablet,' he said. I can't describe the relief I felt; I know it wasn't good but I thought the worst was coming.

Andrew is relieved that the lie he has been living has been set free and I know he is looking forward to what is ahead. As a family, we are even closer now.

CHAPTER 13

MY ROOM-MATE FORM GUIDE

When I sat down with the calculator and did my sums, I realised that during my 14-season career I must have spent over 450 nights holed up in a hotel room, mostly sharing the experience with a footballing 'roomie'. That was almost 14 months of my footy career spent 'in camp'.

At Newcastle we usually stay the night before an away match at a hotel to save on travel on match day. In State of Origin you can spend a week to 10 days in camp with the Blues, then there are the overseas tours with the Kangaroos or even, say, five days at a time in camp for domestic Test matches.

So I'm well qualified to talk about footballing compatibility, which is pretty damn important considering how vital the right preparation is in these times of professionalism and competitiveness at all levels of the game.

Not that it's all that serious, as I'll endeavour to explain.

My very first room-mate as a professional footballer, in 1994, was the tough Knights front-rower Tony Butterfield. Tony is a front-rower, an intellect, a philosopher ... and a nudist. I grew to accept that nudity in hotel rooms was a peculiar habit of many footballers over the years, including 'Butts', and let me tell you, Tony Butterfield in the raw is not an attractive sight.

I was partnered with Butts for the first round game against Souths down in Sydney, my debut run-on game, so you could imagine how excited and nervous I was: literally bouncing off walls. Anyway, we came in after dinner and I was sitting on my bed reading the game plan which, coming from our coach of the time David Waite, was fairly complex — two or three pages worth. Buttsy said, 'I'll give you some advice, youngster,' then stood up and proceeded to snatch the game plan out of my hand and throw it out the window. True story. I didn't know what to say.

We went on to win the game by 43–14 and I scored two tries, seven goals and a field goal, so it probably wasn't bad advice.

I roomed with Butts for a few years, and he was sensational, well, except for his penchant to get his gear off too often. For an impressionable guy in his late teens and early 20s it was a daunting and unsettling time for me, but he was always great for advice, always steered me in the right direction and prepared me well for games, so I am indebted to him for that.

Some nights he used to keep me up late, though ... without even realising. I'd know, if we were down at dinner and Buttsy started to whack into the broccoli, that I'd pay for it late at night when he would be dead-set ripping the paint off the walls with some of the farts he used to exert, some sounding like he was tearing bed sheets apart. I wasn't game enough for probably the first 12 weeks or so to say, or do, anything, but towards the end of that first season, I'd learned to try to remind him of his 'problem' when he went to dinner, and if I saw too much broccoli on his plate, I'd try to clear it just a little when he wasn't looking.

I'll go back to the days on the road with the Knights later, but first I'll take you through my times with the New South Wales and Australian teams, and hopefully give you an insight into some of the better-known figures in rugby league.

I was partnered with my brother Matt for my first Origin game, which was great as we were making our debuts together. But for my second Origin game I had the interesting experience of being thrown into the room with none other than the infamous John Hopoate, which turned out to be his only Origin appearance: game two of 1995.

'Hoppa' truly is one of the great fellows of the game, great to be around. Now he hasn't drunk or smoked in quite a few years, which is to his credit, because he used to go a bit mad on the drink, and be a real pain in the arse with his chain-smoking habit.

The accepted protocol if you smoke is that you leave the room and go outside onto the balcony for a puff. Hoppa refused outright to do this with me; he'd just lie on his bed, inhale and smile. I was a devoted non-smoker so I didn't cop this too well and I'd whinge and beg him to step outside to indulge in his filthy habit. He'd reply with 'shut up, you little prick', and who was I to argue with a bloke with Hoppa's reputation for being able to look after himself? So, I generally had to sit quietly in our room, which soon began to smell like a nightclub. Eventually I'd nag him so much he'd arch back and suck on his cigarette as hard as he could, hold it in his mouth, go up to my bag and blow all the smoke into it so my clothes would reek. Talk about an initiation into rep footy rooming!

Other than that, I had no complaints about rooming with Hoppa, who is a genuine, family-orientated, good bloke. And he took his clippers there with him and used to cut my hair: how good is that?

My next Origin room-mate was Jim Dymock in 1996, one of my favourites; just an all-round really nice guy and really funny. It was at that time when I was still wet behind the ears, straight out of Newcastle, not long out of Cessnock really, and I thought the only place in the world you could buy jeans from was Just Jeans. When Jimmy was showing me all his collection I probably had a $60 or $80 pair of jeans; he had $600 pairs, even a brand called Diesel which I'd never heard of, plus a $700 and an $800 pair. Luckily we were pretty much the same shape so he used to let me wear them out on our bonding sessions, and I used to think I was the King of Sydney wearing his gear. It didn't help me attract any members of the opposite sex, but it improved my self-esteem just the same.

Then we have Brad 'Freddy' Fittler, who I had the pleasure of sharing a room with in Origin one season, although the two of us took the saying that 'this room looks like a bomb has hit it' to a new meaning. We are both pretty untidy and there would be week-old training gear on the ground, smelly shoes, and clothes hanging off everywhere. After a day we would forget what colour the carpet was, because you couldn't see it through the litter.

Rooming with Freddy wasn't particularly good for my diet either. We would have dinner about 6.30pm or so and by 9.30 or 10 we'd be getting a bit peckish. So Freddy would look at me and say, 'Are you hungry?' and I'd nod but my conscience would be saying, 'Keep your discipline,' because in camp it is often spoken about that you can over-eat and over-drink, and easily put on two, three or four kilos. Well, Freddy and I would look at each other and, to clear the guilt, Freddy would say, 'How'd you train today, Joey?' and I'd bullshit to him and say, 'Oh, look, I trained really tough and I did an extra session on the rowing machine,' and we'd both agree we deserved a late snack. So, usually every night around 10 o'clock, we'd order up some chips and gravy and some crunchy hot bread rolls.

During that particular camp I put on three kilos and you don't have to be Einstein to work out it was around my rump and the top of the legs. So Brad Fittler may have been fun to room with, but his influence wasn't good for my 'barge arse'.

Now Laurie Daley was one of those players I idolised when I was coming up through the ranks, so to actually get to room with him in Origin camp in 1999 was a real honour ... and an experience. To this day, I still call Laurie 'the nudist' because, dead-set, the whole time we were rooming together for the whole 10 days, Laurie would just take his clothes off as soon as the door was closed and leave them lying around the whole time. Sometimes I'd be on my bed and he'd be standing next to me talking to me, and I'd feel like I was having a conversation with, not Laurie or that big nose, but something else.

Laurie had a chat to me after the first-game loss in Queensland, when both of us were under a bit of heat to keep our positions. Our coach Wayne Pearce sort of told us we were on notice after I'd hit the bonding sessions a bit too hard during that first camp. So when we came into camp the second time, Laurie dragged me aside and said, 'We are going to look after ourselves and show everyone how good we can play,' vowing that he was going to watch what he ate — and let me tell you Laurie is the best eater I've seen in my life. He was just a glutton for punishment with those big buffets that were put on for us; he would fill his plate up two or three times. It was a running joke amongst the boys, even later when he was working alongside Ricky Stuart on the coaching staff, how much Laurie would pile on his plate.

But this particular time in '99 we made a pact that he would watch what he ate and I wouldn't drink at all. The first night in camp we went out on a bonding night and I refrained from having a beer, just sat in the corner drinking water; it was one of the most boring bonding nights of my life, although I got up the next morning and trained really well and I thought to myself, 'Gee, this isn't too bad, there might be something in this.' That afternoon I told Loz I was going down the Coogee Beach for a swim, but when I got downstairs in the hotel foyer I realised I'd forgotten a towel, so I went back up to the room. I went in nice and quiet because I thought Laurie might be sleeping. To my absolute disgust, I realised he'd smuggled a packet of those wafer biscuits into his gear bag and here he was, quite contently lying on the bed (nude, obviously), stuffing the whole packet of wafers down his throat. He looked like a kid who had been caught licking the spoon with the chocolate icing.

So that night, with our joint vow of brotherhood defied by a bloke who was a legend in my eyes, I felt I had no choice but to break my promise and get on the drink. A few days later we won the game, the first-ever played at Stadium Australia, 12–8 in front of an Origin record crowd of 88,336, and one L. Daley was man of the match!

In the days before iPods came in, I'd always ring ahead to the manager and make sure I had a CD player in my room, so I could take my choice of music and not listen to Laurie's choice of radio. During that series I remember we were just playing Offspring over and over again in our room. It must have made an impression on Lozza too because his wife Michelle told me that when he got home to Canberra, he went out and bought the Offspring CD.

I roomed with Paul Harragon in Origin camp one year, and if there could be the perfect — or make that imperfect — 'Odd Couple' in rugby league, we were it. If you took the spectrum of behaviour that was possible from players in camp, Chief and I would be at opposite ends. Chief was happy to just sit in his room and 'veg', and while other blokes got excited about getting into camp and having all the fun, Chief's excitement amounted to going to a restaurant called Danny's Seafood and overdosing on crustaceans.

He was also obsessively neat, and forever stretching in the room, lying on golf balls or tennis balls to loosen his 'glutes' (the gluteus maximus and gluteus medius muscles around the buttocks). He is also a real deep thinker, our Chief. There were times when he'd ask me what the meaning of life was and I thought he was talking about the Monty Python movie. I really didn't have a clue what he was on about. Nah, he was a good man to room with, although it really was akin to getting all excited about heading off on your annual family holiday, then finding out you were sharing a bedroom with your grandfather ... sorry, big fella!

While I go through my Origin log book of accommodation arrangements, I notice I was also paired one time with Roosters fullback Anthony Minichiello. 'Mini' was without doubt one of my favourites when it comes to football roomies. We were like two hyperactive schoolkids on an excursion; we tended not to get much sleep because we were chatting and laughing all the time. He gave me a real complex, though, about my body and made me get into shape, because the sight of Mini with his shirt off is like a snapshot of Mr Olympic or a Greek statue, he doesn't have an ounce of fat on him.

Now Mini was single at that time and his phone was constantly ringing (must be a Roosters thing, come to think of it), mainly from male friends, but also a few female admirers. I couldn't work out how Mini had the ability to ask the same questions to every person — his repertoire was restricted to 'how ya going?'; 'what's been going on?'; 'you been going out much?'; 'you been having much fun?' and with every question he'd attack the phone with his laughter. If you've ever had a conversation with Mini you would have realised he ends up about six inches from your face, attacking you with this laugh. During that time rooming together, we really combined well on the field and had a great understanding, and I think it was because we got on so well. The music we were playing in the room at the time was the White Stripes, real rock music, and Mini loved it; he'd put it on, blaring it up and dancing around the room. I had some great times with him.

When it comes to Test match room-mates, I cut my teeth on the 1995 World Cup tour to England with none other than Terry 'Tezza' Hill. How can I best describe that? Well, let's just say there was never a dull, or a quiet, moment. Terry and one of our trainers, Brian 'Sheriff' Hollis (the Manly trainer who has since sadly passed away), were the best scammers I've ever come across. They used to get theirs and everyone else's tracksuits and they'd have all of the north of England staked out, and go to the best shops and trade our tracksuits for different clothes: big warm jackets, different sorts of shoes and the latest English fashions. Every day we would train and then Terry and Sheriff would head off and go shopping for everyone. I would come back to my room and there would be so much gear it was ridiculous. My wardrobe really kicked a goal from on that tour.

Terry was sensational to room with, on the go all the time, would never stop talking. It was a cesspit of energy in our room and considering we were away for over eight weeks, it was a real fun time.

Another Australian Test team 'roomie' was the redoubtable little halfback Allan 'Alfie' Langer in 1999. I loved the idea of rooming with 'Alf' because we never discussed footy at all. Well, he didn't, all he talked about were racehorses, and that's all we watched on television, even if they were racing at Cessnock or Ipswich or whatever. Jockeys were coming into the room all the time; Glenn Boss called in a few times, he and Alfie were obviously thick and forever talking horses. Alf was just one of those absolute geniuses; I don't know if he thought about footy much because he certainly didn't talk about it at all. He just got there and went from joker in the dressing room to genius on the field, like he just flicked a switch and let all the talent and focus take over as he switched into football mode.

Allan Langer is also, along with my silly brother, one of the funniest blokes I've met; he takes nothing seriously. And it had such a positive effect on my football when I roomed with Alf, I suppose it relaxed me and I was so happy and buoyant once I got to the ground. I had an absolute ball rooming with him; I knew what horse was going well, what jockeys were going well, what trainers were training well. Problem was, all that 'mail' from Alf didn't always convert to our bank balances, but I never stopped laughing being around him.

Darren Lockyer is another I was assigned to as a room-mate. Now how do I describe 'Locky'? Well, unfortunately Locky is like Teflon, absolutely nothing sticks to him. I've got nothing on the bloke; he's just an absolute champion. The only thing I can say is he talks like Patty Bouvier off *The Simpsons*; you know, Homer's awful sister-in-law with that husky voice. He's also got more shoes than Imelda Marcos and they'd be lined up around the room in order of colour or style.

I loved the time we spent together during the 1998 tour of New Zealand when we were young and didn't have a care in the world. Invariably he used to get back to our room a lot earlier than I did, so I used to rock in and for no apparent reason I can think of, I always used to jump into bed and give him a big wrestle. I also tried to make him pack my bags a few times when we were leaving, but he never did — you know what Queenslanders are like! I tell you what, though, I feel proud to say I've roomed with an absolute legend like Locky — a legend as a bloke and as a footballer.

Talking about great blokes brings me to Robbie Kearns, who I linked with in 2001 when we went to England for the Kangaroo tour. Anyone who has met Robbie would know he is the best conversationalist in rugby league. He could have been a first-class detective or counsellor; he just sits there and asks you questions all day and is so up-beat about everything. During those awful times away in England when you can get homesick and the weather is lousy, and you might be bouncing off walls or kicking stones, Kearnsy would talk you out of it, and by the end of the chat you'd be up giving him a hug or high-fiving him and just be in a frame of mind that you're loving life again.

The boys used to call him Eddie McGuire because he would ask so many questions, like on *Who Wants To Be A Millionaire*. When we'd wake up in the morning I used to give Kearnsy a brief: I'd say, 'Righto, Kearnsy, today you are allowed 20 questions, that's all you are allowed, so use them wisely.' Well, he would have used up his 20 by breakfast. So we'd get back to our room and I wouldn't talk to him. He was also unbelievably neat and an absolute nature's gentleman. Touring can be really tough but he really helped me through some hard times over there, and I'd like to think that I squared the ledger a bit and got him up to a bit of mischief.

Jason 'Toots' Croker was my room-mate for the 2000 World Cup — and that was different. When I first met Toots, he was a pretty quiet sort of country bloke from Crookwell. But I soon learned that after a dozen rums he would loosen up. The first night we roomed together he decided to come home relatively early. The Canberra boys apparently are big on wrestling so he decided to match his gorilla frame against mine, literally throwing me up against the wall and around the room, before becoming an imaginary shearer and shearing me as if I was a sheep, before hitting me on the arse and releasing me back to the yard. He was so strong he could throw me around like a rag doll.

Next day I told him the wrestling had to stop, that I didn't mind a cuddle or two if he came home, but nothing too rough. It was during that trip that all the metrosexual stuff was coming out, and blokes were starting to clipper their chests and get all the hairs off their back and what not. Darren Britt came into our room one time and Brittie is like a yak; he is covered in hair from his cheek bones to his toes. So Tootsie got the clippers out and decided to clip Brittie in our room, which must have been the smallest hotel room in England. So here we were, clipping Brittie, and it was hilarious watching him get it done, with Toots' style being sort of half-pied shearer, half Jose Eber (the Hollywood celebrity hairdresser, for those not as up to date with the fashion pages as me). For the next three weeks I'd wake up at night coughing up fur balls and all this red curly back-hair in my mouth — it was awful.

Tootsie is also a mad golfer (as well as lover of hot cars) and at times we'd tee up a ball in the room, open a window and he would drive the balls into the car park. At that time we both had young children — he had a daughter born pretty much the same time as Samuel — and it was our first time away from them. There were times when the photos would be out and the bottom lips quivering and we'd help each other get through the homesickness.

As I mentioned before, I would always have a CD player in my room blaring away. Well, my music and Tootsie's had no similarities whatsoever. He was asking where my Charley Pride CDs were; I thought Charley Pride was a horse trainer. I remember specifically that Powderfinger had their CD called *Odyssey Number Five* out at the time and we just played it all the time. By the end of the trip, Toots was putting it on himself — another graduate from the Joey Johns School of Superior Music Education.

On that 2000 World Cup tour about a dozen of the players took time out for a break and we flew to Dublin, with my Newcastle team-mate Matthew Gidley and I rooming together. Now let me ask you — what else is there to do in Dublin but sample the Guinness, to be sure?

We had a couple of real big days on the beautiful Irish brew and I got back to my room on the second night and found

'Gids' sound asleep. We'd been away about six weeks by this time, my son Samuel was 14 months old, and I felt like I was bordering on a complete emotional breakdown. Matt woke up to find me standing in the middle of the room in a sobbing mess, saying that I wanted to go home, that I missed my family, blah blah blah. Gids was so worried he called up my brother to ask what to do. I even gave him my mother's number, and after talking to Matt, she was thinking about flying over. Anyway, being the good brother that he is, Matthew said, 'Just put him to bed, and get in with him and give him a cuddle.' So there we were, Australian Test players at the time, lying in our underpants, and Gids spooning me from behind, whispering in my ear that everything was going to be alright.

When I woke up in the morning it was a bit of a haze. I couldn't open my eyes because they were stuck together, so I assumed that maybe I'd been sobbing like a baby. I vented some anger and frustration, kicking a hole in the wall, so we ended up getting evicted from that hotel. At least Gids left Dublin with it on his resume that he helped an international team-mate through a potential nervous breakdown. We still laugh about it now, and he takes off my sobs pretty much to a tee with the bottom lip quivering and the crocodile tears coming out.

I could be a leader on tour, though, and possibly the best example was the following year. The 2001 Kangaroo tour happened just weeks after the tragedy of 9/11 in New York and the tour, after being initially called off, was reduced to just three Tests on successive Saturday nights.

We'd go out after the game and have a few, being Saturday night; nothing too drastic, though, because we had training the next day, before which we'd have a recovery session at about 8am. The coach was Chris Anderson and he'd say after Sunday's session, 'Look, I don't mind if you have a few beers today but don't start too early; you know, do some extra training, go to the gym, work some soreness out, or go for another swim and do some cardio work. But I don't want you getting on the drink too early.'

Anyway, I summonsed everyone to my room, which was right across the hallway from our captain Brad Fittler's, and told them to each bring their kettle and teacups from their rooms. There we were, the whole 25-man touring party, about 11 in the morning, and they're all wondering what the hell I was up to. I told them I had a carefully thought-out plan and asked who wanted to have a few beers. Pretty much everyone's hand went up, so I sent the youngest guy on tour, I can't remember who it was — the youngest is usually the designated gopher — and he went down and got a couple of cartons of beer out of the touring room — a sort of activities room set aside for us with pool tables, table tennis table, jukebox and the like, so we had somewhere just to hang around. Once he arrived back with the supplies we opened the kettles, tipped in the beer, which was methodically poured into the nice China teacups, and we sat around my room enjoying a few quiet ales … a real English tea party with a twist.

We had music playing, were chatting about the game and life generally, blokes would do different skits, and a good time was being had by all. Our conditioner Billy Johnstone would pop his head in and say, 'What are you guys doing?' and we'd just say we were having a chat and a couple of cups of tea; he was none the wiser. A few times Chris Anderson came in and he had no idea either what we were up to; in fact, he was probably delighted the boys weren't having a beer and how responsible a leader I had become as a senior player! We christened these times 'The Captain's Tea Party' and for the rest of the tour it would happen every Sunday. I don't know if the coaching staff ever 'jerried' to what was going on, but we sure thought it was pretty clever.

The next year the Kangaroos toured England again but unfortunately I missed it through injury. Every Sunday though, I used to get a phone call and it would be from Darren Lockyer's room and I was happy to say the tradition lived on, as I could hear 20 of the guys in the background yelling out, 'Tea party, wish you were here.' It was hilarious, just good harmless fun, with no one ever getting into much strife.

Now, playing for the Newcastle Knights, hotel life becomes a big part of the season, seeing as we stay the night before a match interstate or in Sydney at a hotel, usually the Crowne Plaza at Parramatta or Coogee (or the Rydges at North Sydney in earlier years). So you spend a hell of a lot of time bunked up with a team-mate on the road.

Now after being 'sworn-in' as a Knights stay-away footballer by Tony Butterfield, I had an array of roomies over the years. Danny Buderus was a partner in crime for a long time, and everyone in rugby league knows what a champion fella he is.

But 'Bedsy' is also a real 'clean freak', bordering on being 'obsessive-compulsive' — I mean, he's someone who really needs help (I hope you're reading this, Bedsy!). I would unpack my bag sometimes and my Speedos might not have been washed from the week before and they would stink the room out. He'd be absolutely horrified. In contrast, he would get to the room and everything would be folded, everything would be put away, his bed wouldn't have a wrinkle on it, and when it was time to leave, he would pull the sheets and bedspread back and make sure it was folded to perfection again. I don't want to let the cat out of the bag completely, but Bedsy is so obsessed with cleanliness that when he goes to the toilet he likes to take all his clothes off, because he thinks any odour from the toilet will get on his clothes.

Bedsy used to always give me a hard time about my side of the room, because everything would just be tipped out of my bag and thrown around the room; I'm sure this used to keep him up at night. He always used to give me the lecture: 'Nugget, clean your side of the room, this is disgusting,' and I just used to laugh at him and make it even messier. Somehow he remained my roomie for a long time without bailing out. I often wondered if he was like that at home or whether it was just the nervous energy coming out of him before a match. Well, you go to his house these days and everything is labelled; he's out cleaning his windows twice a week, he is just an absolute clean-freak. Now, Daniel, you have given me a whole load of advice over the years — about football, life, my bad habits and my lack of order. Well, now it's my turn — get some professional psychological help, mate!

I'll never forget the one time I roomed with a player from the Knights called Brett Grogan, a pretty talented centre. We got to the motel at about four o'clock that afternoon and 'Groges' immediately turned the air conditioner up as cold as possible, so it was dead-set freezing in the room. He then got under the covers, pulled the doona up to his throat and slept until seven at night. Then we went down to dinner and when we returned after our meal about 8.30, he was back under the blankets with the doona up, with the eyes closed again. I wanted to watch a bit of telly, or read, but Groges wouldn't let me have the TV or the light on. So I laid there still for about three bloody hours looking at the ceiling! I got up about eight o'clock next morning, went to breakfast, had a bit of a chat with the boys, went for a walk, then headed back to our room about 10; only to find my room-mate still asleep. I was amazed a man could sleep so long before a match. It was 10.30 before he came to: that's 14 hours of shut-eye. He wandered down to breakfast, then, can you believe, hopped back into bed again and didn't rise until 1pm. Then he had a shower, got on the team bus, and went out and played ... and had an absolute howler!

A regular Knights fellow boarder was one of my best mates in footy, Mark 'Boozy' Hughes. Let's just say he didn't get his nickname from being a teetotaller, but he's one of the best blokes you will ever meet in your life, with a real dry sense of humour. To be honest, I've got no real stories on Boozy from when we roomed together, except the time we were in England for the World Club Challenge in 2002, and stayed in Leeds. It was hilarious; similar to sharing with Alfie Langer, just constantly funny with Boozy's dry, quick wit having me in stitches.

During that trip I was lucky enough to be awarded the Golden Boot; a real honour, I might add. Well, Hughsie wanted us to have a special memento to remember the occasion. So he got us to both strip naked and I had to hold the Golden Boot in front of my most valuable organ and Boozy got a pair of his best John Karandonis dress shoes and covered his old fella. I've still got that photo of us and I really should have it framed and put above the bar. The one noticeable thing about the shot is that the Golden Boot is a pretty big 'trophy' which was necessary to cover my crown jewels, while Boozy's got a smallish shoe which was more than enough to do the job.

If there was an award for the most hazardous roomie I've had in over 14 seasons in first grade, Kurt Gidley would have to be a firm favourite. We're great mates now, but he sure didn't pick up many of his older brother Matt's good habits. I've only ever roomed with Kurt when overseas on holiday or when we'd go up the coast surfing — you'll soon read why I'm too smart to have him in the same room the night before a game.

We roomed together in Hawaii one year on a trip away, and there was myself, Kurt and Billy Peden. Well, Kurt got home after having a night on the drink and we soon found out he's a terrible snorer ... and I'm talking about picking the worst snorer you know and putting the loud-hailer in front of his nose: that's how many decibels Kurt Gidley can discharge. He wakes people in the adjoining rooms or the floor above, that is not a word of a lie.

Anyway, we came home this one night in Hawaii, Billy and I, and Kurt was already asleep. We had two double beds, and with Kurt being the touring rookie, he was assigned the fold-out bed. His snoring was that bad that we got three or four towels and wrapped them around his head, before Billy picked him up and threw him around on the bed. Yet he still wouldn't wake up. It was the worst night's sleep I've had.

Another time, Kurt, Adam Dagwell — a good local footballer — and I decided, at the drop of a hat, to go up to Byron Bay one Boxing Day to have a few days' surfing. None of us are great forward planners so we got in the car and just drove up the coast, but when we got to Byron Bay we quickly realised what a popular holiday spot it is; there was not a hotel room or holiday flat available in the whole place. The only place we could get a room was at a tiny backpackers' joint, sharing with two Norwegian guys who seemed obsessed with oranges. This room was absolutely tiny, somehow squeezing in two double bunks and a fold-up, and here were the five of us and somewhere between 100 and 200 oranges they'd stashed on their beds. It was bizarre but we couldn't ask for an explanation as they couldn't speak our lingo. So the three of us thought we'd head to the pub that John 'Strop' Cornell owned across the road from the main beach and have a good time. We rolled home about three or four in the morning and Kurt got up to his old trick of snoring with megaphone volume; he even outdid his Hawaiian feat.

The next morning, when we came out of the room, it seemed like every backpacker in the joint was outside shaking their heads, looking at Kurt, me and 'Daggy', pointing fingers.

We only lasted that one night; they turfed us out. So here we were, 500 kilometres away and homeless. Kurt said, 'Let's go home.' I said, 'I'm not going home, we've come all this way up here, and I'm not turning around because of your bloody snoring.' Kurt was clueless, so I thought for a while and said, 'I know what we'll do — we'll go to the pub tonight, tell someone the story, and who knows, they might feel sorry for us and put us up.'

So we took the car up the beach and went straight back to the pub at about 11 o'clock in the morning, had a beer, looked at each other as if to say 'action', and at that moment one of the barmen who was a footy fan came up and asked us what we were doing in town. We proceeded to tell him our hard luck story, which after a couple of beers we thought was pretty funny, and he offered us some hospitality. He opened his house to us and the three of us ended up sleeping on the floor of his lounge room for a week. I don't know how much sleep he and his partner had, because Kurt was in fine form, but it was one case where being well known sure was an advantage.

Another word of serious advice to a mate here — Kurt, you have to get an operation, buddy, or you'll end up never having a long-time relationship with a woman and being black-banned by every major hotel chain. It is that serious, mate.

In this chapter, I have intentionally left the worst for last. The worst room-mate I've had is definitely my older brother Matthew, who I have had to room with too many times. Now think about it: I shared a bedroom with him my whole life as we grew up in Cessnock, so why would I want to room with him when I go away?

When he was playing, Matthew was the ultimate stress-head, and an incredible creature of habit; everything had to be the same. When we'd go away for matches — and people won't believe this but I swear it is true — he used to take upwards of six pairs of boots, and he would lay them down in the room and think about which ones would be lucky for him. If he played in a new pair of boots and didn't do well, he would burn them. Now I know he seems such a stable character on television and people laugh at his alter egos, but he has so many weird habits. For some reason, he used to carry around different things, like one of those round rims that a hose or length of string or cable would wrap around.

He would always be stressing about things and, honestly, he'd be on the phone constantly to his wife Trish, telling her how much he loved her and what she meant to him. OK, that last bit might not be totally true, but I just thought I'd put that in to give him some brownie points.

No, he was truly awful to room with, constantly worried about how he was going to play the next day and you had to tread on egg-shells the whole time; it was like rooming with a big baby. And my own brother was another of these weird footballers who had the idiosyncrasy of parading his naked body around the room. He left me with a complex, that's for sure; not about the shape of his finely tuned body (which has been let down badly since his playing days) but his more manly attributes, if you get what I mean. What a specimen ... but you might have noticed that already from those shorts Reg Reagan wears!

CHAPTER 14

SOMETHING FISHY ABOUT TOMMY

Now that I have spilled the beans on the peculiarities of some of the blokes I have encountered 'in camp', this book wouldn't be complete without spinning a couple of stories about probably the greatest larger-than-life character I have come across, my State of Origin coach in 1997–98, Tommy Raudonikis.

Tommy has more yarns to spin than anyone I've known and is one of the funniest blokes you'd meet, a true legend of the game. He tells it pretty much just as it is with his raspy voice and abundant expletives, and certainly isn't one for political correctness.

Going into the third game in 1997, we had already wrapped up the series with victories in the first two matches in Tommy's first year as coach. So he decided to whip up all this hysteria to keep us focused despite it being a dead rubber. He came up with a plan that when we got to a scrum, he wanted us to spark an all-in brawl, so he created a call called 'cattle dog'. Now, I wasn't real keen on the idea because I was playing hooker at the time, not halfback, where I would have fancied my chances of at least an honourable draw against Adrian Lam. But Tommy kept going on about it and every day he kept winding the forwards up. Chief and 'Spud' (Mark Carroll) were our front-rowers and my minders, but something happened during the game that led to my opposing hooker Jamie Goddard and I being involved in a bit of a fracas and a few punches were thrown; I think he hit me late or something. Talk about setting the scene for mayhem!

Come the next scrum, Spud said to me, 'I saw what went on back there, I want to call "cattle dog".' It was right on the halfway line, so Spud was all pumped up, calling, 'Cattle dog! cattle dog!' Steve Menzies was in the second row putting his head in, going, 'No cattle dog! No cattle dog!' and I looked over at the bench and could hear Tommy screaming at the top of his voice, 'Cattle dog! Cattle dog!' So as we packed into the scrum, Spud let fly with a punch and hit Craig Smith and a brawl started. We all squared off against each other, according to the 'plan'; leaving me eyeball to eyeball with Jamie Goddard. Now as a kid I used to knock around the police boys club and do a bit of boxing and so I thought I had a bit of Danny Green in me. Unfortunately, Jamie Goddard must have done the same thing growing up, but with a better teacher.

We were soon trading punch for punch and it was all about to blow over when Goddard said something not too complimentary and, like an idiot, I decided to go on with it. So I stepped around the touch judge and told him where to go in no uncertain terms. He went at me again and, as I charged in for him, he saw me coming and landed one of the sweetest right handers that's ever been launched in State of Origin ... and knocked me out. My one saving grace was that at least it was only State of Origin and not many people were watching it; well, other than 33,000 at the Sydney Football Stadium and about two million via television! I have never since been able to live down that brief moment.

We were both sin-binned and I was left with a split from my lip right up to my nose. My senses slowly returned in the sheds while Dr Nathan Gibbs was stitching me up, and I sort of blurted out: 'What are you doing, mate?' The good doctor told me I'd had a fight, so I inquired innocently enough, 'And how'd I go?' to which he replied, 'Well, I'm stitching you up, aren't I?' I think he put 21 stitches on the outside and threw in six interior stitches for good measure. My lip was killing me — it had swelled badly and I was naturally feeling sorry for myself and thinking what a stupid plan the 'stink' was — when, shit, I opened my eyes and looked up and, through a cloud of cigarette haze, I was greeted by the sight of Tommy, blowing smoke in my face, saying I was a weak bastard and had better get back out there and play the rest of the game. So I did, not that it helped me or the team; Queensland won 18–12, I had a sore face for weeks and was suspended for two matches (along with Goddard and Wayne Bartrim).

The mere mention of 'cattle dog' still gives me chills up my spine and there would hardly be a time since, when I was doing a boxing session in training, thinking I was going alright and throwing them pretty crisply, that the name Jamie Goddard wasn't thrown across the room by a team-mate.

Another story involving Tommy was when he organised to take the NSW team to the home of his good mate, well-known media magnate, racehorse owner and fellow ocker John Singleton.

We piled onto the team bus one evening and headed off from our permanent Origin base, the Holiday Inn at Coogee, with none of us having any idea where we were going ... other than it was a surprise created by Tommy, who by the way, was nowhere to be seen.

Next thing, we pull over on millionaires' row beside the harbour at Vaucluse and all the boys are pointing out the unbelievable real estate. We paraded single file into one of the nicest houses I've ever been in and there was this big table and beautiful big spread of food on it. The word soon filtered down the line that we were at 'Singo's house, although he and Tommy weren't there — apparently they were still out having a few beers. Eventually they lobbed — fashionably late — about an hour and a half later with, it was apparent, a few ales under their belts.

By this stage we'd eaten dinner and all was great when Tommy and Singo started reeling off the stories and had us all rolling around laughing. When it got towards the end of the night, Tommy started telling his infamous story from one of his early tours of New Zealand as a player with the Australian team, when a couple of front-rowers were egging him on to put his hand into the goldfish tank, pull out a fish and eat it.

Tommy, all in the order of getting his team-mates' respect, did what he was asked and then apparently pulled another one out and ate it, by this time with 'Dallas' Donnelly matching him. He reckons from that moment he had the respect of his front-rowers, who looked after him.

Something must have clicked inside Tommy's mind and he looked straight at me and said, 'Well, you are our halfback, aren't you ...' and he proceeded to run through Singo's house, which had this stream about a metre and a half wide. In the water there were these massive Asian-looking carp, these bright red ugly fish. They had these rotten growths on them, big spots about the size of a 50 cent piece growing out of their skin. I didn't know until afterwards, but Singo's wife said they were cancerous.

That didn't deter Tommy. I looked him in the eye and said as cautiously and calmly as I could, 'No, Tommy ...' He was in jeans and shoes but decided to jump into the stream and was suddenly up to his knees in water chasing these fish around for about 10 minutes. By this time I was terrified, even though he was so full of drink I thought there was no way he was going to catch one. Lo and behold, he emerges drenched but holding this ugly-looking fish about 30 to 40 centimetres long, and looks at me daggers and declares, 'Righto, you've got to eat this fish.' I said, 'You ate a goldfish, mate, look at the growth on that thing's head.' Then Singo walked in closer and I looked at him, thinking, he knows how mad Tommy is, I'll get some support here and he'll tell Tommy to settle down. Instead, Singo ordered me to eat it too. I said, 'I'm not eating that, no way in the world.'

Tommy called me the weakest so and so under the sun before, thankfully, Singo's wife came in and told Tommy to put the fish back in and to stop being an idiot — that I'd be sick if I ate it. Everyone was absolutely pissing themselves laughing.

We left soon after, thanked the Singletons for their hospitality and hopped on the bus to go back to the hotel. Tommy immediately held fort and announced that there was a moral to the story: that he put his mind to catching the fish and he succeeded and that is what he wanted us to do in two days' time ... then he called me a weak prick and said that I'd let him down, and that I'd better play my part in a victory or else. (Unfortunately we were badly hit by injury and were beaten 19–4 by Queensland; Matthew played hooker with Geoff Toovey out. It was also Tony Butterfield's only Origin game for NSW.)

Singo actually wrote a personal letter to all the players wishing them luck and describing what playing for NSW must mean to us. It was a great night and a great touch by Singo.

Another funny story from my State of Origin experiences happened in 1996 when all the Super League players were welcomed back to the rep teams after losing the court case, which stopped them starting a rebel competition that year.

For some reason, the first night of camp before Game One was pretty tame, which, in those days, was rare; normally you would go out and have a good night together to 'bond' as a team. Next morning, Laurie Daley, who was one of the senior players, had a word to our coach Phil Gould and said he was disappointed with the previous night's bonding session and that he felt we really didn't get to know each other very well.

So Gus got us all in and advised us that it had been planned for us to go for a walk then the movies, but he said he was going to knock that on the head. He then said something like, 'I understand last night wasn't one of the great bonding nights. I want you to go out tonight and enjoy yourselves and not come home until you love each other.' There was a cheer, because obviously we were going back out to have some good fun again — all endorsed by the team management.

So we headed off to the bottom bar to have a second 'bonding session' and there was a piano player there, so we started singing along and getting into a jolly mood, before hopping on the bus and heading up the Kings Cross. The night turned into a long one and everyone came home around three or four in the morning ... or so I thought.

We had to meet at 9am next day to get on the bus for training and we were two players down. So we all looked around and counted the numbers, and Brett Mullins and Jason Croker weren't there. We went back to the foyer and were sitting patiently until about 9.20, hoping the two AWOL culprits were going to lob, when a cab pulled up and they both got out, in their good jeans and shirts.

Gus immediately called them over and was really giving them a dressing down, asking what the hell happened and what their excuse was for not coming home with the others. 'Mullos' piped up, saying that they were at the casino playing black jack and 'I looked at the clock, realised it was 8.30 in the morning, I looked at the bloke next to me ['Toots' Croker] and I said to him ... you know what, I think I finally worked out I still don't love you. So let's have a couple more cards, a couple more drinks and then we'll go home.' It was the perfect explanation in a sticky situation.

Now one of the great things about Origin is that no matter what happens in the match you invariably catch up with opposing players out on the town afterwards, particularly in Brisbane. You would arrange to meet at a club or pub to have a drink and all would be forgotten. After the third game especially, when the series had ended, you would let your hair down together, even if you had disagreements during the series.

We'd get back to our hotel at all hours, usually not in the best shape. Our team manager was Geoff Carr, and part of his job was to make sure we were up and on time for the departing flight next day; often you'd have to leave the hotel at eight o'clock and have a wake-up call at 7.30. Very early on I worked out that sleep was extremely precious, so I devised a very clever plan.

'Carry' would do the rounds of the rooms and all the bags would be numbered and he'd check off everyone's luggage. 'Two number seven bags primed [if I was halfback wearing the number seven jersey],' he'd shout to the porter and there, sitting in the hall half an hour before the wake-up call, were our bags, ready to be taken onto the bus by the porter. We used to think, 'Gee, he must be well organised,' until I realised he had a master key that would open all the rooms. So he'd come in while we were out to it and put out our bags to avoid any chance of delaying our departure.

He used to tell me how he'd go back to the rooms after the group wake-up calls had been put through and bags put out and check for stragglers. He'd always come into my room, find me still all snugly tucked up in the blankets and think, 'This is going to be a challenge.' He'd half wake me up and ask what the hell was going on ... only for me to pull back the blankets and spring to my feet in my full kit — suit on, tie done up, shoes on, ready to walk out the door.

I used to come home from town at whatever time, jump in the shower, give myself a good wash and then put my official uniform on — just to give myself an extra 20 minutes' sleep in the morning, which I felt was absolutely crucial. 'Carry' conceded it was an absolute masterstroke, a routine I maintained the entire duration of my career, right up until I retired from rep footy.

CHAPTER 15

ONE CLUB MAN ... WELL, ALMOST NOT

I am proud that I played for the one club, my local club the Newcastle Knights, for all of my career. I'm one of a lot of local boys who did that (not including career-ending stints in England), including Paul Harragon, Mark Hughes, Matt Gidley and Billy Peden. Then there were blokes like Tony Butterfield, Marc Glanville and Robbie O'Davis, who came to Newcastle very early in their careers and never left. I'd hope Danny Buderus, Steve Simpson, Kurt Gidley and Jarrod Mullen will add to that list before they hang up their boots.

But twice I was very close to not being a 'one-club man'. The first was in 2000 when I very seriously looked at an offer from Brisbane, and then there was the well-publicised option to go to rugby union in 2004 (see chapter 18).

I received numerous offers over the years to leave the Knights and could have conservatively earned $100,000 to $150,000 more a season. Extra cash was never enough to entice me away. Money was never an issue during my upbringing and hasn't been a major one since. After only one season in first grade in 1994, I was earning more than I would have ever dreamed of, and I always thought, 'When is enough enough?' I wouldn't know how much money I have in the bank, how much I have earned on or off the field over the years, or even how much I have in assets — other than the fact that I'm well off.

The first time I had to make any real choice of clubs came in 1997. Matty and I were unsigned when we won the grand final and, through John Fordham who had become our manager the year before, we had a heap of approaches. I think 'Fordo' has it recorded that 12 clubs came in for us that year, as well as rugby union, which Matty treated more seriously than I did.

We weren't on big money at all — still on the $350,000 a year ARL loyalty payments (after getting the $255,000 up-front payment) — while there were plenty of blokes getting $600,000-plus. So while Fordo felt he had to do the right thing and get 'market value' in the first contracts he negotiated for us, I was always going to stay in Newcastle; I was 23 and had just bought my place at Merewether. So we both signed for three years — 1998–2000.

At the end of that contract Matthew wasn't even offered a renewal, an issue which split the town, devastated our family and left me pretty bitter at the time.

A lot has been said and written about how Matthew was treated by the Knights that year — including a pretty pointed column I did in the *Sunday Telegraph* when I said they insulted him just as much by not offering him anything, as they would have by making him a reduced offer. We both look at it now and say it was the best thing to have happened to Matty, although it was the toughest few months of his life, a period that made him a nervous wreck and sent him into depression.

He was struggling with bad hamstrings and an ankle problem and wasn't playing very well with the stress that that created. And he and Warren Ryan were fighting all the time; after one training session they were embroiled in a really big slanging match. I stayed out of all the politics as usual and tried to stay right out of Matty and 'The Wok's issues. Warren didn't have the best bedside manner and at one stage the players sent Tony Butterfield and Matthew to see the board about Warren's tough attitude with the players. But Warren was a great coach who taught me a lot and it's good to know that he and Matty get on well now — there are no grudges held at all about what happened then.

They clashed over tactics, plus Wok used to play mind games with Matty all the time, and other players too, to be honest; that's Warren being Warren. Matty was our main tactician on the field under Malcolm Reilly and contributed a lot to how we did things at training, but Warren, who coached us in 1999–2000, was much more his own man and was harder on Matty. Matt played for Australia in 1999 under Wok but by halfway through 2000 had lost his confidence and enjoyment from the game. He was a mess.

The whispers had been around for a couple of months that the club wouldn't be able to keep both of us under the salary cap, but when they decided at a board meeting on 3 May — 13 rounds into the season — that they couldn't even offer Matty a contract that wouldn't 'embarrass' him, all hell broke loose around Newcastle.

None of us anticipated how the issue of Matthew not being re-signed was going to be such a big emotional public debate. I remember going to a meeting at the club, and one of the hierarchy said something like: 'With this whole affair about Matthew and Andrew, the best indication of what the public feels is in the letters to the editor in the *Newcastle Herald*; there hasn't been one letter with a negative comment about the club's decision.' I thought that was a bit arrogant. Then next day there were four or five scathing letters, and I was laughing, saying, 'It just shows how little you know.' I just thought that with what Matthew had done for the club on and off the field — he and a few others had transformed how the team played into a more attacking style — I thought he deserved better.

Then my parents got caught up with the emotion of it all, which forced me to have a go at the old man and tell him to back off. Dad became really outspoken about it and was being quoted in the newspapers and getting into a war of words with Warren Ryan; to be honest, it gave me the shits. The supporters organised a rally against the club's sacking of Matthew before the home game against the Warriors at the end of May and the old man got up and spoke, telling them I was 100–1 to re-sign and that Warren Ryan 'could burn in hell'.

That's when I'd had enough. I was turning up for games trying to get myself mentally prepared and all this shit was going on and distracting us. So I got on the phone and told Dad, 'Matthew and I aren't 14 year olds, we are grown men. I know it hurts you, but it's also hurting us seeing you doing this; you've had your say, just leave it alone now.' I know he was upset about what I said, but he didn't enter the argument from then on. I felt people were using him up for their own agendas, even though I knew how passionate he was about his sons' football — any father would be, considering the circumstances. That was the only time I felt he stepped over the line in our careers.

Matty couldn't have played in the NRL against Newcastle, or especially against me, so he didn't want to go to another club here. He had approaches from rugby union which he seriously looked at, but he also got offers from Wigan and Wakefield in England and decided to go to Wigan. It was the best thing that could have happened; he went overseas and really found himself, then he came back to Sydney, had one season with the Sharks, and kicked on brilliantly with his media career. He laughs about how such a dramatic time in his life turned out to be his biggest turning point.

He loved living in England, although his youngest son Cooper struggled with asthma in the cold weather and Matty struggled on the field because of injuries. He met Brian Carney who became a lifetime friend and he loved being able to go to Premier League soccer matches and enjoy the English culture. And there is no doubt it did him a world of good getting away from the familiarity of Newcastle, and that has been in my own mind ever since.

When Matty came back he was a totally different person. In 2000 he was depressed, had become a real loner instead of the life of the party, and he'd lost his confidence and self-esteem. When he returned at the end of 2001, he took to being on camera with Channel Nine and Reg Reagan was born, he moved to Sydney and has stayed there, and his life and post-match career have kicked on unbelievably. He was also able to have one more season in the NRL, adding experience to the Cronulla side when he played under Chris Anderson in 2002, but he just wasn't fit enough because of his hamstring and shoulder problems, then a bad neck injury convinced him to retire.

It was during all the turmoil surrounding Matthew's contract at Newcastle not being renewed that I seriously looked at a change of club myself. What made me consider leaving was that not only was I going to lose my security blanket in Matthew, but at the time there was a lot of uncertainty surrounding the Knights: a new coach to replace Warren Ryan — who was departing the club after two seasons — was yet to be appointed, Paul Harragon had retired in 1999, and leading forwards Tony Butterfield, David Fairleigh and Peter Shiels were also leaving the club. It was the first time in my career that I'd been uncertain about what was next with my football. I didn't know whether the Knights could remain competitive without the players we were losing.

It was difficult confronting life without Matthew. He'd become such a crutch, and a convenience, for me. I was living with Renae but we had only one car, so Matty would pick me up for training every day and we'd go kicking together and do extra practice; and I'd take Samuel up to his and Trish's place while Renae was at work. We lived in each other's pockets and he was my chauffeur as well as my brother and most influential team-mate. Neither of us had ever contemplated playing anywhere else and thought we had at least two or three more years left together at Newcastle.

When he decided to go overseas, I realised he wasn't going to be around for the first time in my life and I somehow had to look after myself. I was scared that my safety net was not going to be there; someone to tell me to pull my head in, or drag me to do extra training, or tell me to do this or that. But in other ways I was excited that I had to prove myself and get out of the 'Johns Brothers' stigma, the belief that neither of us would be as effective without the other.

During that period I called Wayne Bennett — who I got to know reasonably well when he coached Australia in 1998 — as I knew he was looking for a halfback, with Kevvie Walters retiring just a year and a half after Allan Langer had left for England. I actually rang to recommend Justin Holbrook, my understudy at Newcastle, a bloke I reckoned was a genuine first grader but who hardly got a run with me missing few games that season. I had never given the slightest thought to going to Brisbane myself.

Wayne said something like, 'What about the other halfback at Newcastle — would he be interested in joining us?' It took me aback a bit and I said, 'I'll get back to you,' but when I thought about it, the idea really started to grow on me. The Broncos were still the best team in the NRL, and went on to win their second grand final in three years that season; Bennett was a great coach; and I thought it might be good to get out of Newcastle, which would force me to become more independent without Matty around. Plus living in a place like

Brisbane, which was more laid-back than Sydney but was bigger than Newcastle, had appeal. The Broncos had the most powerful pack in the competition, with Shane Webcke, Gorden Tallis, Petero Civoniceva, Dane Carlaw and Ashley Harrison, who was looking like he'd be a super player, even with Brad Thorn and Kevin Campion leaving; then they had Darren Lockyer, Ben Ikin, and the biggest wing partnership in Wendell Sailor and Lote Tuqiri in the backline.

I thought that playing under Wayne Bennett and in such a great side would be perfect for my career at that stage, given the uncertainty about how a much younger and inexperienced Newcastle side would go.

I'd just about made my mind up to leave; I felt no loyalty to the Knights after what they'd done to Matthew. It got to the stage where my partner Renae and her parents were looking for employment and housing in Brisbane. But a heart to heart with Matty and some clear thinking convinced me I was better staying put and taking up the challenge myself at Newcastle. And Michael Hagan getting the coaching position for 2001 was also a big influence. 'Hages', who had been at the club in 2000 as reserve grade coach, sat me down and talked about his plans and the added responsibility he wanted to give me. Straight away we struck it off and I thought I would really enjoy playing under him.

It turned out to be the best decision of my career; a heap of young blokes took us to a new level in 2001 and I was able to captain Newcastle to the premiership. And Wayne Bennett was great when I told him my decision — he virtually said he was glad I wasn't leaving if my heart was truly still with Newcastle.

There were often times I thought getting out of Newcastle would have been the best thing for me but when push came to shove, I couldn't leave the Knights or, in latter years, my son Samuel. I haven't got any regrets about that now. I've often read about plenty of players being on over $500,000 or $600,000 a year, and much more in the Super League and post-war years in the '90s. Well, I never ever had a contract worth more than half-a-mill a year with Newcastle. And it has never been a sore point with me; as I've said, money has never motivated me.

Other than offers from rugby union in 1998 and 2004, the biggest offer I received was probably from Souths, also in 2004 when I was out after having the knee reconstruction. While the rugby union thing was always in the paper, Souths had also offered me something like $150,000 to $200,000 a year more than I was getting — according to our manager John Fordham, the Rabbitohs also offered Matt and me $600,000 a season each in 1997 for the 1998–2000 seasons. I was really looking for a change in my life in 2004, and for a while it excited me that I might be able to play a role in sparking a revival of one of the two most famous traditional clubs (with St George). But, with all due respect to their team at the time, I just didn't think they had the personnel, especially in the forwards, not to struggle on the field and decided — at age 30 — I just didn't need that sort of pressure.

CHAPTER 16

2001 — SIMPLY THE BEST

The year 2001 was when I knew I had to step up to the next level in my career and take ownership of the Newcastle Knights' fortunes; I had to take a lot of responsibility that I had shied away from previously, when Matthew and other senior players were there.

That was the season I really learned how to — and fully believed that I could — control a game of football and my team's performance and take them to a new level with me. Around 1999–2000 I started to get the blueprint of how it could be done — I remember just taking command in some games and thinking, 'Beautiful, I'll sit back and kick and stay out of the game for a long period, but still control what's happening if our forwards are doing their job.' It just came from years of experience out on the field. It doesn't matter what sport it is, whether it is boxing, cricket or whatever, the time out on the field is where you learn these things.

With the retirement of Tony Butterfield, I'd also been made captain, and that seemed to bring out the best in me in a fairly young team. I'd rate 2001 as my best season for Newcastle, considering the circumstances. I captained the Knights to a premiership, scored the most points in a season in all my career (279) and came second in the Dally M count to Preston Campbell, despite missing eight games (although I became ineligible after being suspended for a forearm to Adam Dykes at Cronulla late in the season).

The worries I had about whether we could compete after the departures of Matty, Tony Butterfield, David Fairleigh and Peter Shiels ended up being unfounded. I rate the 2001 side as the best I played with during my 14 seasons with the Knights. That's something that Brian Smith, who was Parramatta's coach that year, spoke to me about when he came to coach Newcastle late in 2006. He received plenty of criticism after the Eels lost the grand final to us in 2001 after dominating all season, but what he was disappointed with was how the Knights didn't get the accolades we deserved as one of the great teams of the modern era. I agree with him that it was one of the most talented premiership-winning sides in the last couple of decades.

In our backline only five-eighth Sean Rudder hadn't played, or didn't go on to play, State of Origin or for Australia (Mark Hughes and Darren Albert played Origin and Robbie O'Davis, Matt Gidley, Adam MacDougall, Timana Tahu and myself also played Tests). Unfortunately, Alby was injured three weeks out from the finals after scoring 16 tries in 22 games, but we still had enough class to win the competition without him. In the forwards we had internationals in Danny Buderus, Ben Kennedy and Steve Simpson, plus Clinton O'Brien, who had played Origin for Queensland, Josh Perry, who went on to play for New South Wales, and Paul Marquet, who had won a competition with Melbourne and was one of the most underrated workhorses in the NRL. It was just the perfect blend of experience and very good emerging players, along with Matt Parsons, Billy Peden and Glenn Grief adding experience and toughness, and Daniel Abraham in the best form of his career probably, while John Morris came through that year as an interchange player and filled in brilliantly for Danny Buderus.

The season certainly wasn't all plain sailing, but it showed more than any other the importance of having the right sort of momentum at the back end of the season. From a couple of weeks out from the finals we were dead-set firing, and while everyone was blown away by Parramatta setting all sorts of records as runaway minor premiers, I knew what we were capable of on our day and that we had their measure. In our last four-and-a-half games of the season, before we clocked off a bit after leading the Eels 24–0 at half-time in the grand final, we scored 182 points to 52!

We didn't start the season all that well, winning two of our first five (and drawing 28-all with the Bulldogs), but we then got a roll on and won our next eight straight.

During that period, in round 11, I tore my medial ligament against St George Illawarra, just when I thought I was probably in the best stretch of form in my career ... with the State of Origin teams to be chosen that night.

I was out for 10 weeks, missed the entire Origin series, and when I was fit to play — against the Broncos at home — I was itching to get back into the team that had gone from first on the ladder to fifth and been flogged by Parramatta 40–0 the week before, and by the Bulldogs 46–18 the week before that.

My comeback game was probably my best individual performance for the Knights, which I go into in the chapter 'My 10 Most Memorable Games', and I was so happy to help the side to a 44–0 win against Brisbane who were second on the ladder. That put us on a four-match winning streak, during which I kicked the most extraordinary goal of my career.

It came against the Warriors in Auckland. We had the game won when Adam MacDougall scored the last of his four tries, just inside the right-hand touchline, a minute before the end to give us a 35–30 lead. I'd been practising a banana/reverse goal-kick at training and I'd shown it to Daryl Halligan, who was giving me some specialist kicking tuition that year. Daryl was in the commentary box for Sky TV New Zealand that day and I signalled to him to watch what I was about to do. When I took the ball back about eight metres from the try-line and stepped almost straight back from the ball — rather than to the left as most right-foot kickers do — all the Kiwis spectators nearby starting laughing and stirring me. Daryl immediately knew what I was up to and apparently said so on air. Bill Harrigan was the ref and he stood behind me wondering what the hell was going on. Somehow I nailed the goal, just screwed it around the upright, and I couldn't stop laughing at myself. Billy has said since it was the most amazing thing he's seen on the football field.

Our winning run ended at Cronulla in a game in which I was put on report and later earned a two-match suspension. It was a stupid act, which came from frustration; I'd scored a club record 34 points from four tries and nine goals against Canberra in a 54–26 win the weekend before and I think I just assumed I'd get a bucket-load of points again. When things didn't go our way I reacted ... and we went down 49–30.

We finished third and had to face the Roosters at home in the opening finals match. Paul Harragon never used to come to training but the night before the game he appeared out of the blue, got us together and said, 'Look, this is what's coming out of Sydney [from the Roosters camp]; they're saying that Newcastle are soft, they don't like the hard, physical games, they can't handle the arm wrestle, they are flamboyant and like high-scoring games but won't handle the pressure of finals.' Chief was so passionate about it and then said: 'If they think they are going to come up here to our club and do that, they're kidding.' Everyone pretty much went, 'Boom, let's show these bastards,' and the next night we blew them away, winning by 40–6. I didn't need any extra motivation; I hadn't forgotten the intercept I threw to Brad Fittler that cost us the final the previous year, meaning they were in the grand final instead of us — which is my biggest on-field regret from my career.

Late in the game I stepped through and put Ben Kennedy in to score next to the posts, and as BK was running back and I was about to line up the kick, I looked up towards the coach's box and eyeballed Michael Hagan. Against the tradition of the coach always keeping his cool, Hages was real animated. I remember thinking right then, 'We are going to win the comp, this is our year.' We got to our rehab session the next day and everyone was just bubbling and, when the conversation got to who we would play next, the feeling was: 'who cares?' As it turned out the Dragons (seventh) beat the Bulldogs (second), which gave us a week off.

We had to beat Cronulla to make the grand final and we were behind 10–6 at half-time. But we scored two tries in the second half from kicks — Mark Hughes went over from one of my banana kicks — and then Ben Kennedy sealed the game when he leaped over Preston Campbell to claim a bomb from Sean Rudder. We won 18–10.

'Ruddsie' was everyone's whipping boy and copped a bit of criticism about his inconsistency. I used to say to him all the time, 'You're either diamonds or stones,' but he worked up a good combination with Danny Buderus and myself that year, and the next week in the grand final we didn't have a better player than Sean Rudder.

On my first sighting of the Parramatta side, though, at the grand final breakfast the Thursday before the Sunday night game, I wasn't so sure our opponents were in the right mood.

A lot was said at the time about whether Parramatta 'choked' with nerves before the grand final after blowing everyone away with 17 wins from 18 games. Well, I have no doubt there is some degree of truth to that.

My first signs that they were very beatable came when a few of us went to Mark Hughes' place to watch them play Brisbane in the preliminary final, the day after we'd beaten Cronulla. The Eels dropped a lot of ball in the first half and there were clear indications to me that they were feeling the pressure —

they were minor premiers and the talk of the league, and there had been a lot of expectation about them making their first grand final since 1986, and winning it. A few of the blokes went, 'Oh we've got Parra' — they'd beaten us comfortably twice that year (32–14 and 40–0, although we had players missing both times) — but I was saying, 'Hey, I would rather play them than Brisbane.' The Broncos were like us, they had plenty of big-game players. There were areas of Parramatta's game that I felt we could exploit. It was just a matter of building everyone up, especially our least-experienced players, and getting them on the same wavelength by the time we got onto the field. I thought if the others could see how confident I and blokes like Ben Kennedy were, it would help them relax. Hages, for a bloke who was in his first season of first grade coaching, was extremely relaxed all week too.

On the morning of the grand final breakfast (you're up at six and at the function by seven, so we stayed at a hotel at Darling Harbour overnight), we were so relaxed; I thought then maybe too relaxed. I remember vividly how both teams had to line up, enter the room and go up onto a long table on stage while the teams were announced, and I looked at the Parramatta players and started grinning; they were just so obviously nervous and uptight. And their mannerisms didn't change the whole morning.

On the bus trip back to Newcastle I was saying to the boys, 'Did you see how nervous they were?' and we went into the mode then of talking it up as much as we could. We were saying, 'We are going to get out there and absolutely blow them off the park,' and when we got to training everything clicked so well, we were so relaxed and fluent. I just knew we were going to win.

We would normally stay at the Parramatta Park Royal the night before a game in Sydney, but the club's administration wanted us to stay at Coogee because they thought it would be off-putting staying in the heart of our opposition's territory with their supporters giving us heaps. There was a bit of drama about it as the team didn't want to change our routine and in the end we won the argument; so we stayed right in the middle of the Parramatta CBD. The morning of the game we went to Richie Benaud Park at North Parramatta and played cricket; everyone was kicking back and laughing and joking and people were hanging out of cars and giving us some stick — I think they couldn't believe we were staying there. But it was fun, if anything.

That was the first night-time grand final and the wait was murder. We had a whole day to fill in. I roomed with Danny Buderus and neither of us could sleep after lunch, so we flicked to see what was on TV ... nothing ... so we put on an in-house movie. It was about this female dancer who was deaf and dumb and her brother was also her manager, as well as being a drug dealer and an addict. Somehow, we sat through it for an hour and 45 and when it finished I looked at Bedsy and said, 'That was the worst movie I've ever seen in my life' — and he totally agreed but didn't want to say anything while I was watching it. Great preparation for a grand final!

We wiggled back and just flicked through the TV channels until we had a pre-game meal at 4.30; then the bus left at six. The night grand finals are the pits as far as I am concerned, especially an 8pm kickoff as it was then (it is now seven), and I haven't met any player or fan who doesn't think it should go back to an afternoon kickoff.

Again when both teams appeared and lined up for the national anthem I could see how nervous the Parramatta boys still were, while we were so relaxed. Plenty of people have asked what our specific tactics were and whether it was to expose their halfback Jason Taylor, a noted soft defender. But honestly, there was no extra point made of him at all. The talk all week was just that we had to be physical in the forwards, really take the game to them early, try to force them into error and get into our own rhythm. I knew we had the talent to get them if we just set a solid platform.

As it turned out we blew them off the park to lead 24–0 after scoring four tries in the first 22 minutes; we completed 20 out of 21 sets in the first half. It was near perfect; one of those games where everything just clicked. Our big props Matt Parsons and Josh Perry would start the momentum, then Ben Kennedy and Steve Simpson would come at them wider of the ruck and spot their smaller men. They were giving me so much room to kick, I was just finding the dirt and kicking into the corner every time. I couldn't train much all week because of the hip flexor problem and I couldn't kick the ball properly during the game. If I kicked with a normal motion with my right leg it would pinch the muscle, so I had to kick with a more rounded, wider arc where I would use more the outside of my 'glute'. But it was fine.

We went in at half-time still leading 24–0 and we had a circle of seats in which we all sat. It takes probably three minutes after the players arrive for the coach to get down to the dressing room at Telstra Stadium. Before Hages got there, there was all the hyperactive, bullshit talk starting, so I got up and said, 'C'mon, I don't want to hear anyone talk. Sit there, drink water, take your shirts off if you want, cool off, and no one talks except Hages and me.' It became nice and quiet — you don't need all the shit talk in that situation; people start panicking and getting overanxious. I remember sitting there grinning to myself, thinking, 'We've got this won,' and Hages was really relaxed too and just kept it to brief, controlled messages. We said all we had to do was score first in the second half and they would fold.

To Parramatta's credit they scored first and came back fairly strongly, but despite the final score being 30–24 there was no way we were ever in danger of losing; we would have found another gear if we had to.

I have a much clearer memory this time of the after-match events than in the 1997 grand final. Being captain and having to go up and receive the trophy was really special; then to win the Clive Churchill Medal was just unbelievable, although I still reckon Ben Kennedy should have won it (not that I'm giving it back, BK). It's funny actually — we went into camp with the Australian team a week or so after that and Wendell Sailor kept yelling out, 'When are you going to give that medal back to BK?'

I saw one of my best mates Kris Lees in the crowd while we were doing our victory lap and I'd told him earlier to back me for the man of the match award. I spotted him and he was holding up five fingers, screaming, 'I got 5–1, I got 5–1,' and I was yelling, 'Is that all you got?' By the time we were back in the dressing room I grabbed two beers and I met Brian Smith on his way out of the media conference when I was on my way in. I gave him one of the beers and said, 'Bad luck, mate,' and all that. You could see the devastation in his eyes.

When I got back to the sheds Prime Minister John Howard and Opposition Leader Kim Beazley were both there fighting for a photo opportunity. I said to them, 'How about we get one of you either side of me and we'll get a photo together?' which seemed to be the pragmatic thing to do. It ran in the papers next day.

Being such a late kickoff, it was after 1am when we returned to Newcastle and we were told we were going to drop into the stadium first. To see over 15,000 people who had waited up that late to greet us was absolutely unbelievable; that was the moment it really hit home to me how special our supporters were and how much our success meant to them. It was almost as special as winning the match itself. I'd taken it for granted in 1997 when the town went wild; I was just a young lair then who carried on like an idiot and rode the wave. This time it meant a lot more to me.

All things considered — that it was my first year as captain and my first without Matthew outside me as five-eighth; it was Michael Hagan's first as coach; the fact we had lost so many experienced players from the year before and didn't have one senior signing from outside, plus the fact Parramatta broke so many records that year — it was the best season I had at Newcastle. Sure, I wish Matty had stayed for one more season and played in another grand-final winning team with me, but that's no big issue now. It was just a dream year.

CHAPTER 17

KING OF THE CASTLE

The positives of having been able to live in Newcastle and play in the NRL from there far outweighed the negatives. I feel lucky I could do what I have in the area where I grew up, an area I am so familiar with, an area where I am around a lot of my friends and family. I love the culture of the place, how laid-back it is; it is not a big city, it is probably like a big country town but with all the attractions you need and beautiful beaches.

I think it's a great place to raise a family, although I have reservations about how it will be for Samuel growing up there as my son. Samuel will be eight soon and is not interested in rugby league or playing it himself, which I'm happy about really. Don't get me wrong — I think it would be great for him to play any sport he chooses, but he would just be under such incredible scrutiny from such a young age and kids don't need that.

Generally, I know I am blessed. Sure I've worked hard, but I've just had so many lucky breaks. I live in a beautiful house in a spot right on the beach; people would kill for that and I don't take it for granted. I know also how fortunate I was that I was protected from any off-field scandals becoming headline news by the general public and media during my playing career, and the way the Knights have handled things. I'd say that's part of the Newcastle culture too, not dumping on each other. You know, 'Hey, he's one of us and look what he's done for us — let him go.'

People in Newcastle and the Hunter absolutely love their league team, and they love the city. You talk to anyone from Newcastle and they say how great it is and they'd never live in Sydney; they are just so incredibly proud of the city and what it has achieved. I don't think any other place in Australia has the parochialism and loyalty to match Newcastle's. There isn't much bullshit in the place either.

And it's not just Newcastle that I love but the surrounding areas too. Port Stephens is just up the road; that's where a lot of my best childhood memories belong and I still go up there in summer, get in my dad's boat, moor it and swim; there is no one around and the water so crystal clear, you could be anywhere in the world.

Even though I grew up in Cessnock I've spent little time in the vineyards, but when I go out there now I realise what a beautiful place it is. We took Brian Carney there — the visiting Irishman and Knights winger of 2006 — and he reckoned it was one of the most beautiful places he'd seen in the world. I sat back and thought, 'Yeah, it is, but it's been in front of me my whole life and I've just taken it for granted.' The beaches here are beautiful too. Those who still think of Newcastle as an industrial city are behind the times; they haven't had heavy industry here for 10 or 15 years.

But there are certainly downsides of living in a 'fishbowl' like Newcastle. And I haven't ever got used to being one of the biggest fish in the bowl. I think with anyone who is relatively famous and whose face becomes easily recognisable, people are black and white in their attitude towards you: they either love you or hate you; there is no grey. I know that's the case with me. And I know I've brought a lot of that on myself with things I've done to give people reason to dislike me. I can be short with people because I genuinely don't find it easy to communicate with those I don't know, and I've already mentioned my ridiculous behaviour when I'm out on the grog.

What a lot of people don't understand is that on any given day I could get home at night having been asked the same question by 50 different people — 'how's your knee?' or 'how's your neck?'; 'where's your brother?'; 'how are the Knights going to go this year?' If I'm a bit short with someone, they'll tell 100 people I'm 'a rude prick', whereas if I'm pleasant to someone and answer them, nothing is said.

Now I know it's nice for people to recognise you and be interested in you; for you to feel as though you're their hero and that what you and the Knights do each weekend has a real big effect on how they feel about their lives. And they are not to know that 50 other people have said the same thing to me in the previous few hours. But I've never become used to the fact that I'm a sort of human exhibition. I'll drive past the shop when I need to get some food and if I can see there are a few people in there, I won't go in because I just can't face all the attention I know I'll get. I know that maybe it's my problem more than anyone else's, but I just really crave my own space and to be anonymous sometimes.

You become very guarded with people. You don't let people in. I can be somewhere and I dead-set know what someone is going to ask me. I wish I was much better at the public side of being a well-known footballer but I'm just not; I don't thrive on being the centre of attention and I do have trouble making conversation.

And there is the bipolar side of me that makes me really suspicious of what people who may be staring at me or whispering about me might be saying. It really used to do my head in, to the extent that I went to a psychologist and spoke to him about it. I told him I just wasn't coping with it; I didn't want to leave my house because everywhere I'd go people would be looking and it could be so off-putting. I'd be out getting some groceries and I would hear someone whisper my name and I'd be thinking, 'What are they saying about me?' It didn't help sometimes that I might have been on the grog all weekend and didn't know where I'd been.

My oasis is The Burwood Inn at Merewether; it's one place where I'm treated as Andrew Johns and not Joey Johns, and I love it. The Burwood's probably not a lot different to any other unobtrusive Aussie pub, but it's my home away from home to an extent, where I can just be me, and even if I have a few beers and become a bit silly, the locals just accept me as any other drinker. There are some pretty down-to-earth regulars there and they take the piss out of me more than give me any adulation!

The Burwood Inn is run by Barry and Debbie Bradley and daughters Sian and Rae and they are just great people. They really look after me and the Knights boys when they go there.

Matt Hoy first introduced me to The Burwood, or 'The Zoo' as some locals call it, over a decade ago. I introduced the Knights boys to the pub and we started to get back there late after a home game. One of the best nights of the year is 'Surfest Sunday' after the annual surfing contest finishes, when all the surfers and footballers mix and it goes off, with dance challenges and everything. The Gold Coast's Mick Fanning won Surfest one year and invited everyone back to The Burwood and it became an annual institution from then on. One year there were 10 world surf champions there, including Kelly Slater.

Another time, cricket legend Dennis Lillee walked in on Surfest Sunday. He was in town on a speaking engagement and must have gone down to the beach and heard everyone was going back to The Burwood. He came in and sat down, said hello and had a drink with everyone — what a great down-to-earth bloke. I had a good chat to him; you wouldn't meet a better knockabout Aussie guy.

Whenever we have anyone come to town and stay over, I generally take them to The Burwood. When we had Samuel's 'wet-the-head' session in 1999, David Furner, Laurie Daley and Jason Croker came up and stayed three days there (I don't think their wives were too impressed).

There are some interesting regulars at The Burwood. 'Howie' has lived upstairs for about 20 years, and probably hasn't changed the sheets in all that time. He looks like the Abominable Snowman with his long hair and wild beard and I reckon he holds the world record for the most gout in the one body; his toes are bent every which way. Then there's 'Changa', who writes his own songs, some of which are hilarious when he sings them in the bar. Changa also fancies himself as a rock and roll wrestler, although he has one setback — he weighs about 45 kilos. One night, my brother Matty got in a wrestle with Chang, Matt fell on a broken schooner glass and got about 20 stitches in his knee; our coach at the time, Warren Ryan, wasn't too happy with Changa, nor was the club with Matthew, who got a stern 'please explain' letter.

Barry has done it up a little bit the past few years, put in a good bistro with good steak; I'm generally down there a couple of nights a week and often watch *Monday Night Footy* with Baz and have a couple of lemon squashes. Sometimes I ride my skateboard there, put it in the corner and have a few beers; if I have a few too many Baz will drive me home. Almost anything goes within reason at The Burwood, except there is one golden rule — the old guys drink at the western end of the bar and the younger blokes sit at the eastern end, and if the 'west-enders' come up to the 'east-enders' territory or vice versa, there is hell to pay.

My other 'local' at Merewether is the break just outside my house on the Dixon Park end of the beach. Surfing is my most common release from the fishbowl existence. Out on the waves I'm just one of the boys; I am just a mere mortal out there. If I'm in a spot and they want to take off, I get no special treatment in the water; they certainly don't say, 'You kicked six from six on the weekend — you get the first wave of the set.'

I'll surf anywhere where the waves are good around Newcastle or, when I have more time to do it, I love getting in the car with a couple of boys and heading to Forster, or half an hour south of Newcastle to different spots. Having Wednesdays off when I was playing, there was often no one in the water so we would get it to ourselves really; it's just sensational.

I surf every day in summer; sometimes I'd get up early and surf before training during the footy season too. Even if I only had 20 minutes to get out there and catch four or five waves I'd do it, and I'm blessed to live a 20-second jog to the beach. On a normal off-season day I'd get up at six, surf until seven, have breakfast and go to training.

I love to look over the ocean from my house. I'm lucky I have such an expansive view, but I have this thing where I can't stand thinking people are looking or pointing at me from the street. Being on a busy road, people come past bipping their horns and screaming all the time. My house gets 'egged' probably twice a week and letters would be left in the letter box or under the windscreen of my car when I was in the old house. Some were pretty weird and threatening, which makes you feel fairly vulnerable. But that was before we knocked the house down and had a new one built with pretty good security and a front wall.

The only time I've been vandalised was when I was living in a unit around the corner while the new house was being built. The *Newcastle Herald* did a spread in the paper listing the details of the place I'd just bought, so, great, it told every potential lunatic my address. I was away playing in Townsville the next weekend, and when I got back the sliding glass door had been smashed and my plasma TV stolen.

The most chilling experience came in 2004 when two women from Orange in western NSW became obsessed with me, and supposedly would go to Newcastle to see Knights games and sort of stake out my place. The ordeal started when my mum received phone calls from this woman saying she needed my phone number; her sister was sick and she needed to talk to me. A few days later — this was in my old house — I was out in the front yard and these two girls, who were in their early 20s, came over and were asking all these weird questions, so I quickly retreated inside. Then Cathrine started getting phone calls at Sony. She left her mobile number on her voicemail message so they obviously got that number and left over 50 messages calling her a slut and a prostitute. One time, one of them said, 'I'm watching you ... stay away from Newcastle and stay away from my boyfriend.' Another time, Cath just heard a long scream at the end of the phone and then they hung up. They also sent a letter in red and black type, saying, 'I see people!!! Dead people see you!!! You are a bad woman,' which shook us up a fair bit. We informed the police and the calls were traced straight away to the house where the women lived. Police went there and there was Knights paraphernalia everywhere and 'I love Joey' on their mobile phones.

Apparently they'd been on the internet on a chat line and someone had pretended to be me, and they were completely fooled by it. The funny thing was that at that time I didn't even have a computer and wouldn't have had any idea how to use one if I did. They were telling people they were going out with me; and they used to drive to Newcastle all the time. Cathrine was at a game at Penrith one day and they were calling her name and giving her the death stare, so that's when she first recognised who they were.

Eventually we applied for an Apprehended Violence Order and they were charged with stalking Cath, but both their cases were dismissed on the grounds they were suffering from mental illnesses at the time. They were ordered to have treatment and to stay away from us.

What shook me up most was that Cathrine was exposed by it all. I used to get worried enough anyway about Samuel playing in the yard at our place when you wouldn't know who was hanging around, but this episode made me more paranoid.

Early on, it was a buzz to be so well known. I'd go to a nightclub and there'd be a line-up and I'd be ushered straight in. Then I'd get free drink tickets and wouldn't have to line up for drinks; or I'd go to a restaurant and there wouldn't be any tables available, but room would be made for me anyway. It was fun to get out and about and get attention from the girls and become a bit of a man about town. But in the end, it became part of a false sort of reality; it's wonderful that people just bend over backwards for me and you do tend to take it for granted, but the 'Oh it's Andrew Johns' reaction can become too 'in your face'.

Often when I am at a restaurant, people come up and put stuff in front of me to sign when I'm just about to take a mouthful of food. It sort of makes me laugh — people say, 'Look, I'm sorry to be rude but ...' when it is being rude not waiting 10 minutes until I'm finished my meal or walking out of the restaurant. Then if I sign one thing, it can be the prompt for other people to come over, thinking that the ice was broken by someone else. Don't get me wrong — I'll sign something because I am conscious of how rude I end up being seen as if I don't; ultimately people would tell 20 of their friends and the story would grow into me blowing up at the waitress. Maybe I should learn to say politely, 'I'd be happy to do it for you a bit later, but would it be OK to finish my meal first?' It can get pretty tiresome, especially when deep down I so much want to be treated like everyone else.

When the NSW cricket team played at Newcastle's No. 1 Sports Ground once and Steve Waugh was playing, he was quoted as saying something about how ridiculous the fan attention was in Newcastle, that he couldn't go anywhere without people being in his face and how he was caught signing autographs for an hour and a half. I'm happy to sign autographs, for kids especially; the only time I wouldn't was before a game when I was trying to focus on the match an hour or two away.

Then there were moments when people might grab me after a game and say, 'We drove four hours to see you play and it's great to see you play in the flesh.' I remember being introduced to a boy by his dad at Campbelltown one day. He said he'd always talked about me to his son and finally he had got to see me play in the flesh, and it meant a lot to them. It's great to know the positive impact I can have on people and think back to when I was a kid and what it meant to me to meet rugby league players I looked up to. You can get a bit blasé about it and want some peace, but moments like that give you a reality check.

It doesn't seem that long ago that I was a kid who met Steve Rogers, Brett Kenny, Peter Sterling and those sorts of players who were more than my heroes — they were like superhuman. When Donny Schofield would take us down to Balmain games and we'd meet Wayne Pearce, Benny Elias and 'Blocker' Roach, it was 'stars in your eyes' stuff. These blokes were bigger than Hollywood stars to us; their pictures were all over my wall.

So while you'd want to get into your car or the team bus instead of being stuck signing autographs for 40 minutes, I'd try to think about what it means to kids and tried to always do that after games, even when I was feeling down or carrying an injury. I'd say, 'Think back when you were a 10 year old. If someone had said one day you were going to play Friday night football against Brisbane, there were going to be a million people watching and you were going to be the focal point of the game, you would have done anything.'

And the real upside of being a well-known sportsman is the joy you can bring to people, especially sick or disadvantaged kids, by just turning up and giving them some of your time, or giving them a memento from your career. It's the side of all sportsmen not a lot of people see — I'm no different, although I wish I had time to do more. I admit it makes me sick, though, when you see sportsmen or entertainers at a hospital and there are cameras in the background; if you want to do it, you don't have to let the media know and get recognition for it.

I am a patron of Ronald McDonald House in Newcastle and I'm in awe of the fantastic job Ross and Rohan Bingham (a husband and wife team) do there. When you have kids of your own you realise how vulnerable families are when kids get sick. I couldn't imagine the burden of having a terminally ill or critically ill child, especially people who aren't well off. Newcastle's Ronald McDonald House covers the area from Newcastle to the Queensland border and there are always so many kids and their families there; it's a cause I'm proud to support.

One of the most touching experiences I've had was one year when Danny Buderus and I saw a girl called Emma in hospital; it was arranged by the club and she didn't know we were coming. It was just great to see her face light up when we walked up beside her bed. That night we were playing the Roosters and I told Emma to make sure she watched the game and I'd win the man of the match for her and mention her. Well, I was fortunate enough to win the award and said hello to her on Channel Nine while she was sitting up watching with her family. Sadly, Emma died later that week and I received a touching letter from her parents.

A person who really inspires me is a teenager from Hull in England called Scott Walker, who suffers cerebral palsy. He and his family are dead-set rugby league fanatics and the town raised money for Scott and his dad Terry to come to Sydney to watch an Origin game in 2004. They came out to Origin training and I was just so impressed by their enthusiasm for the game and how positive they were all the time. After the game, I arranged to give Scott my jersey and wrote on it, 'Your enthusiasm for the game inspires me.' Cathrine brought Scott and Terry to the after-match function and she took him around to meet all the boys, which was a massive buzz for them.

We kept in touch with them and they returned to Australia in 2006. They came up to Newcastle and we put them up — they stayed for the Tri Nations at the end of the season. Matt King gave Scott his winning Tri Nations Medal, which was really special.

Whenever I might have been struggling for motivation in the latter part of my career and thinking, 'What am I still doing playing?' I'd only have to think about Scott, who loves footy as much as me but has never been able to even run.

Footballers generally are fantastic with people who deserve a lift. One guy who is just amazing with kids is Willie Mason, but unfortunately he gets publicity for the controversial parts of his life, not the good things like that.

So, as you can see, there are upsides and downsides to being someone 'famous' (I hate using that word really), when my address is no secret, people can be invasive but equally as supportive, and their rugby league team is such a big part of the city's culture.

I don't know where my next journey will take me but I think I will leave Newcastle, for a while at least, whether to escape the 'fishbowl' or just to experience something different. Western Australia would be perfect, but then I have to face the reality of my media commitments with Channel Nine and News Limited and the chance to earn a living doing specialist coaching, so that may not happen unless I can just get 12 months off to live a life of anonymity before I go into the next phase. It would be perfect if I could pull that off, but then again I have to think of Cath and her needs in life and her career too. We'll have to see.

I will always have a home in Newcastle because that's where Samuel will be and it will always be home to me; I was brought up just down the road in Cessnock and all my mates will be here. Matthew has moved away and lives on Sydney's northern beaches, but he still gets up here a lot and he was even talking about whether to move back at one stage. But I know I couldn't cope with taking on the F3 in the two-and-a-half-hour trip to Sydney too often.

Overall, I feel blessed to have grown up and lived where I have and to have played for the Newcastle Knights for my entire career. There is not a shadow of a doubt the Newcastle supporters are the most devoted and loyal in the NRL, and I never underestimate how special it was to run out to a packed EnergyAustralia Stadium with the locals right on our side.

The Knights really gel the whole Hunter community together and it has been great to have been part of that.

But I've always wanted some sort of balance, to be able to slink away and be myself and not be noticed. I know that's not a reality of my unreal world. Newcastle is a place where everyone feels you're one of them, that you can be as successful or famous as you like, but you shouldn't lose touch with the common man and they have the right to own some part of you. That's really earthy and special ... but in my case I've also found it hard to deal with.

CHAPTER 18

I WAS GOING TO RUGBY

If the Australian Rugby Union had opened their arms in welcome instead of being cautious about my age and fitness, I would have finished my football career in rugby union. There is no doubt about that.

But for those in rugby still pointing the finger at Brett Robinson, who was then the ARU's high performance unit manager who recommended they shouldn't sign me, I have no hard feelings. In fact, when I look back on it now, he was just doing his job and made the decision that probably anyone in his position would have under the circumstances.

The events of 2004, which became a five-month saga played out almost daily in the media, was one of the toughest times of my life. The first story I can recollect, from the clippings I have gone through while doing this book, was in the *Sun-Herald* on 11 January 2004, when

Danny Weidler reported: 'Johns has told friends he would like nothing more than to take on [Jonny] Wilkinson in the 2007 World Cup, even though he would be 33.' The whole 'will he or won't he go to rugby?' issue didn't finish until days after I made a decision on the morning of 25 June to re-sign with the Newcastle Knights and finish my career in rugby league.

How close was I, truly, to defecting to the other code? I was on my way — twice. That was even though the main reason I stayed in Newcastle, to be close to my son Samuel, played on my mind heavily. I was desperate to tackle the challenge of playing rugby union. I had no doubt whatsoever I would have been successful and would have gained a place in the Wallabies squad as a number 10 (five-eighth). If there was a situation where I could have taken Samuel on at least part of the tours, and the NSW Waratahs would have allowed me a couple of days off every second week to go back to Newcastle to see him, I was going to rah-rah land.

I was pretty keen on the idea by the time I first sat down for informal talks with Wallabies coach Eddie Jones in April 2004 and told him I wasn't using the discussions as a bargaining tool; I genuinely wanted to play rugby union. Eddie genuinely wanted me to go across and, to be honest, I was pissed off when he didn't get support from the ARU.

This is the true story of how it all evolved, which I want recorded because I know there are some people in rugby union who still think the whole affair was a great con by John Fordham aimed simply at increasing my income from rugby league. It was never ever about money — the money on the table from both parties was about the same. It was about me taking on a new challenge.

If it was about money I would have gone to rugby union years earlier. Matthew and I were first approached in 1997, just after we'd won our first premiership with the Knights. 'Fordo' tells the yarn about having dinner with John O'Neill and John Laws (who he also manages), and their wives. Fordo and O'Neill had had informal discussions about what it would take to entice Matt and me to rugby, and as O'Neill was leaving Otto restaurant (one of Fordo's regular dining houses, in Woolloomooloo), he said something like: 'Let's make it easy for you — we're offering $600,000 each per season for three seasons.' That was unbelievable money for those days, even with rugby league players still on Super League-inflated contracts — the size of which, by the way, were on the way down as the NRL salary cap became fair dinkum.

Now it was obvious that, with Fordo's strong rugby background, he would not have been unhappy if we became high-profile rugby signings, but I never considered it for a minute then, even with the amount of money involved. I was 23 and had a lot still to achieve in rugby league, despite having played Origin for NSW, Tests for Australia and having won a competition with the Knights. But Matthew really did think about it, to be honest, before deciding he also had too much to enjoy in league.

I've always enjoyed watching rugby — on a Friday night I'll watch a couple of Super 14 games before the NRL match goes to air. I like it when they play ad lib footy. To be honest,

I think rugby league has spoiled rugby union because the rugby league coaches have gone over and improved their defensive structures, if not their one-on-one defence, so now teams just defend too well. In rugby union 10 years ago, they would play one ruck at a time, shift the ball and throw it and loop around; nowadays you see eight, nine or 10 rucks and they still don't make any ground. It's too structured, but I enjoy watching the way New Zealand teams play; they have a great attitude to their rugby — they like to throw the ball and they don't keep the ball in tight too much. You see the South Africans play, they are just massive and love the collision but they just play around the rucks, where New Zealanders play it wide, they like to use their pace outside.

Anyway, I never thought about playing rugby again until Matty and I were guests in the Sony corporate box at Stadium Australia in Sydney for the 2003 World Cup final — that unbelievable game in which Jonny Wilkinson potted an extra-time field goal to win the game for England 20–17 over the Wallabies. I had to go into the Channel Nine studios early the next morning to do comments on the third rugby league Ashes Test in England, so I wasn't drinking that night and I took in the whole amazing atmosphere. Matty was pissed and he turned to me during the second half and said: 'If you're not a part of the next World Cup, you are crazy.'

I don't know how it crept out that I had an inkling about trying rugby union, but I wish it hadn't. I became sick of my life being played out in the media and people second guessing around the half-truths or dead-set untruths over the ensuing months.

I had finished the 2003 season with a neck injury after suffering back fractures the year before. Then, after working my arse off for a big season in 2004, I wrecked my knee at Parramatta in round three, which meant I needed a reconstruction and was out for the season. I was in the wilderness, depressed, and had doubts about myself as a footballer for probably the first time since becoming a first grader. During 2004, Kurt Gidley had come up to play halfback and was playing really well — and proved how well he could influence games when he won the Knights the match against Brisbane at Suncorp Stadium in round 10 with a field goal in extra-time. I had just turned 30 and people were questioning that I could come back, and I know there was talk around town that maybe the Knights didn't need Andrew Johns any more. I seriously started to question whether I had a future at Newcastle and thought maybe it was time to move on.

I don't know who sparked rugby's interest, whether it was ex-Wallabies coach Bob Dwyer, who John Fordham also manages, or Eddie Jones. I'd met Eddie the year before when Wendell Sailor introduced him while I was in Origin camp and the Wallabies were staying at the same hotel. Wendell had previously told me Eddie had huge respect for the league players and he loved watching rugby league. Anyway, we sat and talked for a while, about tactics and the similarities and differences between the two games, and they were picking my brain about this and that. I played really well during that Origin series; whether that had an impact on Eddie or not I'm not sure, but we certainly struck a chord with each other. He seemed a really down-to-earth sort of bloke and a smart coach.

Anyway, in April of 2004, John Fordham told me that rugby was interested in talking to me and he set up a meeting at his place with Eddie Jones and Brett Robinson. That's when I told Eddie I was serious about looking at union. I told him what I thought of the game and how I thought it worked, and I think he was impressed with how much knowledge I had of the basics of why you keep the ball in tight, that sort of stuff. I had a good dinner with them and the negotiations started after that. It would have been such a big learning curve for me, but that was the attraction, getting out of my comfort zone and learning something all over again. I would have been under enormous pressure, I know, but I wouldn't have let myself fail; there was no way I would have let myself go over and given the critics ammunition to have pot shots at me. I still know to this day that I would have handled it fine. There was talk of me playing number 10 or inside centre even, although I thought there was no way I was fast enough to play in the centres. But I just thought number 10 would have suited me down to the ground.

At that stage I really felt I needed a change; whether it was just getting out of Newcastle and playing somewhere else, or going as far away as playing in England, which would have been tough with Samuel back home. The big jewel for me was playing a whole different sport like rugby. I wanted to play against Jonny Wilkinson — I wanted to outdo him, that was a big driving force. Looking back now, he's hardly played a game since then, but other challenges have come up, like All Black king Carlos Spencer and then Dan Carter, who has become such a dominant player for New Zealand. It was the opportunity to play on the world stage that really excited me.

Fordo was into this secrecy stuff so he made sure that in any correspondence or phone talks I was referred to as 'Player Y' ('Joey' ended in Y), and apparently about the same time he was talking to rugby about 'Player X', who was Roosters centre Ryan Cross, who eventually signed with the Western Force two years later.

I spoke to Wendell a few times and a bloke called Simon Atkins, the Wallabies masseur, who also used to massage me. I was worried about what the reception would be amongst the players, whether they would think, 'Shit, here comes another "leaguey" crossing over and getting this sort of money,' but they said everyone was really positive and hoping I'd come over, which was good to hear.

We had a second meeting with Eddie Jones and Brett Robinson, and Eddie seemed pretty keen. Then there was a meeting with Waratahs coach Ewan McKenzie one night at a restaurant near John Fordham's home in Woollahra; Bob Dwyer attended too. I remember getting a bit wound up that night, holding court about how I would play rugby and some things in rugby that could change and I think Ewan McKenzie was thinking, 'What is this bloke talking about?'

From then on it became a soap opera, on the front or back pages every week bar none. There was never a quote from anyone, but it went on and on and just did my head in. I deliberately don't read the papers if I know I'm going to be in there, but I'm sure the over-hype about the whole thing made people think, 'Geez, this bloke just loves getting his mug in the paper,' when it's totally the opposite.

Negotiations began between Fordo and the Waratahs, who

knew they had the backing of the Australian coach. I don't know the politics involved between the NSWRU and the ARU and I don't really care, but there was some friction there and it all went pear shaped very quickly. John O'Neill had left to take over as Soccer Australia boss and apparently there was a rift between the two bodies over who they wanted as his successor. Matt Carroll was acting ARU CEO at that stage before Gary Flowers was appointed. I let Fordo worry about all that and he organised a meeting where both parties were there. He left pretty fired up, and called me to say the ARU wouldn't support the Waratahs in getting me to go across (the Waratahs could offer only $155,000 and needed further financial input from the ARU), so we put out a release saying that I was staying in league. It looked like all bets were off.

The same day, the ARU released a statement that they had decided not to support the Waratahs' bid to get me. That's when it came out that they thought I was too old and, with the injury problems I'd had, too big a risk. And all the fingers started pointing at Brett Robinson who, I admit, never appeared as keen as Eddie Jones. The irony to me was that their freakishly talented number 10 Steve Larkham was born the same month as me, May 1974, and had had more than his share of injuries, but I was considered to be too old and injury-prone.

Look, the ARU high performance unit was asked for its view and Brett Robinson gave them his expert opinion from all the facts he had. He's been portrayed as a bit of a bad guy in all this, but if I'd gone over and in the second game I'd done my knee again, he would have been the fall guy. I had complications with my knee at that time; it wasn't the run-of-the-mill reconstruction recovery. I couldn't straighten the leg, I'd had the blood clots after the operation — which were pretty scary — then I had an infection in it, so not wanting to pay big money for a 30-year-old player who had a recent history of injuries — neck, back and knee in the previous three years — I can understand his point of view. He was only doing his job and I'd like to think it was nothing personal. I later had an MRI scan on my knee which showed I had a 'cyclops lesion' and, to be honest, it did worry me a bit, although it didn't affect me greatly on the field. I had an operation on it about 16 months later when I pulled out of the Tri-Nations tour of England. So the ARU could see there were complications with it and I can't blame them really. It didn't stop my manager, however, sending Brett Robinson every press clipping after I played what I regard as my best game in my return to State of Origin the next year, but the 'gesture' didn't have anything to do with me.

When the ARU pulled out I thought that was the end of the subject. But then some influential figures in NSW rugby, led by Bob Dwyer, established a Friends of the Waratahs group to arrange third-party sponsorships in a last-minute bid to get me across to rugby. With the help of Mark Ella's company Horton Ella, they ended up raising more than $400,000, I believe. But the whole affair had left a bad taste in my mouth. I thought, 'If the ARU don't want me, and I go over and I play as well as I think I can play and make the Wallaby squad, all of a sudden the ARU would be back-slapping me and it would be so hypocritical.' Plus, after talking to people around me who knew what a loose cannon I was off the field, I thought that if I did anything wrong and it got out, they would just hang me out to dry.

It's ironic that reports have come out recently that one of the reasons the ARU didn't want me was because they'd heard rumours about my alcohol problem and, supposedly, a drug problem. I still don't know if it is true or not. After it hit the papers, Eddie Jones said my off-field lifestyle was never mentioned. People have been saying Brett Robinson was the one who brought it up when questioned, after I hit the headlines with the London ecstasy tablet incident. I don't know what the motives were, but if that was the case, I found it a bit like kicking a dog when he was down.

I had no idea my reckless lifestyle was an issue but if it contributed to the ARU's decision to shun me, I understand and accept it. Personally, I have no problem with anyone in rugby union. I'm not a vengeful person; it's water under the bridge.

Despite all the complications associated with me switching to rugby union, I was desperate for a change, and the challenge of having a crack at it just wouldn't go away in my mind. The only thing keeping me in Newcastle was the fact that Samuel was there, so I had to weigh up that if I went to rugby I'd be away from home a lot, I'd have to base myself in Sydney and wouldn't be sure how often I'd be able to see my little boy.

I was down at The Burwood, having a feed on my own one night, when Phil Gould called me on my mobile. We were talking generally when he said, 'Are you alright?' and I said,

'Mate, I'm not, to be honest, I'm really struggling with this decision but I think I'm going to rugby — I'm going to announce it in the next couple of days.' The line went quiet and Gus said, 'What are the reasons?' I told him I needed a new challenge and that I just couldn't handle the fishbowl existence in Newcastle any more. That it had gotten to the stage that if I drove past a shop and some people were in there, I didn't feel like going in. Plus I didn't know if the Knights needed me any more ... I just needed a change of scenery. He said he could relate to that and asked if it was a money thing. I said, 'No, not really, although I could probably get a bit more in union.'

The pressure I felt I was under and the things that played on my mind, like the guilt of leaving Newcastle and Samuel and being branded disloyal by the rugby league legends I idolised, weighed on me heavily; it tortured me. I asked those who were close to me that I respected, like brother Matt and my parents, what they thought I should do; they all came back with 'whatever you decide we'll support you, it's your decision'. If someone had just said, 'Go to rugby, you've done all you can in league, take on a new challenge,' I wouldn't have hesitated and would have signed long before then. I just needed some reassurance from someone.

Next thing, the wheels were in motion for News Limited and Channel Nine to kick in a little bit to help me stay in league. It was funny how that story grew a ridiculous amount of legs too, like Kerry Packer coming to Newcastle and picking me up in a helicopter, which was absolute garbage. Extensions and upgrades of my agreements with News

Limited and Channel Nine were negotiated by John Fordham with John Hartigan (News) and David Gyngell (Nine), which increased the income I could receive in league to near what rugby and the peripheral payments offered. NRL boss David Gallop was also in the background, offering support to keep me in rugby league. As I said, money wasn't that important to me really, but that's what a good manager does, makes sure you're not financially disadvantaged and have good contracts away from the field.

I was at the Fordhams' office on Thursday 24 June, and had to go on *The Footy Show* that night. I knew Channel Nine and News Limited were expecting me to make a decision and give them exclusive stories, but I wasn't ready. My stomach was churning, I was going to the toilet and vomiting, the pressure was killing me. At that stage, I was going to go to rugby union. I really wanted to prove people wrong and go across and take on a whole new challenge, play for Australia in the World Cup and in Tests all over the world; but in the back of my mind, I thought I was letting Samuel down.

I actually had a medical examination with the NSW Rugby Union that day, and a contract from the Waratahs was sitting on John Fordham's desk, waiting for my signature; that's how things were progressing. When I was backstage at *The Footy Show* that night, people were coming up, saying, 'Why don't you announce it tonight, what are you going to do?' I was saying, 'I don't know what I'm going to do,' and they'd say, 'You've got to know.' Matty came up and saw me and said, 'Mate, don't be pressured into saying anything if you're not comfortable with it.' I asked him again for his opinion after telling him I was thinking about going to union, and he said, 'Mate, if you do that then I'll support you all the way.'

I got on the show and I felt under that much pressure I could actually sense the weight bearing down on my shoulders. I'm on telly all the time now and I never get nervous any more, but this night I was sweating, I could feel myself shaking all over and I had to grab the table to keep my body still — I felt like I was going to break down. I also knew everyone was sick of reading about it, just like the Lote Tuqiri affair in 2007 when NRL clubs tried to win him back from rugby. I just had to be honest and say I hadn't decided what I was going to do.

I stayed at Cathrine's in Sydney that night and didn't sleep a wink. I went from league to union and back again a dozen times. The next day I was driving back up to Newcastle, feeling that I finally had the time and space to myself, and it just hit me — you can't let Samuel down; he needs you. He was four and we'd had some health problems with him and he was going to start school the next year, so I thought of things like 'what if I'm not there for his first day of school?' I decided then and there I wasn't going to rugby union. The one reason, the only reason, was my son Samuel. I was driving up the Pacific Highway and I pulled into the Pymble Hotel car park, called Fordo and said, 'I'm signing with Newcastle, get the deal done.' He asked, 'Are you sure, have you thought enough about it?' and I said, 'Yes, I know it would eat at me if I left my boy at this stage of his life.' But, as I've already stated, had the ARU been keen and offered a deal a month or so earlier, so many doubts wouldn't have entered my mind and it would have been a different story.

The more I've thought about it since, it has turned out to be the best thing that happened, although I do often wonder about what might have been. I owe everything in my life to rugby league; I live in a great house and all the material things, and the wonderful life experiences I have had, plus great people I've met, were mostly created by my success in rugby league.

After we got the new deal sorted with Newcastle for the 2005–2006 seasons, I just needed to get away. I was still out with the knee problem and felt physically and mentally exhausted, so Cath and I went for a holiday to Britain — which caused more drama, can you believe, with people questioning why I would be allowed to head overseas during the football season. I couldn't train and was of little use to anyone in the frame of mind I was in, so I asked Michael Hagan if I could get away for some 'R and R', and he thought it was the best thing for me. And it certainly was. We went for two weeks and Cath got back to see her friends and her family in Wales and I enjoyed getting about.

I still keep a keen interest in rugby union but I wish they would open the game up a bit. The great difference is that in league each team is kept at least 10 or 15 metres apart, whereas in rugby they are just on top of each other. That's the first thing I would have had to change in my game, having defenders in my face so much. But the games are similar in that you want your forwards going forward to make room for you in the backs; in rugby union, teams rely on those rolling rucks to get them over the advantage line and they constantly suck defenders in, which creates room for the backs. It is hard to go wide in rugby union too early because you get isolated at the ruck and your breakaways can't get there. That's why you have to play it so tight.

I think they just need some rule changes to open the game up. They need to have less kicking and encourage the fullback to bring the ball back. And they need two referees on the field to keep both teams apart, by standing the attacking and defending teams back five metres, so you have some time to put some plays on.

I have massive admiration for All Blacks number 10 Dan Carter and it has been one of my great honours that we have struck up a good friendship. He is without doubt one of the top three players in the world if you pooled all the players from both codes.

The link started when Daryl Halligan, my kicking coach who also spends time with the All Blacks, told me Dan Carter wanted to come to Newcastle and have a kick with me. He was out with injury at the time and when he came to meet me we practised under Daryl's tuition, knocked a few goals over and then went to lunch and exchanged phone numbers. We have talked from time to time ever since — not just about footy, but we do discuss kicking; what sort of kicks we can do in different situations.

I'll never forget one of his Tests, against the British Lions in 2005, when he scored two tries, four conversions and five penalty goals for a record 33 points. For one of his tries he got the ball around halfway, beat someone, grubbered through and regathered to score this unbelievable try in the corner. Then he lined the ball up from the sideline and went *whack*, kicked the conversion. Any goal-kicker knows if you do a 50-metre 'exertion' you are knackered, so to then kick a goal from the sideline, that was outstanding. He didn't do it once, but twice in a row. I remember thinking, 'This bloke is on another planet.'

I'm also mates with the Irish centre Brian O'Driscoll, who I met in rather bizarre circumstances in Auckland. I'd learned a bit about him from Brian Carney when I was playing for Warrington in 2005. Brian Carney is good mates with my brother Matthew from their days playing at Wigan together, and Brian was telling me how he knew the Irish rugby trainer and he raved about this O'Driscoll character. Not long after, I read a *Sydney Morning Herald* story on O'Driscoll that Fordo passed on to me, and in the interview he said how he loved watching NRL games on TV because 'they have more flair, none of that run, tackle, stop stuff', and he thought I was a legend.

I told Brian Carney about it when he came to play with the Knights in 2006. The Irish team was touring Australia and New Zealand that season, so Brian rang a guy called Mick McGurn, who worked with Brian in the Irish rugby league team and is now the Irish rugby union strength and conditioning coach, to see if he would arrange for me to meet O'Driscoll. As it turned out, Newcastle played the Warriors in Auckland in 2006, the day after the Irish touring side played the All Blacks at Eden Park. The Knights players watched the rugby Test and Brian Carney and I got to go into the Irish dressing room and met O'Driscoll briefly. We were beaten by the Warriors next day, and after a couple of quiet beers at a pub we decided to have an early night and were walking back to our hotel. We were passing this Irish pub when Carney said, 'C'mon, come in and have a Guinness with me.' I wasn't fussed and said, 'I'll have just one,' so we walked in and there was this bloke in the corner with a hood over his head, blind drunk like an Irishman on St Patrick's Day. Carney ordered a couple of drinks and next thing I felt someone grab me on the shoulder. I looked over and it was Brian O'Driscoll, with the hood almost covering his head.

If I ranked the best nights out with a couple of mates, this night ranked in the top five. Here we were in this tiny Irish bar, full of Irishmen and Englishmen and O'Driscoll and I were dancing around having a wow of a time, singing along to old Irish songs. Someone took a photo of the two of us — he had his shirt off — and it ended up in the newspapers back here, plus on the front page of *The Irish Times*, apparently.

The following Saturday the Irish completed their tour with a Test against the Wallabies in Perth and O'Driscoll, the winger Shane Horton and Mick McGurn hopped on the midnight 'red eye' flight to Sydney, hired a car and drove straight to Newcastle and stayed a night.

It is incredible how the DVD I did in 2002 has infiltrated into the rugby ranks and given me some sort of profile there. In 2003 I was invited to speak to the Welsh team before their World Cup quarter-final against England. There was an obvious connection there in my great-grandfather being Welsh and current Wallabies attacking coach Scott Johnson being the Welsh assistant coach. Scott put my DVD on in the team bus one day, and I don't know if he was exaggerating, but he

ABOVE: 30 September 2001: one of the best nights of my football
career. What a proud moment, captaining a Knights team to the title.

ABOVE: I had a great relationship with Knights coach Mick Hagan. The highlight of our time together, premiers in 2001.

BELOW: Where the hell is Pauline Hanson? Flanked by 'pollies' John Howard and Kim Beazley after the 2001 grand final.

ABOVE: Fifteen thousand fans at EnergyAustralia Stadium about
1 a.m. — I got slapped in the back of the head by 10,000 of them!

RIGHT: Grand final
celebrations — I don't
think I look too bad

ABOVE: I'm pretty sure Freddy and I were about to rip in for a few days after winning the 2001 Ashes series in England.
LEFT: Two Origin greats — that's how Finchy describes us.

ABOVE: BK and me — I loved playing with him on and off the field.
RIGHT: Captaining Australia in 2002 — a great honour and a great night — a record 64–10 victory over Great Britain.

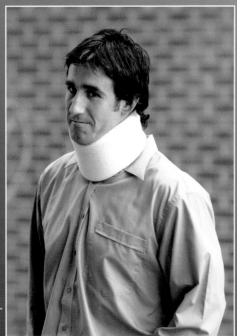

LEFT: I was especially self-conscious wearing the neck brace for eight weeks in 2003. Now I know why.

Newspix

RIGHT: 'Your attitude stinks — go away and fix it.' Phil Gould being honest with me during the 2003 Origin campaign; not many people would tell me the truth.

Newspix

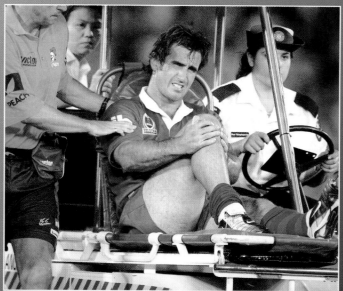

ABOVE: The worst pain of my life. Moments earlier my knee collapsed from under me, causing me to have 12 months out of the game.
BELOW: Warrington 2005 — what a wild ride. Loved every minute of it.

ABOVE and RIGHT:
An emotional day —
the media conference to
announce my retirement
on 10 April 2007.
Trying hard not to
blubber my eyes out.

said the whole bus was quiet, so that's when he contacted me and asked me to address the team. It was more Johnson asking me questions about how I trained, what philosophies I had on the game, what I thought about rugby union and different players and would I ever consider playing their game.

My brother also tells the story about when he was in Brisbane in 2005 for a State of Origin match and the French rugby union squad were in town for a Test against the Wallabies. A couple of the French players bailed him up in Queen Street Mall and said, 'Aren't you Andrew Johns' brother?' They said they'd recognised his face from my DVD and thought I was great and all that. It's pretty humbling really — the French rugby players are superstars in Europe.

Another time I was at Sydney Airport going to play away somewhere with the Knights and four or five of the South African rugby union players came up and asked for my autograph, including their star goal-kicker and number 10 Andrew Pretorius. I was thinking, 'I should be asking you for your autographs.' In 2006 I received an offer to go over and coach one of the South African Super 12 teams, the Bulls, for two or three weeks, doing some specialised work with some of their players. So it's quite remarkable how far that DVD has spread my name. It has also given me some hope that I might be able to play some sort of trouble-shooting coaching role in both rugby league and rugby union. But after the dramatic events of 2004, that was the closest I was ever going to come to defecting to the 'other game'.

CHAPTER 19

MIND OVER BODY

I know there has been concern about how my body will be in retirement, after what I put it through on the field. That is an obvious worry with any modern-day footballer, considering the weekly physical intensity of the game, how much players put their bodies through to get back out there and how often they play with injury. I'll go into that later but first I wanted to paint a picture of just how tough and resilient a lot of footballers are these days and give you an insight so that before you next criticise someone for not putting in a great performance, you might ask, 'I wonder what he is going through just to be out there.'

Few players would go into a game in the last quarter of a season without some sort of injury that would ideally do with some rest. There are so many aspects to that, particularly gaining the acceptance from your peers that you're tough enough to play with injury, something that is certainly alive in the Newcastle Knights culture, although it is not something which is discussed or subject to any great pressure from anyone in the club.

In 2006 I couldn't believe how Jarrod Mullen, who was only 19 and in his first year out of school, played with a busted sternum and was getting upwards of a dozen needles to play. I said to Jarrod, 'Look, mate, you've got so much of a future in front of you, you shouldn't be getting these needles in your chest.' He just shrugged it off and played the last month of his first season in first grade with his sternum fractured. He and I knew how hypocritical I probably was, which was the case every time I lectured the young blokes on lifestyle or looking after their bodies; I certainly didn't treat mine as a temple for most of my career.

Danny Buderus is a bloke who can consistently play with unbelievable discomfort and pain. At different times he carried an Achilles injury, broken thumb and a painful arthritic problem in his foot, yet would hardly miss a club game or State of Origin or Kangaroo tours, at the end of the season, until he stayed home for the birth of his and Kris' first child Ella instead of playing in the 2006 Tri Nations.

When I first came to grade there was a catchcry that you always 'had to show a jersey', and there were stories of guys who broke their arms but stood up and showed their jersey — in other words went into the defensive line — whereas if they laid down the opposing side could physically see a hole there and would attack that space. That was the motto that reflected the toughness the Knights were all about. Players who were always spoken about in high regard in the early years were Tony Butterfield and David Boyd; they weren't flashy but were tough as nails. I had the chance to play with Boydie when I was a kid coming off the bench in 1993. I remember him giving me a massive spray one game because I didn't chase my marker or something. I just think that is the way the club is built; it is about your own pride in your performance and not letting your mates down when the heat is on. I know people will rate me on the fancy stuff I might have done on the field, but I knew I was playing my best when I was playing really tough; getting into defence and ripping in. I'm sure my team-mates respected me more when I did that, when I tried to lead the way, although it was sometimes to the detriment of my body. Too often I probably wore myself out getting in and making two or three shots in a row in defence, but that was all part of carrying the load, being tough and living up to the culture of the club.

We've all had examples of when we had to play on with an injury when we should have gone off the field and had treatment. I remember playing one game at the Gold Coast in 1995, my second season in first grade, and I had a cork and couldn't run in the warm-up, couldn't even jog, and I was thinking, 'There is no way in the world I can play today.' But once you get on the field and that adrenalin hits you, you find that other whatever per cent you are missing. We ended up winning, which was a positive, but I've still got calcification in my leg from that injury.

There are so many players who play with injuries these days. Ben Kennedy was just freakish how he could get himself on the paddock when he could hardly walk the day before a match, and Steve Crowe in the '90s was another one; he was like a pin cushion before a game. He'd have needles in his sternum and it got that bad he had to get them through the back, his elbows, his shoulders, but he kept playing; it was just the nature of the game.

People point to the injuries I had which were pretty serious — groin, neck, back, knee — but again, other than the neck, which I couldn't take a risk with in the end, I overcame them and don't expect any great inconvenience when I get older if I manage them right.

Without argument, the toughest to come back from was the knee reconstruction in 2004. It was a nightmare straight after it happened and when I returned to the field, it caused the biggest self-doubts of my life about whether I could hack it any more as a footballer; for the first six weeks or so in the 2005 season I was bereft of confidence and it showed in my performances.

Let me take you back to the 2004 season first. After suffering the neck injury in 2003 I don't think I had ever trained harder than I did in that off-season. I didn't have a drop of alcohol for four months and was very conscious of what I ate; I was as light as I'd been for years and we started off the season by beating Penrith, the defending premiers, on their own turf, then beat Melbourne away. I remember talking to our coach Michael Hagan on the plane on the way home from Melbourne and saying how good I felt about the year. We were playing with confidence and I was injury free and really keen.

The next Saturday night at Parramatta, we were leading 14–6. It was 21 minutes into the match, I was second receiver and got the ball. I went to step on my right foot and my body went one way and my knee went the opposite. The rest of that night is a blur; I just remember being in absolute agony, screaming at the top of my lungs, coming off and being in tears knowing all the hard work I'd done had just been wasted. I'd ripped my anterior cruciate ligament and was out for the season. To make it worse for the club, our fullback David Seage wrecked his cruciate the same night, so we were down two players for the entire season.

Cathrine was in tears after the game and 2UE's Johnny Gibbs, who is a champion bloke, came past and asked Cath how I was. When she told him I'd done my knee, he was shaking his head, saying, 'He will never be the same player,' and that sort of stuff. I knew a lot of people were thinking that and saying I'd have to alter the way I played after such a bad run of injuries, but it just drove me on to prove them all wrong ... which fortunately I think I did.

A few days later, I got a package in the mail from Steve Crawley, the boss of Channel Nine sport, and inside was a book on Seabiscuit, the champion American racehorse who overcame so many crippling injuries, with his jockey 'Red' Pollard also coming back from a shocking leg injury to ride him to glory. I read it and drew a lot of motivation from it; I still haven't seen the movie, but the book was sensational.

Again there is a funny story to tell from an otherwise agonising part of my life. One of Australia's top surfers, Beau Emerton, was staying at my place and there was a maze of cameras out the front waiting for me to come out. So I got Beau to dress up in my Knights gear, put bandages around his knee, put a cap on him and sent him out on crutches. He came down the front steps and pretended to be playing with the dog and then hobbled up the steps, holding his knee and putting on all the theatrics. We were in the lounge room pissing ourselves laughing. Not long after, it was all on the midday news bulletin. I still don't think anyone who was camped outside that day realises it wasn't me.

There wasn't much to laugh about after that, though. I had the knee reconstruction done and was home for only two days before I picked up an infection. I went back into hospital to get it drained and they were worried I had golden staph. I went home again, was sitting idle for a week, then one morning I woke up about five, and I could hardly breathe. Cathrine was with me, thank God, and I said to her, 'I'm really sick, I've done something bad.' She reckons I'm a hypochondriac at the best of times and told me to go back to sleep.

I went into the lounge and sat back on the recliner bed, put my leg up and watched TV for a couple of hours, but it just got worse. Cath woke up at about 7.30 and came out and saw me sitting there with sweat dripping off me. She went white and took me straight to our physio. Luckily, Neil Halpin was also there. He came in to say hello and when I told him how I felt, he told me to get straight up to the hospital. I rushed up to John Hunter Hospital and tests showed I had a blood clot that had lodged on my lung. They put me on a drip and told me I was very, very lucky; if it had lodged on the brain I could have died from it.

Next thing I was in hospital for another week, sharing a lung ward with all these old ladies that must have smoked three packets of Marlboro a day. All night they'd just be coughing their lungs up; honestly, I was just that depressed. After a week I'd had enough. Cathrine came in and I said, 'I'm going home, get me out of here,' and she replied, 'No, you're not.' I grabbed the doctor and insisted, 'I'm going home today and if you don't let me, I'm going to walk out of here on my crutches by myself.'

So they let me go home and the long recovery process started. I had to take medicine called Warfarin, which thins the blood; they say it's a real dirty drug, like Ratsak. You have to monitor the dosage and your blood count. I think I took the drug for three months and had to have daily blood tests for a month. It was just horrendous. I would occasionally go to training but I was like a black cloud hanging around the joint, so Hages ended up saying in a nice way to stay away.

Ever since then, if I'm going to travel on a plane for two hours or more, I have to get injections, take Clexane (an anti-clotting medication) and wear tights. And when I go for operations now, they have to give me all this stuff to stop clotting.

An ironic part of the tale was that David Seage, who had his knee operated on the same day as me, was out of hospital three days later, but when he went home he fell over in the shower, landed on his knee and ripped the graft off. So he had to go back in to get the graft redone, and then he got staph in his too and was in and out of hospital. We were both hit by the same curse. I have never seen a man sicker than 'Seagie' and, to his credit, while I whinged and kicked stones, he never complained and worked his arse off to get back.

We developed a pretty special bond, Seagie and I. We spent a lot of time together in rehab and respected how hard the other had trained and how intense our recoveries were. He's had rotten luck — he came back from his knee injury, then tore his hamstring and broke his hand, had to have a back operation, but that didn't deter him … only for him to need another knee reconstruction in 2006. When he hurt his knee the second time, in the game against Manly, it was the only time I saw players from both teams come into the room and say, 'Oh no'; everyone knew how much bad luck he'd had. I can still picture Ben Kennedy, who had moved from the Knights to Manly, patting him on the head saying, 'You poor bugger.' True to form, Seagie never complained and just got on with the lonely life of rehab again — two or three hours of physio, gym work and pool work every day for six to nine months.

I was right for the start of the 2005 season but I really struggled with confidence and cohesion in my game. We lost the first match in Melbourne 48–10 then went to Canberra and were dusted up 39–14. I was sitting in the sheds after the game. Everyone had showered and was getting on the bus but I was still in my playing kit, with my head in my hands. I remember speaking to Michael Hagan and saying, 'Look, mate, I think I am embarrassing myself. I'm doing nothing for the team and I'm worried I'm going to undo all the good work I've done during my career because I can't compete any more.' Hages was great during that time — he reassured me that things were turning around, we'd start winning again and I'd start playing better. Quitting was in the back of my mind. My confidence was absolutely shot — every time I got the ball I was thinking my knee was going to blow out and every time I was going to tackle someone, I thought, 'This is it; if I drive too hard my knee is going to buckle under me.' I got so frustrated with it on the field I was screaming at my team-mates; it was awful.

That was the time I realised how badly the lack of the right resources at the Newcastle Knights had really affected us as far as how many injuries we were suffering, how they were recurring when players got back on the field, and how long we seemed to be out compared to players at some other clubs with similar injuries. We didn't even have a full-time physiotherapist; had little state of the art equipment other clubs took for granted, and were pretty much left on our own to do rehab training with just the basic instruction. I'd go to training and rip into weights, but it was the same weight program everyone else was doing, not specifically designed for my injury.

I was at the annual NRL Captains' Dinner in Sydney, which raises money for breast cancer, and Wayne Bennett came up and asked how I was going. 'Shithouse' was my answer if I remember rightly: 'I've got no confidence in my knee and I'm not playing well.' Wayne could obviously see how frustrated I was. He told Michael Hagan and me about how the Broncos halfback Brett Seymour had been through a special rehabilitation program with Scott Dickinson and Suki Hobson at the Queensland Academy of Sport and they had got him back on the field early and in really good shape.

Wayne couldn't believe I didn't have someone supervising my rehab and was saying what a joke he thought that was, that it was a waste a club paying so much money for its talent, then investing bugger all in keeping them on the field.

The next week Hages arranged for Scott Dickinson to come to Newcastle and he got me in the gym and flogged me for two hours. He said, 'Mate, I know you like a beer and I know you like a good time, but I'll give you a tip — don't even try in the next six weeks because you are going to train that hard.' As it turned out I think I lapsed once. I had a big weekend and turned up under the weather and he didn't go easy on me. Scott and Hages had planned for me to go to Brisbane every couple of weeks for two days and for Scott to come to Newcastle the alternate weeks, but I broke my jaw against Auckland a fortnight later and ended up spending most of my weekdays in Brisbane — in the 'concentration camp', as I called it. It was bloody torture — but the best thing for my knee, and my career. I stayed in a hotel while we went through daily torture sessions at ANZ Stadium under Scott and Suki. I started doing weights on my leg, including all these one-legged squats and hopping and holding routines. What I had to do was build up my 'glutes' and 'quads', strengthening muscle around the injured knee. We'd also do horrific fitness sessions, and after every one of them I'd spew my guts up — it was that hard. Seagie was still playing so he'd come up for one or two days a week; but I bunkered down in a suburban hotel for most of the six weeks and pretty much got up and trained in the morning, rested up and trained in the afternoon, then I'd go to the movies just down the road from ANZ

Stadium, go back to my hotel and go to sleep; and it would be on again the next day. It was a lonely time as I shut myself off, but I was so focused and motivated on getting fitter and making the knee stronger. Hell, it was worth it.

The most ongoing problem I had during my career, and the worst injury I had to carry, was a groin/hip flexor injury. I had three groin operations from 1998 to 2000 and it really hindered me for a long while — I had little power in that region at all. If I'd had the right rehab when I first did it, it would not have been near as big a problem, although in that case it was mostly my own fault, because I went back to training too early and was doing sand hills and stuff when I wasn't supposed to; but there was no one there supervising me, telling me what to do, and a lot of scar tissue built up.

My groin/hip flexor problem worried me right through the last five years of my career, and in between games I really had to manage it. I had to be careful when I was doing goal-kicking practice; I'd do a session with Daryl Halligan once a week or once a fortnight and I'd only have 10 or 15 kicks but make sure the session was all quality. After a goal-kicking practice session and a general play session, my groin would get sore and the first sign was that it would tighten up in my glutes in my backside.

From 2002, I started seeing an osteopath and chiropractor called Kay McPherson in Sydney. My brother Matthew put me onto her after he came across her while playing for the Sharks. I saw her once a week from then right through to the last week of my career in 2007. She'd get in all around my glutes and was a big reason why I was able to stay on the field so often. If I didn't get down to see Kay or do sessions with our physios, I'd really have trouble.

Before Kay came along I relied too much on painkilling injections before matches at times. I was getting constant pain in my 'perineum' — the area between the base of the 'old fella' and the rectum — and I remember lying there one day getting an injection, with Matty holding my legs, and I was thinking, 'This is outrageous, you can't be doing this.' The pain was so intense I almost passed out. But I was the one who put the pressure on the doctor to do it, even though he was extremely reluctant.

Sometimes I had to get through without my little friends, the 'needles', when I played for Australia. The Australian doctor Hugh Hazard doesn't believe in players playing with painkilling injections. In 2001, when we toured England, I was in real pain with damage to my rib cartilage I'd carried for the last six weeks of the NRL season. I got another knock on it during the first half of a Test and I said to Hugh, 'Mate, I can't get through unless you needle me,' and he said, 'Well you aren't playing, simple as that.' Somehow I got through. Ben Kennedy broke his hand on the same tour. He came in at half-time and Hugh said, 'You've broken your hand.' BK replied, 'I know I've broken it, just needle it,' but Hugh refused. Canterbury (Hugh has been their club doctor for about 30 years) and Brisbane are two clubs I know of who won't needle players; I wonder how I would have gone if I had signed with the Broncos in 2000?

The thing that hurt the most during my career was the timing of my injuries: in 2002 and 2003 I thought we had sides with a real chance of winning another grand final, but I finished both years on the sidelines; then in 2004 I was out from round three. So, after we won the premiership in 2001, it was only 2005 and 2006 that I was fit come finals time. In '05 we gave the rest of the teams too big a start due to a horrendous injury toll in the first half of the season, but stormed home. Then in 2006 we finished fourth but had our two incumbent internationals Danny Buderus (suspended) and Steve Simpson (injured) out, along with fullback Milton Thaiday; if it wasn't me, it seemed one of our other leading players was missing when it counted most.

The broken back I suffered in '02 was, in fact, fractures in what are called the 'transverse processes' — the little wings that come off the spine. I fractured three of them 10 minutes into our finals match at home against the Dragons in 2002 when Luke Bailey came over the top as I was going to the ground and accidentally got me with knees in the back. There was a fair bit of controversy about the tackle and 'Bails' was cited to front the judiciary, but anything intentional is completely against his nature and I never suspected there was anything illegal in it.

Sorry, but there was another funny hospital story here too. I was taken straight from the ground to hospital for x-rays and only had the playing gear I was wearing. So one of the nurses gave me these old grandfather pyjamas, you know, the long ones with the tie-up around the waist; they were 10 sizes too big and had this big open fly. Next day, I had to be transferred to the Lingard Private Hospital at Merewether and was full of morphine to kill the pain as they pushed me outside in a wheelchair to get me in the ambulance. There were three or four photographers lurking, and here I was, no shirt on and wearing nothing but these baggy, loose PJ-pants. As they were going *click, click, click* I looked down and my dick was sitting out the front of these pants. I was horrified the photos would be in the paper next day. Mum called in and I said, 'Get the papers and tell me my old fella's not hanging out, Mum.' Luckily the photos were cropped.

I was crook for two or three months with the back injury but I didn't require surgery, because so much muscle around there presses on the spine and it fuses itself. It hasn't given me any trouble since and I started the next season on time.

The neck injury the following season was really the scary one and, to be honest, that was when the word 'retirement' hit the radar of my brain for the first time. It happened against the Sea Eagles: I went to step Sam Harris, I fell into him and he accidentally got me around the head. I pretty much got bent in half and the back of my head nearly hit my heels. I've seen photos of it, it looks horrific. It wasn't his fault at all, even though he gave me a call and apologised.

We were playing the Cowboys the next weekend in Townsville but despite my neck being really stiff and sore, I was determined to play. It was round 22 and we were equal eighth with the Dragons and I was desperate to play in the finals again. I knew my neck was crook when I was in the plane heading north. I was in the window seat with our football manager Mark Sargent in the middle and this bloke was half-pissed in the aisle seat; it was absolute torture. I was trying to sit there and read my book and he kept asking me questions. I had to look around 'Sarge' to answer him and every time I'd get a sharp pain in the back of my neck and think, 'This is not good.'

Before the match I asked Hages if I could have an early mark if the game was in hand and he agreed. Well, we led 48–0 at half-time and 60–4 halfway through the second half and I had pretty much played in a dinner suit. I passed the ball this one time and someone hit me — not even high or low, just sort of touched me — and I got this incredible pain down the left side of me; it went all the way into my thumb. So I put my hand up to come straight off; it terrified me.

When we got back to Sydney, I remember it was the day the City to Surf fun run was on. I stayed in Sydney the night at Cath's, had a few beers with Matty and was really worried about how bad the injury might have been. Next day I went to see Professor John Yeo, the esteemed neck specialist, and I was sent away for MRI scans. When he saw them he apparently told Neil Halpin there was never a more obvious case of an MRI showing the disc protruding and pushing on the spinal cord. It was around the C4/C5 vertebrae.

Professor Yeo told me how serious he thought the injury was and gave me two options — to have fusion surgery (where they fuse two joints together) or immobilise the neck in a brace for eight weeks and hope the disc would settle back off the spinal cord. He sees it from a doctor's point of view and has to be ultra-conservative, but it was still pretty chilling when he told me, 'Look, Andrew, I see so many of these injuries that go bad and people can never walk again. If you have a fusion I would like you not to play again but it is your decision.' He is one of the leading specialists in the world, so I knew I was in safe hands and I was prepared to leave the call up to him — I wouldn't have argued with him (isn't that ironic now, considering he had to make that call three and a half years later?). I took a punt on a couple of months in the neck brace and fortunately it did the trick. Mark Hughes suffered a neck injury a week later and for eight weeks we hung out together with these stupid neck braces on, which would be filthy dirty after a night out.

It seems crazy, I know, that I didn't get tests done in between the Manly and Cowboys games when the neck was so tender, but I got plenty of physiotherapy on it and thought that as there were only five rounds to go, and I really believed we could win the competition, I'd just battle through. But I soon found out I was kidding myself.

I still thought we could have won the competition after we beat St George Illawarra at Kogarah 42–8, but injuries to other players killed us in the end. We finished seventh and were knocked out by the Sydney Roosters 36–8 the first week of the finals, when we were without Timana Tahu, Matt Parsons, Clint Newton, Mark Hughes and myself.

While on the subject of injuries, I'd like to mention a guy who was a godsend for me at times — the man with 'magic fingers' called John Munroe, from a place called Mulbring, which is between the F3 freeway and Kurri Kurri. He hasn't got all the standard certificates or done courses, but just about every sportsman from the coalfields would know about him. My dad was going to him before I was born, and if I ever got a soft tissue injury, corked thigh or corked bicep or a strain, I would go out and see him.

When I was carrying my groin trouble for a while I was talking to journalist Neil Jameson, who co-wrote the autobiography of Craig Johnston, the Newcastle-raised Liverpool soccer player. Johnston apparently had an awful injury in his legs and had gone to all the great physicians in Europe. Then he went and saw John Munroe who got him back playing after about six weeks of treatment. I sometimes went out there when I appeared no chance of playing and his magic hands and the psychology he used on me ('You'll be right, mate, I'll get you back on the field') would work wonders. And he never once charged me. I don't know how many jerseys and other things I've given him over the years and I think he gives most of them away. He is a greyhound owner and trainer and sometimes I'd spend the morning and afternoon out there, on all sorts of machines he'd use on the dogs' injuries and getting all these sorts of weird remedies thrown into me, but he'd invariably fix me up. On his wall are photos of Johnny Sattler, Johnny Raper and Chad Reed, the motorcyclist, and heaps of Knights players who have all been treated by him. Leo Pinczewski, one of the top knee surgeons in Australia, got up at a tribute night for John and gave him massive praise about how they couldn't teach people at universities what John knew about injuries.

For most of my career Knights players even had to foot the bill for massages, which meant some blokes wouldn't bother at $50 to $60 a session. That can cause small injuries to later become major ones and that showed in 2005 when we had five times the amount of missed games through injuries to our players than some other clubs. Tony Butterfield demanded in the late 1990s that the Knights put on a full-time masseuse, but it didn't happen until 2006. I had to drive two and a half hours each way to get the special treatment I needed from Kay McPherson. Looking back I wonder how different players could have been with better facilities all those years. When Ben Kennedy signed with Manly everyone jumped up and down saying how injury prone he was, but when he got down there with all the Department of Sport and Recreation facilities at Narrabeen, he hardly missed a game for two seasons.

When we went into State of Origin camp, our physio, Liz Steet, would always complain, saying, 'Every time I get to camp the only people in our room are the Newcastle boys — your bodies aren't looked after, you've got too many little niggly injuries that will become big injuries.'

It was interesting that our coach Michael Hagan and our football manager Mark Sargent were so determined to get our rehab and training facilities changed after they saw the benefit the visits to the QAS did for Dave Seage and me in early 2005. They put pressure on the board to assign some money to that area of the operation and were pretty outspoken when they didn't get much of a response. Ultimately, it cost Sarge his job and probably went towards the club not re-signing Hages too, but it was a cause worth fighting for. From the end of that year we had a full-time rehab officer for the first time — none other than Scott Dickinson, who came down from Brisbane — a full-time physio and, with Wests Leagues Club at Lambton backing us, we gradually saw our facilities improve out of sight.

I am so glad that Newcastle at least now has facilities comparable to those of other clubs when it comes to training, medical and rehabilitation facilities. The guys now train at a gym called Balance, part of the Club Phoenix complex at Mayfield. The gym was built for our needs and there are hot and cold baths, steam rooms, massage areas and a pool to train in. On the playing fields next door they took the cricket pitch out and turned it into a training ground for us. Before, we used to have to go out to Glendale about 25 minutes from the city — for sprint training — and drive back in for gym work at Mayfield, which would be another 25 minutes' drive. Before that we would use the university's facilities; sometimes we'd struggle to even get a ground. Since 2006 the Knights have also had a full-time physiotherapist and every player gets two massages a week; they have a rehab officer to look after injured players one-on-one and watch everything they do. I think it will extend the careers of the Knights' good young players and I hope it will see someone like Danny Buderus get another two years, after battling injuries without the right back-up for too long.

In my last season and a bit (2006–2007) I hardly missed a game and I was getting massaged twice a week in Newcastle, plus when I went to Sydney to see Kay, I had the benefit of specific training for my complaints and enjoyed better access to physiotherapy — it was like a whole new world. I can't believe there was a faction in the club that thought Wests Leagues coming on board wasn't a good idea; that's mind blowing.

I was criticised for a long while for playing too physically for my size and trying to do too much on the field, which was valid. But I did become wiser in the latter years of my career, becoming conscious to stay out of the early battle — that that was what front-rowers were for. My coaches used to say to me all the time, 'We want you to be strong in the last 20, not the first 20,' but I used to go out and rip in; that's how I used to play. I used to put everything in the first 50 or 60 minutes and then try to blow them away. It wasn't until I made it to Origin in 1998 and Laurie Daley and Ricky Stuart grabbed me and said: 'You know we want you firing in the last 10 when the game will be won or lost. Look at what Alfie [Langer] used to do, look at Wally Lewis, he used to sit back sometimes for 75 minutes, and in the last five minutes he'd go bang when everyone was tired and win the game for them.' It wasn't really until later in my career, though, that I understood tempo: if it's a slog, get out of it and let the forwards sort each other out. I used to like getting in and getting involved in the slog, which was to my detriment.

Once the neck heals, I reckon I will have ended up OK physically compared to a lot of blokes. Look at Laurie Daley — he can't train because of his knees; he does his fitness work all on the rowing machine and that's the price you can pay for pushing your body too much.

I consider myself as being pretty lucky.

CHAPTER 20

THE REAL STORY ABOUT GUS AND ME

Phil Gould is the best coach I had during my 14-season rugby league career. I also regard him as a good friend and a man I go to for advice when I need it.

Having said that, we are both strong personalities who haven't always seen eye to eye. One of those times — the only 'paparazzi' type episode in my career, where newspaper cameras tapped into a private conversation outside a restaurant during the 2003 State of Origin campaign — led to all sorts of speculation. It created a string of headlines, with journalists coming up with their theories about what happened that day, and that week. I was supposedly going to walk away from Origin football; had refused to play under Gus; we had differences that couldn't be resolved and the whole camp had been thrown into disarray.

Here is the correct story.

It was a period of my life when I was depressed and, as a result, on and off the field my attitude was terrible. I thought I was playing OK and the reports of the time said I had been too, but Phil wrote in his *Sun-Herald* column that I was out of form and that I looked distressed on the field because I was overweight and unfit. He'd said much the same on Channel Nine as well. I thought, 'I don't think there is a real need for this,' even though I was a bit underdone after going into the season without doing a lot of running and needed to get my fitness level up in the gym and on the rowing machine.

In the round seven game against Wests Tigers I was put on report for a head slam, which typified my frustration about my life at the time, and I was subsequently suspended for two weeks. In that period I went up to Port Macquarie for a break with Cathrine and Samuel. I was looking at photos later and saw how chubby I looked, so I must have been carrying a bit of lack of condition. I came back against the Sydney Roosters and we went down 36–14 (the day after I'd scored the winning try for Country, late in the City v Country clash at Gosford in the rain). The Roosters pack, with Adrian Morley on fire, smashed us so I didn't get much chance to be dominant. Gus, who was still coaching director at the Roosters although they were coached by Ricky Stuart, obviously watched me closely in those games and thought my attitude wasn't right.

That year the selectors had picked a provisional New South Wales squad and had got us together earlier in the year. Gus arranged for a sort of pep talk and lunch at the Crowne Plaza at Coogee — which was the team's base when we were in camp — the day after we played the Roosters (and three weeks before the first Origin match). Even though I was New South Wales and Australian captain, I thought getting the squad together was a wank. Turning up unshaven and disinterested only typified how I was feeling generally. My eyes were on the ground — I couldn't look at anyone. In front of the whole squad Gus pretty much told me that he'd been watching the way I'd been playing and that I was 'kidding myself'. He also said I'd been using my *Daily Telegraph* and *Sunday Telegraph* columns to generate publicity by comparing players who were under consideration for selection and pushing my Knights team-mates. He sort of said, 'That stops now, do you agree on this?' so that I had to acknowledge it in front of the whole group. I said, 'Yeah, no problem,' without much enthusiasm.

When the meeting finished we walked down the road for lunch to a restaurant in the main street. I thought Gus' crap was out of order and I said I wasn't going to the lunch, but then I thought, 'No, I'll have it out with him.' So when we got to the restaurant I asked Gus if we could go outside and have a chat. That's when a photographer snapped away without us knowing.

I told Gus I didn't think I deserved the humiliation he'd just put me through, and he said, 'OK, and what else?' I replied, 'What do you mean?' and he told me there had to be something else, that he'd never seen me 'like this' before — meaning demotivated and undisciplined, I suppose. I opened up a bit and he said, 'Go away and work on your attitude, rip into training in the next month. Come back with a better attitude and pick that lip of yours up, it's dragging on the ground. Do that and I promise you that you will have the best six weeks of your life.'

The bagging in front of everyone else was Phil's way of motivating me and shaking me up, because he knew I needed it … and he was right; not that I was ready to concede that just then. He also wasn't happy with how a few of the leading Blues players were going and obviously thought if he was prepared to give it to the captain, other blokes would realise they'd have to lift their games as well.

On the drive back to Newcastle I was still fuming about how he'd spoken to me. I don't know whose idea it was, but after the media then went crazy with Joey–Gus rift stories, I was asked to head down to Sydney for Gus and I to meet with NSWRL chairman Colin Love to 'clear the air'. We had a 'kiss and cuddle' which was all nice and civil … then sat in a room with a chalk board and talked about how we were going to beat Queensland. The 'feud' was over, although the media kept us on their radar looking for a drama right through the lead-up to Game One.

If it was all part of Gus' mind games, it worked. After that blow-up I went straight to King Edward Park when I got home and trained hard. Over the next three weeks, I did extra drills and really got a heap of miles in my legs, thinking every minute, 'I'll prove that red-headed prick wrong.' I trained my arse off by myself every day.

So, as unorthodox as Phil Gould's tactics were in getting the best out of me and the others, it worked — we won the trophy back from Queensland in the first two games, winning

25–12 and 27–4; I won the man of the match in the second game and was more than happy with how I played in the opener. The upshot of the home truths he bluntly told me was that it led to two of my best performances in State of Origin.

That series also revolutionised the way everyone started to play in State of Origin. We had devised a plan to centre our attack around the 'scrum lines' (then 10 metres in from touch where scrums are set), then using two-pass shifts, or we'd get our quick players bouncing quickly out of dummy half from the scrum-lines and jog around three or four defenders, then pass to direct runners hitting holes in the middle of the field. It would put immense pressure on the opposite edge in defence and we destroyed Queensland. From that I reckon players went back to their NRL clubs, saying, 'You should see the way Gus had us playing,' and the game followed right across the NRL.

I first met Phil Gould in 1995 when he came to Newcastle, as the Super League war broke out, with the express objective of signing the Knights players for the Australian Rugby League. I came across him as a coach a couple of months later in the New South Wales Origin camp. I was instantly blown away by how good a coach he was. Technically, he is a genius.

He knows, for instance, what edge to attack, what shoulder a player doesn't tackle well on, what player fatigues, what angles to run at different times on the field, what player to 'bomb'. It's like he knows every strength and weakness of every player. And personally, he was great because he was a real straight shooter with me too.

He also had the ability not to over-coach. He had the right ego to sit back and say, 'Hang on, I don't need to put my special touch on this team — I'm just going to give the players these guidelines and let them do it.' He knew what players needed a structure to play to, but he was wise enough to understand that it wasn't a structure a club team might employ where all 17 had to play to a pattern. He would let the outstanding creative players follow their instincts and put their own stamp on the match plan. That's where Gus was so good — he had the ability to get great players to play even better, which is a special gift.

I look back at the times he coached me and they were some of the best times in my career. The 1996 series when we had the same 17 players go through all three games and won in a clean sweep was one of my greatest Origin memories; plus 2002 when he came back and coached us to a series draw, and the win in 2003 as captain.

Phil Gould understood my psyche. He knew how to motivate me and how to challenge me. He would never really give me accolades but would always set challenges for me, whether it was at training, or with my fitness, or with what he wanted me to do in a game. One time we were doing a beep test at a pre-Origin camp and he stood one metre away from the mark I had to run up and down to. The beep test stops at 14 (repetitions of 20-metre sprints, each one faster as you have to match the 'beep' and I'd normally get about 13 and a half, then not be able to go any further. This day, because he was standing there, I got to the end and really couldn't stand up I was so exhausted; but I really felt proud that I was able to push myself further than I had ever done before. I looked back and Gus had wandered off and didn't say a word.

Going into games we'd have little chats and he would always give me a challenge like, 'How do you think you are going to win the game for us tomorrow night?' Or there were times when he probably thought I was under pressure and he'd come up and say to me, 'This isn't one of those games where you're going to have to win the game for us. You just sit back and do your job and the rest of the boys will do theirs, and we'll be right.' Specific challenges on the field might have been identifying a certain defender in the Maroons team who would miss tackles when he got tired. Gus would say to me, 'Look mate, this player does this when he's fatigued, you'll see him get tired so make sure you get him,' or he'd say, 'Look, such and such is going to be sitting on your edge and charging you all night — are you going to be tough enough to handle him?' That would get my back up and I'd say, 'Yeah, you sit back and watch.'

Gus must have a psychologist's degree tucked away in his drawer; he knew who he had to pamper and bullshit to, and who he had to be tough on. Sometimes, though, he was too good at it, too challenging — like Warren Ryan, he could squeeze so much out of one player or a heap of players, but then it would tire on them and it would be time to move on. Gus being so intense for six weeks of an Origin series was perfect; two or three years at club level under him would have been a whole lot more challenging for a player. He is a complex guy, he would admit that, and so intelligent and articulate.

I remember one half-time — I'm pretty sure it was the first match of 2003 at the reopening of Suncorp Stadium — and we were ahead 12–6 but absolutely out on our feet; guys had shirts off and couldn't look up and Gus realised we were under duress. He said to everyone, 'I need your eyes, look up at me,' and everyone looked up at him. Then he said, 'Right, hands in the middle here,' and everyone sat closer and outstretched their arms and joined hands in the middle of a circle. Gus had a few catchcries about what we were going to do — he'd repeat things like, 'Where's the ball, what's my job, what do I have to do?' to reinforce our responsibilities in defence. He spoke for four or five minutes, and it was the most uplifting half-time I'd experienced; just simple, short, sharp, tactical messages that picked everyone up. Gorden Tallis scored for Queensland straight after half-time but we stuck to what we'd discussed at half-time and went on to win 25–12.

The night before each match it was traditional to have dinner together, go and get an ice-cream, then walk down to the stadium and Gus would ask you to pick a piece of turf and stand there and imagine yourself doing something brilliant. He'd come up with one of his legendary tales, always with a moral to the story that was meant to inspire us. He'd talk about a famous battle in history or famous person or example of gallantry or bravery. One night it was about the Port Arthur massacre of 1996 when Martin Bryant killed 35 people, and he reflected on the courage of some nurses in the cafe who, instead of lying there on the ground to save their own lives, got up and helped other people while there were gun shots still sounding outside.

I didn't talk to Gus all that often over all the years outside of Origin camps, but when we did we 'connected'. Occasionally, we'd get into an SMS war that could last for hours. I think we're very similar in ways and I just love talking to him, whether it's about football, horse racing — which we both have a strong interest in — or life generally.

These days, I come across Gus a little bit with our roles at Channel Nine. I think he is amazing on TV and great for the game with the insight he can provide. I know some people are turned off by his strong opinions and feel he is a know-all, but when you sit beside him when he gets two seconds' notice that they're going to cross to him, then the camera rolls and he communicates so well and can see a problem on the field so quickly and can so simply portray that to the viewer, you appreciate what a gift he has with words to match his football knowledge.

CHAPTER 21

THE WONDER OF WARRINGTON

The three weeks I spent in Warrington in 2005 was the most enjoyable detour in my rugby league career. The club, the coaches, the players and the fans were wonderful to Cathrine and me during my three-match stint. Having said that, the home semi-final loss against Hull — my third and final match for the Wolves — and the lead-up to the defeat, still rankles me and I regret I never had the chance to go back and set the record straight.

Playing in the English Super League was an opportunity I thought I would never have. After Matthew's season with Wigan in 2001, he raved about the lifestyle and the people, even though injury ensured he didn't have a particularly enjoyable time on the field. I'd toured England three times with the Kangaroos — the 1995 and 2000 World Cups and the 2001 three-Test tour — as well as going over with the Knights for the 2002 World Club Challenge against Bradford. I like the place; the culture, the history, the English Premier League and the scenery. The biggest disadvantage the place has is lack of surf, but you can't have everything.

In July 2005 my manager John Fordham was attending the Lord's cricket Test between England and Australia. He was a guest in the Sony BMG box with his good mate from Sony, Denis Handlin, and ex-Aussie skipper Mark Taylor. Denis told Fordo there was someone who wanted to meet him, a rock promoter who also owned Warrington rugby league club, Simon Moran. Simon was in the box on the Saturday when he whisked Fordo away for a chat and asked if I'd be interested in a short-season stint with the Wolves. Fordo guessed I might be up watching the cricket on television and sent me an SMS asking if I was interested in a brief stint in Super League. I messaged back 'yes mate' and next thing the phone rang, and he put Simon Moran onto the phone explaining that he was keen for me to play the last few weeks of their season after the Knights' commitments had finished (we weren't going to be in the finals). I said, 'Mate, I've always been interested in playing in England ever since I watched Ellery Hanley and Garry Schofield play out here in the 1980s, but with the seasons running parallel since 1997, I thought it would never happen.'

I remember it was after we'd beaten Parramatta that day at Parramatta to start a six-match winning stretch that should have got us off the bottom of the ladder, but Souths and Penrith also had a flurry of wins to stay in front of us. The same night in England, Warrington went down 46–22 to Leeds — who were my first opponents after I arrived in England. Simon had to leave the cricket just after lunch to fly back to watch Warrington play that night.

Fordo gave him an outline of what money and conditions he required, subject of course to clearances from the Newcastle Knights, the NRL and ARL. Showing how efficient Simon was, he had a draft deal back to Fordo by 4pm that afternoon (English time), which was very, very lucrative, I might add; all while I was asleep back home in Newcastle. Unbelievably, within a couple of weeks a deal had been done, with the Knights agreeing to release me on the proviso I extended my contract with them — which was due to end after the 2006 season — by an extra two years. One clause was that I could cut that contract short by a season if I wanted to play out my career in England.

I was just so fortunate for the way the circumstances made it possible for such a one-off situation. The Knights were out of the finals for the second straight season, the English season finished two weeks after ours did, which meant I was available for their last two competition matches, then for the finals. It was no coincidence my form went through the roof in the last six weeks of our season, because I was on such a high from being able to play in England and take Cath with me. I always felt it would be too hard to do a whole year in England because I couldn't take Samuel, whereas by going there in September–October it meant I had the added bonus of being able to miss training with the Kangaroos train-on squad under Billy Johnstone — what a relief!

As usual, though, I was the centre of a drama played out in the media. There was a Tri Nations series at the end of our season which meant Australia had two games here against New Zealand before the team went to England; and if Warrington were to make the grand final it would coincide with the first Test against the Kiwis. I was accused of putting a lucrative private stint in the UK before my duty to play for Australia. As usual, everyone came out of the woodwork giving their two-bob's worth and we had to get around it by saying I would put Australia first. Thankfully, the Australian Rugby League decided it would not pass any strict ruling until they saw how far Warrington progressed. It might have ended up being a heap of hullabaloo about nothing, which is how it turned out, so the ARL refused to be pressured into a decision. Some people thought there should have been a hard-and-fast rule put into place to stop an NRL player registering to play in England the same season after a certain date, or if any player did head over for a 'guest stint' like I did, that they could only do so if it didn't coincide with any Test matches they had to be available for. If it was applied straight away, it would have stopped any situation where I could get to England and refuse to come back and play the Tests that October.

I was disappointed Warrington didn't get past the first week of the finals but at least it averted another headline-causing drama ... because there is no way I would have turned around and missed the Super League grand final. I know that would have meant putting an English club game in front of playing for Australia, but that's what I would have done. Now that might sound like I'm devaluing the honour of playing for

Australia and had expected special treatment, but I felt that after all the service I had given the game at representative and club level, it wasn't too much to ask as it was such a unique opportunity that would never crop up again.

All I knew about Warrington before I got there was that it was where Cath did her university degree and that Allan Langer had played there for three seasons. It was ironic that the head of Cath's university, Steven Broomhead, ended up being on the football club board (as deputy chairman) when we were there. In the weeks before our departure to England, Simon sent me details from coach Paul Cullen about how they played — I spoke to Paul who is a real passionate Warrington bloke and a good coach, once a week before I flew over there and plenty of emails swapped hands. I arrived there on the Tuesday, which gave me enough time to get over the jet lag a bit and be ready for the game against Leeds on the Saturday at their home ground, Halliwell Jones Stadium.

It was like a whirlwind after I arrived. First off, Cath was crook as a dog with the flu and couldn't get out of bed for two days before we left. The plane was overbooked for the Hong Kong leg and we had to be put onto another flight. Instead of going to Dubai then Manchester, we had to go via Frankfurt, but they upgraded us to first class from business class which was great, and that helped Cath get more comfortable; she was doped up on antibiotics and cold tablets. I'd suffered a bad cork in my last game for the Knights, against St George Illawarra at Kogarah, and had ice on my thigh most of the way and, in a rare experience for me, didn't have a drink the whole flight.

The Dally M awards were being held in Sydney on the Tuesday night and the judges obviously knew it was between Johnathan Thurston and me for the major award. I'd been asked to take a replica of the medal with me on the flight — well, it was given to Cath as the NRL thought she was a safer bet security-wise — and I had two hours to get from Manchester airport to Warrington's ground to do a live cross for television.

I just couldn't control myself with the excitement of being there to play in the UK Super League, but I seemed calm compared to how Paul Cullen and Simon Moran were after I walked out of the arrivals gate. There were a fair few media people there and I was dog-tired after getting little sleep on the flight. They took me to where we were to stay, in a picturesque village called Grappenhall, a few miles outside of Warrington. It was a beautiful town house, decked out with a big plasma TV, a fridge stocked with food, and beautiful lounges. They also loaned me a Mercedes-Benz and Cathrine got a flash car to drive around in too. The ladies from the club cooked us lunch and ironed my shirt for the Dally M cross; they were just fantastic in welcoming us. By the stage I got to the ground for the TV cross, I don't know how I had kept awake. As it turned out 'Johnno' Thurston won the Dally M by one point, but they crossed to me a couple of times and it all went OK.

Despite being sleep deprived I insisted I met the senior players that night, so I went to dinner with them at an Italian restaurant. I hit it off straight away with Nat Wood, Lee Briers — who was the captain — the lock Jon Clarke, who would pick me up every morning and take me to training, Martin Gleeson, Logan Swann and Brent Grose. Next day when I got to training it was like my first day in senior football again, like I had to prove myself and get my team-mates' confidence. I remember having to get in and do weights, then going out and doing ball work, and all the players were so accommodating. But my jet lag was so bad that every night I'd wake at four in the morning and I'd stare at the ceiling. Then at about five or six in the afternoon, I'd just hit the wall but try to stay awake.

When we got to the ground for the game against Leeds on the Saturday evening I was pumped. But the talk in the dressing room quickly confirmed what other people had told me: that the Poms can get a little intimidated by success. Leeds were the champions and were, I think, second on the ladder, and some of our blokes were saying, 'Come on, we're playing Leeds, we'll give it our best shot.' I said, 'We're not going to give it our best shot, we're going to smoke these guys. We're at home — let's do it.' I could notice the anticipation in them about me, that I had to prove to them everything that must have been said about me. I felt really nervous about that too; Simon had got me over here, there was a big crowd expecting the world of me, the team was in the bottom half of the top six and it was, like, this is a really big moment for the club.

When I went out for the pre-match warm-up, the crowd went bananas. They were singing a song, of which all I could understand was 'Joey Johns'; I was grinning to myself, thinking, 'What the hell are they singing?' I asked Lee Briers and he said they were chanting, 'Joey Johns, give us a wave.' So I waved to them and it was like the whole roof came off the place; the crowd went berserk. There was a capacity 13,000 at the stadium but it felt like five times that many were there.

Wearing the number 31 jersey, I had to kick off and I couldn't get the ball to stay on the tee — it was one of those telescopic ones. Without a word of a lie, it must have taken me a minute to get it to stick, and all the Leeds fans were jeering. Anyway I kicked off, hit it sweet, really high, their little halfback Rob Burrow dropped it, and our prop, ex-Dragons player Chris Leikvoll, smashed him and we got a scrum. So, 40 seconds into the game, *bang*, Lee Briers hit Martin Gleeson with a great ball and 'Gleece', who is the carbon copy of Matt Gidley, a world-class centre, put Henry Fa'afili over in the corner. I had to try to convert from the touchline and as I lined it up, I could smell the beer coming off the crowd, I was that close to them. The Warrington fans were still going berserk and the noise was just unbelievable. I was thinking, 'If I am ever going to kick a goal, please God, let it be this one.' I hit it sweet and black dotted it and the fans were so elated I thought there was going to be a riot. Not long after that great start we were down their end again and I went to put a team-mate through the line and dropped the ball cold — all the Leeds fans started chanting 'what a load of rubbish!' which made a few of us have a giggle.

The rest of the game was played at a frantic pace, the play just never stopped. I was lucky enough to play a hand in three of our four tries, kicked five from six and a field goal and we won 33–16. It rates with the top five most memorable games in my career, it was just magic — the atmosphere, the fact I was able to live up to the mighty expectations put on me, the fact everyone had welcomed us so wonderfully and we were able to make it a big day for them. We were going around the ground responding to the crowd's applause when someone screamed out, 'Look who's on the field' — it was Simon Moran. He'd never gone onto the field after a game before, but here he was going mad and screaming and jumping; he even gave an interview for Sky TV who were covering the match, and previously he'd never agree to that apparently. I thought: this bloke is a rock promoter who would have witnessed some unbelievable performances in front of big audiences, but seeing his team beat Leeds meant so much to him. As I got to know him I learned how unassuming and painfully shy he was, but that night he was just so excited.

Cathrine and I had the best time over the next few weeks. We'd get in the car and drive to Liverpool, which is 15 minutes away, or drive to Manchester, 20 minutes away, and we were just anonymous. The people in Warrington left me alone, even though my car had massive signage on it saying it was Andrew Johns in a sponsored car.

The next weekend we went to Hull to play and I think they hadn't been beaten there for a year and a half. We beat them 30–10, and everyone was starting to say Warrington were the smokeys for the title. We finished fifth and drew Hull at home in the first week of the finals. From there, we'd have to win three straight if we were to make the grand final.

After thrashing Hull away the previous week, our fans naturally expected us to beat them again at home but we were terrible, going down 40–6 and stunning our fans. That day has stuck in my mind ever since. We really thought we could win it that year but the way we bombed out was a tragedy; I felt really sad for the coach Paul Cullen and for Simon Moran who had done so much for me. There was a capacity crowd again but after blowing a couple of early scoring chances we made basic errors and went from bad to worse, even though a good young kid called Chris Bridge scored two tries.

I didn't play great but I also feel some guilt because our preparation wasn't good enough. There was so much excitement in the team after beating Leeds and Hull that a few of the boys decided to go out and celebrate on the Monday night and I got caught into going with them. It ended up a big night and, even though it was early in the week, it was enough to sidetrack us a bit and physically wouldn't have helped. The coach wasn't too happy, that's for sure. I don't know if it had much to do with the result the following Saturday night, but I'm not comfortable with my last memory of the Warrington Wolves copping a 40–6 thrashing in the finals, when there was so much expected of the team and me personally.

But other than that, it was the perfect three-week working holiday. I'd go to see some of Simon's bands, I was on the TV show *A Question of Sport*, went to the Manchester United–Liverpool Premier League game at Anfield and Renae brought Samuel over for a couple of weeks while she went to Italy with her partner, so we took him to so many places, including Euro Disney. Cath also got to see a lot of friends and family and I met quite a few of them and saw where she grew up in Wales. Simon even got her a job, working for him in the music industry, and all the players' and officials' partners made her so welcome.

I still get texts from the Warrington boys all the time and keep in touch with them and Simon Moran; Martin Gleeson and his younger brother Mark even came out and stayed at my place for a week. The Wolves have some great players. Lee Briers is an outstanding talent; people question his defence but he aimed up when I was there, I think sometimes he just loses concentration. I can't believe he's not picked in the Great Britain team more often — I really rate him.

It is a different game over there — it's more open and the defence isn't as structured as in the NRL. Over here we tend to work towards things, while over there it's like a big game of touch football, they try to score on every play. And generally the players are bigger over there — for whatever reason — and probably stronger. I don't know whether that is because in Australia we do more running due to being outdoors more often, whereas they do their off-season training in the middle of winter, so they are inside the gym more. They certainly love their weights. The facilities aren't as good; I'll never forget how, before the first game, one of the boys at Warrington was strapping another guy's ankles because they only had one trainer. But they can work on that; you know it is not as professional as the NRL and a bit of freedom and ability to relax more comes with that. I love it.

I was contemplating going back for a full season with Warrington in 2008 before my neck injury cut short my career. I had kept in contact with Simon Moran and we'd agreed that I'd give him an answer on a long-standing offer by the end of April or early May 2007 — by which time I would have known how my body was standing up and whether I still had the desire to go on for one more season. I'm not sure I could have left Samuel for a long period and that was the biggest thing to sort out before I could have finished my career in England. If he could have come over for an extended period, or if I could have had a couple of weeks off to go home during the school holidays, it might have worked out OK. I probably wouldn't have gone back though, mainly because it became apparent that physically I probably couldn't have handled the demands of another season. As it turned out, because of my neck injury, I didn't have to make a decision.

CHAPTER 22

RELUCTANT CAPTAIN ... WILLING MENTOR

I had no ambition to captain the Newcastle Knights, let alone New South Wales or Australia. I didn't think I had the personality to have the 'c' beside my name and, as a playmaking halfback, it was my role to make a lot of calls on the field anyway. But that changed one day in circumstances which are quite, well, unusual.

To protect the guilty I can't tell the full story, but it relates to the traditional football team antics on a 'Mad Monday' in September 2000. People within the club had been at me for a while to take over the captaincy from Tony Butterfield, who retired at the end of that season, a year and a half after Paul Harragon had left the game because of his painful injuries. Both were inspirational captains who relished the leadership role, and had enormous respect from within and outside of the club. Matty was the obvious successor but with him not being re-signed, a lot of people felt the responsibility should fall on me.

I was reluctant. I didn't want the off-field duties that came with being captain; fronting all the media conferences, doing promotional work and attending functions (especially in Newcastle, where corporate support is so important with the club not having its own leagues club: so a lot of off-field commitment is required from the skipper). I was also worried that I wasn't always the model player or example to others; sometimes I could turn up to a recovery session under the weather, and not be the perfect citizen off the field, and that weighed on my mind. On the field it didn't concern me — not much would change with how I played, or how I tried to lead the team anyway.

On the Mad Monday of 2000, Paul Harragon and Michael Hagan sat me down and said, 'You've got to be captain next year. It's your duty; it's your time.' I said, 'I don't want to be captain, I'm not the person to be captain, I don't conform to the rules or do this and that, blah, blah, blah.' I don't know why but I softened after a couple more beers and preaching from them, so I said, 'Look, I'm going to do something and if you do it too, I'll be captain next year,' and they said, 'OK, what is it?' Let's just say I challenged them to drink something other than beer from a schooner glass, which they reluctantly did, all in the name of what they thought were the best interests of the club. Then, to celebrate the deal, the glass went around the circle for all to share. And with that 'ceremony' I became captain of the Newcastle Knights. I couldn't go back on my word.

Luckily Billy Peden agreed to be club captain so that took a lot of the off-field responsibility off me. All I really had to do was captain the side on the field, which made the job a lot easier. In effect little changed, other than I had to toss the coin before the game. Being a halfback I controlled most things on the field anyway; and I was never a big talker before the game.

I never aspired to be captain at any level all the way through my career and was happy at the end of 2006 when, after all the expectation and pressure got too much after my run-ins with match officials, Danny Buderus — who by that stage was NSW captain and Australian vice-captain — took over. I relented again when our new coach Brian Smith asked me in 2007, but as it was I only played one full game.

I enjoyed mentoring blokes — it was one of the things that gave me the greatest satisfaction later in my career. Even though I knew I was being a little hypocritical at times, I felt I had a responsibility as a senior player to grab a young bloke and give him some advice on football and preparation. The thing with the Knights is that when we play away we go a day before the game, so when some young players get away from home and into a motel for the first time it can be like a holiday for them. I thought it was important to read them the riot act about being there to do a good job.

Being the Newcastle captain and winning a competition in 2001 obviously led to me being in the frame to become captain of my state and country; not that I was chasing either job. Looking back now though, leading out New South Wales and Australia rate as the greatest privileges of my career.

I found captaining New South Wales (in 2002–03) no great burden at all; it was only for three games a year and I was playing with such great players. There is little a captain has to do at that level, especially with the likes of Phil Gould and Ricky Stuart as coaches. It was a pleasure to run out first with the calibre of players there.

There was enormous debate in 2002 whether Gorden Tallis, who was Queensland captain, me or Darren Lockyer should be chosen as captain of Australia. It was ridiculous; none of us had come out and said we wanted the job because we all had so much respect for each other, but it became a real big him v him argument after Gorden and I were chosen as the State of Origin captains. All the speculation began before the season had even started and went on for months. We were playing Great Britain straight after the State of Origin series, and by the time the Australian side was due to be selected after that series we'd all had enough of the politics and speculation. I know that certain people within the Australian Rugby League were worried about my off-field behaviour after the reports of my antics on the 2000 World Cup tour, and how I would handle the public side of the job, but I knew I was up for it if I was chosen. I can now understand their concerns, although at the time I felt it shouldn't have been held against me, and I know I wouldn't have done anything to cause any dramas while in camp with the Kangaroos. I'd never been involved in any public incident or done anyone else any harm, even though I was struggling with my off-field life at that time. I was confident in my ability to captain at rep level.

For the record, I think it is a travesty that Shane Warne never captained Australia at cricket; he is one of the greats, the best spin bowler ever and the stories you hear are that he has such a great tactical mind, but unfortunately he was overlooked because of his well-publicised off-field activities.

I can say that captaining Australia, even though it was only for two Tests because of injuries, was a massive honour and I was tickled pink when my name was announced as skipper. At the same time, if Gorden had received the job I wouldn't have been disappointed at all and I would have given him full support.

Brad Fittler succeeded Mal Meninga who followed Wally Lewis as Australian captain, so between them they pretty well had the job for about 18 seasons from 1984–2001, before the debate raged on who would be the long-term successor. The way it turned out, injuries stopped Gorden and I playing much Test football, so Darren Lockyer took the mantle and has proved an outstanding Test captain who deserves all the praise he gets. The way he led the depleted Kangaroos to victory in England in 2003, virtually getting them home on his own in two Tests, was unbelievable.

To have been captain when the Knights won the grand final in 2001 is also a huge honour. It was very special to go up and receive the trophy from the Prime Minister, John Howard, although if you watch the video you'll notice Billy Peden and I went up together and grabbed the trophy; he deserved it as much as I did. Billy, who scored two tries in that grand final, didn't get enough credit for the influence he had on the Knights' culture with how he trained, played and conducted himself. Matty badgered the Knights coaches for a couple of years about giving Billy a trial but they kept ribbing Matty about trying to get his Cessnock mates into the club. Billy was 23 before he was graded but went on to play in both our premiership-winning teams and no one deserved the honour more. He also lived with me for two years and is just a champion bloke who is doing well now as strength and conditioning coach at the Harlequins club in London.

I know I received some extra liberties with time off training — all the boys referred to it as 'stress leave'. But I think they understood it and I'd hope it didn't affect their respect for me as captain. In fact it's a credit to Michael Hagan's management how that worked. There is no doubt I played my best football under Hages; with all I was going through over those years I can safely say I would have walked away from the game long before I did if I'd had a less understanding and more rigid coach — let alone being captain and enjoying my football so much.

I must admit I never enjoyed the post-match media conferences. I could handle all the 'raps' after we won but didn't enjoy the scrutiny and the 'what happened' questions when we lost, especially as I felt at times it was too focused on me and not the team; I was a terrible loser. And it was just another vehicle where it was too much 'the world according to Joey' in the papers, rather than comments coming from other players. So sometimes I'd ask for someone else to go and in the end we put in a rotation system for the media conferences.

Irrespective of whether I had the 'c' against my name, I enjoyed being a mentor and it is no secret I loved to pass on advice and knowledge to the younger players. I'd get to training early and stay later and work with certain blokes and I got a real kick out of that. I did a lot of extra work with Kurt Gidley and to see the player he'd become in 2007 and to thoroughly deserve his spot in the New South Wales side was a real buzz for me. He is one of the Knights' leaders now. Jarrod Mullen is another one who has been a keen learner and a pleasure to work with; I've really enjoyed seeing him develop into an Origin player at age 20. I spent a lot of time trying to help him understand the pressures involved and it's been great the way he has handled it.

Unfortunately, whoever was going to wear the number seven Newcastle jersey after my long time there was going to be under unbelievable pressure, just like those who followed Peter Sterling at Parramatta, Ricky Stuart at Canberra and Allan Langer at Brisbane. It's not going to be an easy task and 'Mullos' had the initial job in 2007 — but he is a five-eighth and that's where I'd like to see him play long-term, and I have told him that.

And as I have repeatedly said in the media, I don't know why people are comparing him to me; he does things so much better than I did at the same age and we play a different style. Luke Walsh is capable of becoming a long-term first grade halfback; he was quite impressive in his few games in '07. I just hope if I'm proved right he can handle that tag of wearing my number seven jersey until it dies down eventually. I would hate for it to ever get to a stage where the player who wore it was bitter towards me over the unwanted pressure.

I'm relishing the opportunity to help out the halfbacks and five-eighths at the Knights, from under-15s through to first grade, and hopefully that will help the club identify the right person to carry on with the job. It is hard for a halfback to control a game and for me to teach a young player a certain skill and then see him do it on the field gives me a real buzz. It might be different types of kicks in different situations, patterns of play or how to approach a certain opposing player or team. Sometimes I'll talk to Kurt and Jarrod and I'll say, 'You're playing this player this week and he'll slide, so instead of hitting the fullback or the centre all the time, hit your forward close to you.' For them to come up after a game and say it worked gives me a real kick; I'm looking forward to having that satisfaction in the future as a specialist coach and that's my motivation to keep involved with the game.

Kurt and Jarrod are just terrific human beings and come from great families and it is a pleasure to work with them. Jarrod is under immense pressure for a kid who has just turned 20. I think back when I was 20 I had Matthew alongside me and I just used to play on instincts, whereas Mullos has to steer the side around and suffer the comparisons to me, the poor bugger.

Kurt has always had that ability and his work ethic is probably the best I've seen from any player; I've never seen anyone train as hard nor anyone as fit, other than maybe Robbie O'Davis. Kurt is a bit like my brother Matthew in that he was never a top player when he was young. I remember seeing him play when he was 14 or 15 and he was built like a twig and wore a big headgear. But he kept training and training and eventually made it. He is like a sponge; he just wants to learn and take in information.

I also enjoyed working with Danny Buderus on his game. He was a halfback when he joined the Knights, but when Steve Walters' knee gave in after he'd played only seven games after coming to the club in 1999, Bedsy became our regular hooker. Steve worked closely with him for the rest of that year, but seeing as Danny and I naturally had to create a good combination as halfback and hooker, we really worked hard together.

And I'm lucky the young blokes have always been receptive when I have asked them to do 'extras' with me, concentrating on certain parts of their game or the team's structure. If I thought something needed to be done, specifically with what we'd worked on — kicking or a bit of passing — I'd drag blokes along to an extra session. I'd say it in front of the whole group and leave it up to the individuals concerned to say yes or no. The front-rowers would get together and do their extra boxing sessions and Craig Smith was a great influence in the two years he was at the club (2005–06); it is just a positive mental thing, getting together and training hard, seeing each other doing the 'extras'.

Looking back now it means a lot to me to think I've formed some culture within the club of doing that extra work. I'm sure it will carry on now and when Kurt is older or when Jarrod is towards the end of his career, they'll take guys under their wings; that's a very important tradition.

The role of mentoring, with former players becoming involved in a more structured way, is something the Knights are looking at more closely, and I think it is a great idea. The senior player group has talked about how the club's tough culture developed and how important it is to have past players come to training and games and strike a rapport with current players. The players would get a real thrill out of learning more about the club's history and players before them. There is an old boys system at the Knights where they have a box and every year we have a reunion to coincide with the last home game of the season. The ex-players do a lap of the ground and form a guard of honour as the team runs out. The Knights have lost the last game at home just twice (against the Roosters in 1999 and Cowboys in 2007) in the past decade or so, which shows what it means to current players to play in front of the old boys.

CHAPTER 23

THE 10 MATCHES I'LL NEVER FORGET

If I was to name the 10 matches I'd rank as the most memorable in my career — either for how satisfied I was with my own performance as part of the team or the special nature of the occasion — the following list is what I would come up with.

You'd think they would be all the great victories, but I've thrown in a lost game in the list — the Newcastle v Canterbury finals clash of 1998 — because I look back on that match as a significant turning point in my career and a stand-out game, after which I could say, 'I couldn't have possibly done any more to get us over the line today.'

If I was to list them in order of 'my best game', I'd definitely have my return to State of Origin in 2005 as number one, but it is too difficult to accurately rank my best matches, performance-wise; as that is really something that someone else should judge, not me.

Anyway, here they are (in chronological order):

1. First grade (run on) debut v South Sydney, Sydney Football Stadium, 13 March 1994

It was an absolute dream to score 23 points on debut from two tries, seven goals and a field goal. I remember my first try, in the second half, from a right foot step, left foot step, left hand fend — all from 10 metres, which was a long-range try for me. Late in the game I kicked through a loose ball and scored in the corner.

I'd imagine every player could remember his debut match as well as any they play; I was tingling all over from the opportunity to play first grade and for us to win so convincingly, for me to score 23 points and to have Matthew next to me — it was beyond my expectations. Every good footballer aspires to play first grade and when you do you don't know how many times it will happen again, so you savour that first moment.

2. World Cup final, Wembley Stadium, 28 October 1995

There are plenty of reasons to put this match in my top 10. It was the only time I played at the famous Wembley Stadium, and at that stage of my career the 66,000 who were there was the biggest crowd I'd played in front of — by heaps.

I kicked four out of four, after having the yips before the game, won the man of the match award in the biggest game of my career up to then, and got the most valuable player of the World Cup awarded to me after full-time. I thought 'Freddy' Fittler was outstanding and even though I felt out of my depth at that level, it was still a dream day in my career.

3. Newcastle v Manly, ARL grand final, Sydney Football Stadium, 28 September 1997

I'd never had to go through so much drama for a match and being a grand final just made it even more special. When I first learned I had a punctured lung I didn't think I was any hope of playing in the grand final and Neil Halpin virtually told me that. But to get there after spending three days in hospital and to be able to create the winning try (we won 22–16) — well, I suppose it can't come more dramatic than that.

4. Newcastle v Canterbury, NRL preliminary final, Sydney Football Stadium, 12 September 1998

The game is recorded as a 28–16 win by the Bulldogs in extra-time and the second week in a row we gave up big leads, but only those in our camp knew how 'busted' our team was with injuries. Matthew played with a restrictive hamstring injury and several other players had injuries that should have kept them out; we would have been lucky to field a decent team in the grand final if we'd won.

As I mentioned, it was a pivotal match in my career. I remember going into the game and thinking, 'I am going to win this for us today.' People said to me afterwards I nearly won the match on my own and that it was one of the best individual performances they'd seen, which was flattering. We led 16–0 but ran out of gas, with so many blokes below par with their health. I busted my arse all game; I took the line on, pulled off big tackles, my kicking game was on and when there were times in the game when I thought we needed a big play, I felt I was the one providing it.

Coming off the field I felt so satisfied, even though we were beaten. I remember thinking, 'If I could do that today, there is no reason I can't do that every week if I go out with the same attitude.'

5. Newcastle v Brisbane, round 18, EnergyAustralia Stadium, 6 July 2001

I'd been on the sidelines for 10 weeks after suffering medial ligament damage and missed the entire State of Origin series made famous by Allan Langer returning from Warrington and playing a starring role for Queensland. I was so scared I was going to hurt my knee again. I'd heard other surgeons were bagging Neil Halpin, saying I had damaged my cruciate ligament and should have done this and that. Even my father was freaking about it but Neil was confident I was right; I'd had all the appropriate scans done.

It was fortunate that my comeback game was against Brisbane on the Friday night following the Queensland series victory the previous Sunday, and they had nine Origin players who would have been celebrating and were probably not switched on like they should have been.

We'd lost four straight and had taken a 40–0 hammering from Parramatta the Friday before, and had to win to get our season back on track. The first time I touched the ball I stepped through and put Robbie O'Davis over and, from that moment, all the apprehension was gone. I scored two tries and six goals and had a major hand in six other tries in our 44–0 victory, which was then the biggest loss in the Broncos' history.

6. Newcastle v Parramatta, Grand final, Telstra Stadium, 30 September 2001

It's obvious why this is special: Parramatta were runaway minor premiers but we had them down 24–0 after 32 minutes (the final score was 30–24); I was able to hold the trophy up as winning captain and also won the Clive Churchill Medal. It was my most enjoyable season with the Knights and it had the perfect ending.

7. Australia v Great Britain, one-off Test, Aussie Stadium, 12 July 2002

The fact that it was my first Test as Australian captain, I kicked a record 10 goals in an Anglo-Australian Test and that it was one of the most awesome performances by an Australian team I played in made this game memorable. But as a Test match it wasn't very satisfying; in fact, it was one of the biggest disappointments of my career that a pretty good Pommie side coached by my old Knights mentor David Waite just didn't compete on the night.

They had Kris Radlinski, Paul Wellens, Paul Sculthorpe, Andy Farrell, Kieron Cunningham and Stuart Fielden in their side but travelling out here for a one-off game in the middle of their season was a pretty big disadvantage. We led 34–0 at half-time after they stuck with us for the first 20 minutes, and it was 64–10 in the end, the biggest win by an Australian team against Great Britain.

To lead Australia out as captain in front of my family and friends was pretty special; I only did it twice (the second time being when we beat the Kiwis 48–6 the next year) as I missed the end of season internationals in '02 and '03.

8. New South Wales v Queensland, State of Origin I, Lang Park, 11 June 2003

Considering the run-in I'd had with Phil Gould, and with a supposed big rift between us dominating the newspapers in the lead-up to the game, it was a big game in the context of my career. I didn't look at the papers for a week leading into the match. Cath said: 'If you don't read it, it won't be there,' although plenty of people were telling me about the stories.

Going into camp I was feeling sheepish after what had happened and I knew I had to win the respect of my team-mates. Gus was great, the players were terrific and our preparation outstanding. Before the game, Wendell Sailor came out and said something like it was the worst New South Wales team he'd played against, so we were pumped up. It was also the first Origin game played at the revamped Suncorp Stadium, which is an amazing ground to play at now, so the atmosphere was just unreal.

We won 25–12 after leading 12–6 at half-time and I regard that match as signifying the changing of the guard in the Blues side, with Anthony Minichiello, Craig Fitzgibbon, Josh Perry,

Craig Wing and Phil Bailey on debut and Luke Bailey, Jason Ryles, Timana Tahu and Jamie Lyon playing their second series. I felt I really had to take ownership of the team and lead from the front. I believe that was the turning point of my Origin career; I felt like I really belonged from then on. Previously I'd played well at times and had won two man of the match awards, but didn't think I'd played to the level I wanted to reach. I look back now and can say I only played at a consistent high standard in State of Origin in my last three series — 2002, 2003 and 2005 (I missed 2004 with my knee injury).

9. New South Wales v Queensland, State of Origin II, Telstra Stadium, 15 June 2005

All the circumstances make that my best-ever individual performance. I'd been playing poorly with a struggling Knights team, then broke my jaw — which meant I'd played only one game in seven weeks and eight games in 22 months — and the quality of players I was up against couldn't have been higher.

I'd played OK in my comeback game against the Broncos at home and felt I was ready to play Origin again after getting my fitness level and strength around my knee right at the Queensland Academy of Sport. I was disappointed I hadn't been picked initially, but I understood why. One of the selectors and Ricky Stuart called and said, 'We're not going to pick you but we'll pick you for the third one.'

When Trent Barrett hurt his quadriceps at training, it all changed for me. I was driving home after a massage at

Lambton when my mobile phone rang, and it said 'private number'. I never answer anonymous calls but for some reason picked it up and it was Ricky. He asked, 'Have you got your boots ready?' and I said, 'I'll be there in two hours.'

There were so many doubters, including ex-players, saying in the press that I was underdone and wouldn't perform. I was licking my lips — the more they were writing it the more I could feel myself building up. Whether it was my bipolar I'm not sure, but I was thinking, 'I'm going to show you people.'

The game plan Ricky set suited me to the ground. They had a big pack and we wanted to move them around off the pivot (me), and then, after 20 minutes or so, he wanted me to run and take the line on. The call was 'Wizard'; when I heard that call from the bench it was 'be ready to run'. When the call came I could see the holes in the Queensland defence as they tired. I had a great side around me — Braith Anasta played out of his skin, Anthony Minichiello and I roomed together and struck a great combination, and the forward pack were outstanding. We'd run them around so much the big Queensland boys were out on their feet in the last 20 minutes.

Cathrine was next to me on the team bus when we went back to the hotel after the game, and she told me she was worried about how I was going to be that night, that I might have come off a high into one of my depressions because I was so quiet. I turned to her and said, 'That was one of the great moments of my football career tonight and I'm just taking it in.' I knew straight away how significant it was. I've never been one to boast about what I'd done on the football field but that night I'd never been prouder of an achievement; no one but me knew what I had come back from to put in that performance and how hard I had trained. And I feel the third game of the series was one of my best games too. In that game we defended for five sets in a row, then the game changed and it was 18–0 our way.

After my return in Game Two the Knights beat Penrith away, our first win of the season in round 16, then went on a big run in which we won eight of our last 11 games. The two Origin victories made it 10 wins from 13 for me and I'd have to say that that three-month period produced the best stretch of form in my career; it was the greatest example of how hard work can pay off.

10. Warrington v Leeds, Halliwell Jones Stadium, 10 September 2005

It was just like a wild affair, my in-and-out Warrington experience; just a whirlwind of enjoyment and activity for the whole three weeks. I was on a massive high the whole time.

That opening match, against the reigning world champions Leeds, is one of the very special experiences of my life. And, as a footballer, I felt like I had to prove myself all over again. I was jet-lagged; the expectation by the club and fans was massive; the town was buzzing; and, come match-day, I had never experienced atmosphere like it, the crowd was just going crazy. And I was able to deliver the goods.

In Australia we play with a structure and work towards outcomes; maybe two tackles in a set would you try to bust them, and there is also so much focus on slowing the opposition down at the ruck. In England it's open slather: try to score from every play possible and just tackle and get off them, which ensures the game is so open and fast. I had little time to adjust to all that with just two training runs, but somehow it clicked on the night. To be able to see the joy it brought the Warrington fans made it an even more wonderful memory.

CHAPTER 24

IN THE HEAT OF
THE BATTLE

In the 15 years I was at the Newcastle Knights the game changed enormously in professionalism. Players are fitter and stronger; they are full-time; the training techniques and resources available to coaches have improved tenfold and the analytical and statistical aids are now fairly cutting edge. But, to me, rugby league is still a pretty basic game. If you take the time to study it, to put effort into your self-development as a player and your preparation, you can be successful. Talent will only take you so far.

And to win these days you have to 'play smart' because the distribution of talent around the clubs is so even. The old cliché of 'turning up on the day' is vitally important and will decide the winner and loser most times.

I thought I'd try to provide an insight into how NRL games are generally played out and what I would look for, and see, on a football field during a match. The older I got and the more matches I got under my belt, the easier I found it to 'control' a game from halfback and the more I understood the tempo of a game and what was required to get my team home. I always enjoyed the challenge of steering the Knights, of pushing my forwards and combining the tactics of the coaching staff with using my own instincts as things unfolded.

The preparations of individual coaches are always different. At Newcastle Malcolm Reilly used to set us a basic game plan but he used to put it to the floor, and say, 'Right, you guys have played them before — how do you think we should play them?' So Malcolm would get our input and come back with his match plan that would work well. David Waite would set stringent game plans which really helped me as a young halfback. Then there was Michael Hagan who probably had the luxury that I could control a game once we were out there, so he would just have a simple game plan and we'd go out and execute it as well as we could. Warren Ryan was a great student of rugby league and a master of game plans; one week we could play a certain way and the next week we'd play a completely different way against different opposition. When you look at some teams, they don't change their habits much and worry more about perfecting their own game rather than adjusting it greatly to suit the opposition. Melbourne were a classic example when they won the competition in 1999; all they did was play purely the flat style attack they became famous for, with great go-forward, and Brett Kimmorley and Scott Hill orchestrating moves off that.

These days there is computer software that enables a player or coach to pick up any piece of vision or any statistic to isolate a particular player's game, or specific parts of his game; you could sit and watch what he does over and over. In the NRL now every team generally trains the same, although some harder than others. They do the same weights, similar moves, everyone pretty much has the same philosophy on the game — so it is just that tiny one per cent of things in the execution that makes a difference.

At Newcastle we would generally have a picture in our minds about how we wanted to play and then it was a process of getting together, usually early in the week, and going through the match preview where we would identify the opposition's strengths and weaknesses. I might discuss with the coach certain sets from video vision of the opposition; the danger players, which foot they step off and the areas we can exploit. We might point out a couple of missed tackles, which edge of the ruck to hit; which players get tired, what they do when they get tired and this sort of stuff. So it is pretty analytical but, as I said, after all the years I'd played it became second nature knowing which player did what.

It was also important to know your team-mates' games inside out. For example, with Matt Gidley I used to hit him with a pass early as he could create something out of nothing. Some players were good at getting the ball later (closer to the defensive line), while other players didn't have the best of hands, so instead of passing the ball to them 'in the line', I'd have to get it to them early off a cross play, nice and easy.

In my first few years, I used to get worked up and be extremely nervous and vomit before the game, and feel I had to get out there and rip in; make some big tackles and charge the line. As I got older, I could be reading the paper or form guide five minutes before the game. Then the two-minute bell would come and that's when the energy would appear in the dressing room and all the hyper-talk started and the nervous energy would come out.

The first 10 minutes of a match is all about completing your sets and the big thing for a halfback is to be patient. You want your big boys rolling forward and all getting an early touch of the ball. If I was playing with someone who was making his debut or was early in his career, I'd be conscious of giving him an early touch. If he was a centre, I'd call the ball on the first set, throw the ball wide, and let him dance around and settle the nerves. But generally what you're looking for is to get your game plan rolling, identify the weaker defenders, try to get at them and get into your kick. The most important thing for me was to get into my kick early to try to build some pressure.

Establishing good yardage early in the game is important, especially coming off your own line. You generally get into a rhythm early of your big men punching up the middle. That's why the genuine front-rowers are so valuable: Roy Asotasi plays the first ruck, yet he takes 10 metres, drags two or three defenders in and still plays the ball quickly; Josh Perry, when he was at his best, used to line them up and scatter defenders and our go forward started from there, especially when he was in partnership with such a big bloke like Matt Parsons. I'd always play my best football when Josh and 'Parso' were playing well, because it was so easy to feed off that go forward with the back-rowers coming off quick play the balls.

Once you get that rhythm you start looking for the bad defenders — what everyone now calls 'spot defenders', usually a halfback or a five-eighth or maybe hooker who you find in the line. At the Knights we'd call those plays (bombarding the spot defenders) 'shark sets': if you were playing a certain defender you'd say, 'Right, we are going to shark him,' which would mean you'd find him on an early play, and then you'd just keep criss-crossing him for three or four tackles in a row. Then you might get two quick play the balls out of that, which would enable you to trundle forward 10 or 15 metres each tackle. If you accumulated the metres made, you would be making 50 or 60 metres a set; that would be the objective, allowing you to kick downfield from a positive position (in their half).

As I got older I learned about pacing myself, and the team if possible, although you wouldn't know it looking at the way I played sometimes. Being able to dominate a game in the last 20 minutes was the most important thing; and also learning how to control a game, when to pass, when to shift the ball, when to play long, when to be patient. It really takes a long, long time to learn the craft of a halfback. Counting numbers and getting to different parts of the field ended up coming second nature to me, and once I started doing that more convincingly I realised how much 'time' I could buy myself on the field. There's a fine line for a halfback of knowing 'when to pull the trigger' (as Warren Ryan used to say), and that was probably something that I wasn't too good at for a while. I used to play laterally too often; I was too impatient; I'd try to chip-kick when I shouldn't have, but I learned to have more patience as I got more experienced.

The ruck has become such a big part of rugby league and a game within the game really. I learned about 'ruck recognition' later in my career — how to recognise when you're losing the ruck and when you're winning it. If you're a halfback and your team is slowing the opponents' play the ball and getting quick play the balls yourself, then you're sitting back smoking your pipe, because you've got so much time to do what you want to. You're really in the lap of the gods being a halfback; well, in the lap of your forwards, most of whom think they are gods. I used to always follow different players — when Ben Kennedy ran, he'd drag two or three defenders in, then get up quickly and leave someone behind on the ground. That would give you time and space the next ruck. There are different players who play the ball fast and you work off them. That's 'ruck recognition': knowing when to go 'bang' and making sure you have 'shape' in your attacking formation to take the advantage offered. Next minute there might be a hand on the ball from the defender and instead of being a three to four second play the ball, it's an eight second play the ball, and that's when you've got to fire your forwards up to cart it forward again ... and wait a little longer.

Teams generally work to a sideline and create a thing called a 'channel' — one on the open and one on the blind or short-side — and this revolves around the 'shark set', working over maybe a centre or a five-eighth or halfback. That involves going at him once, going away from him to, say, the open side, then going back to the blind at him again. Most teams generally do this or they get the ball in the corner and wrap the ball all the way across and then kick it.

In 'good ball' a lot of teams work around percentages of field. They might work to the middle of the field, which is called '50 per cent either side' (options both sides of the play the ball), but a lot of teams now work towards scrum line (the line 20 metres in from touch where scrums are set). Around that scrum line you can have six defenders on the open side and four defenders on the short side (plus two at the play the ball and the fullback). It is a great position to attack the open side; if you get a good play the ball it can really strain the centres and the third last defender (in from the touch line). In Newcastle, when my brother Matty and I were together, we used to get to the middle and for the majority of sets we would split and identify a weaker defender. We'd then shift the ball away from the bad defender and use a running forward on the edge of the ruck to hit to around the scrum-line. Hopefully, he would get a quick play the ball and then one of us would swing around to the open side and attack off the second receiver and try to isolate the weaker defender; you see teams do that still. If it's not their weaker defender it is certainly their main playmaker or smaller men who will fatigue quicker from the defensive workload and have less effort left for attack.

Body language and talk are such big aspects of the game. When you play the Bulldogs they never seem to have much chatter in attack — they just rely on their raw power and support. Penrith were similar and played the most basic style of football you would see when they won the competition in

2003, but it was based around their big forwards steaming onto the ball and then completing their sets and being patient until the opposition made an error. The Wests Tigers play a real lateral sort of game where they look like they are playing expansively but they're not doing a lot of passing; they just have a lot of players in motion calling the ball. It is just a master stroke of Tim Sheens' because they haven't got a big dominant pack, but he has three or four ball-players — one of them is usually Robbie Farah who plays like an extra halfback — drifting across field with runners going here, there and everywhere. It looks flamboyant but there is not much ball movement. They won a competition off changing the angles and point of attack and using a pack full of back-rowers who were fast and agile and played the ball incredibly fast. Then there are teams like North Queensland, who have freakish talent in Johnathan Thurston and Matty Bowen who can play ad-lib football off second phase play; they can be impossible to stop. Thurston and Matt Bowen talk in whistles and grunts, it just blows your mind; they have this understanding where they just know where each other is.

If you score a try, the key rule is to complete the next set. Everyone says it — you can hear teams screaming, 'We've got to complete the next set' — but it is amazing how many times teams don't by doing something stupid. So from the kickoff you try to force an error with a big hit because you're conscious of how much it will affect the opposition mentally to have to suddenly defend their line.

Completion rates are important but it's also what you do with the ball that counts; there is no use in completing your sets but not putting the defence under any pressure. Some teams can be as boring as bat-shit to watch; they just hit up, hit up, hit up and kick. When you're going to play those teams it's brought up in team meetings: we'd say, 'Righto, we are playing this team this week, it is going to be an absolute shit fight. We're playing at their home ground, it is a night game, it could be wet, they'll complete 85 per cent and never chance their arm. If we do nothing but the same we'll get beaten 8–6.' In those games, you've got to earn the right to open up your game by playing the arm wrestle for 50 minutes, then playing some footy.

There is a saying in rugby league about 'playing what is in front of you'; in other words, reacting to what the defence may do and following your instincts, rather than relying on the pre-planned moves. The game is generally too programmed these days and not enough players have great football instincts. I think this comes back to players not lifting their eyes up and reading numbers. You have the game plan, and the set might be, for example, to work towards the middle of the field for a certain play. But if on the first play the front-rower carts it up and goes through, then you've got to be looking up, and if their defence is still compressed, you've got to zing it wide. It doesn't matter if it is play-one or play-six; if it's there, then you've got to back yourself and do it.

You see players getting caught into what we call 'ruck watching', where they're constantly watching the ruck and not watching what is in front of them — you've got to be looking at the ruck and counting numbers and being aware. You might think, 'Righto, are we winning this ruck? Yep, OK they've got four defenders in the middle of the field, let's go!' Also, you've got to identify who is in front of you. If there were two big blokes together, say two front-rowers, and they looked fatigued, well I knew I'd have to run. If you put yourself in their situation, and you had a nippy halfback coming at you who is fresh (I won't say I was quick), the last thing you'd want him to do is run — you'd want him to pass. So it's all about identifying who is in front of you, how many numbers they've got and ruck recognition; and it takes a long time to learn that.

Your fullback is as important for his talk in attack, as he is in defence when he calls to players where to stand in the line and where the opposition are going in attack. You've also got to have your fullback tipping who is in front of you. That's why combinations are so important and why teams that are together for a long time are hard to beat. You know they are tipping each other — 'that's so and so in front of you, I'm going to his left shoulder' — or the fullback is there, saying, for example, 'x player won't chase, go through the middle.'

Sometimes you make a 'shark' defender play three plays in a row. When you play against Melbourne you hear them name-dropping from the start of a set: they might call a front-rower's name out, and they'd send a player straight at him; then they'd go one side on play-two then play across at him; then they'd go another side and play across at him on the next play. Then they'd have a trick shot where they go Cameron Smith-Cooper Cronk-Greg Inglis or Billy Slater up the middle and attack that tired marker with a speed man. You know it's coming but it's done so incredibly fast and when you're under fatigue you make the wrong decisions. That is what building pressure is about.

By the way, I think it's bullshit when you see halfbacks defending on the wing or one in; I took pride in defending three-in and when I defended with Clint Newton I used to have to defend four-in sometimes, because he was too tired to get there (sorry, 'Newto', but that's your spot). Like anything, you become familiar with that position. On the edge of the ruck the third bloke in is the most important man: he controls the speed of the line; he controls whether you are sliding, whether you are up and in, and he's the man doing all the talking — it is a hard position to defend from. There is no way of hiding if you're a halfback or five-eighth — you are going to get big blokes sitting on you all game. Darren Lockyer doesn't get the accolades he deserves. He is so tough and gets big blokes charging him all the time, but he stands up to it really well now.

Players like Locky are always the hardest to defend against, just because of their instincts. He could be wide of the ruck setting up play, but he could identify half a break and with his speed go another way and he'd be there in a second; he is just phenomenal with his vision and speed. The great players have that vision: when Laurie Daley was at his best it was frightening how explosive he was. Allan Langer was unstoppable close to the line; with Alfie you never knew what he was going to do. The players who are hard to defend are the fast players, or the big bony guys like Greg Inglis, who is also quick and has got outstanding footwork. You ask anyone and they'll say the bigger blokes are not as big an issue — it's the little fast bony sort of players who are toughest to tackle. Although I wouldn't want to tackle Manu Vatuvei too many times.

At Newcastle we never really played too rigid a style; we used to play a fairly open sort of game, which I enjoyed. People say they love watching Newcastle play. I naturally used to worry about completions but it wasn't the be all or end all. I think the league should think about a rule restricting dummy half running — there is too much and it is boring to watch. Wingers go in as dummy half and (no disrespect to wingers intended) they can't pass, so you know they are going to run. It's an effective, low-risk play and they tire the opposition's forwards out, because they've got whippets dancing around them.

Teams definitely take fewer risks these days. The players are more skilled at catching and passing, but I think we develop more robots than footballers and I don't know how you change that; it is a big debate. There are not many ball-playing forwards and I think that is a by-product of standing teams 12 metres apart; you don't need four or five ball-players to break up the defence, you need big strong robots charging in. Some of the athletes now playing the game are phenomenal — they are big, big boys with agility.

The thing you look for, in your own team and in the opposition, is which players are getting tired towards the end of each half. It was ridiculous when we had unlimited interchange because it took the beauty out of that skill — all of a sudden three or four fresh big men jogged onto the field every 15 minutes or so. With 12 interchanges, you have to be smart enough to sense when the window of opportunity is there with a tired defender, or even a tired attacker who can be forced into error. You can see the signs, like if a player is slow getting back to the defensive line, he's blowing with his breathing, or has his hands on his hips.

I used to say to my forwards, 'You've got to tell me when you are tired.' Sometimes they are too proud to admit it but you've got to be watching your forwards, and if you see they are under fatigue, that's when you call your dummy half sets. I know it is negative but everyone does it; then you control the tempo by putting the ball out and walking to the scrum. I remember playing with Matt Parsons and every second set on the last play he'd be screaming at me, 'Put the *%$!! out, "Cyces", put it out!' and I'd kick into touch and Parso would come behind me and ruffle my hair, going, 'Righto, boys, let's have a walk to the scrum.'

The blueprint when you play the bigger sides, like the Warriors or the Kiwi Test side, is to throw the ball around a bit for the first 10 or 20 minutes, kick early or keep the ball in play, so you can run them around. Then after 20 minutes you bring the speed men into the middle and test out their tired big men.

Kicking is extremely important in controlling a match; and you need a good roll-forward from your forwards to be able to kick from good position. Some teams used to kick the ball towards the posts to catch us off-guard; try to hit the post for the ball to bounce back. I generally kicked the ball to one side all the time; you work on hang time and try to hang off as long as possible before kicking the ball. I used to play around, leaning the ball different ways, try to make the ball banana in the air and bend and bounce for me. Generally, it is simply about trying to buy time for your defence to sprint down and tackle them in their 10-metre zone.

Every team has their favourite plays, most based on decoy runners and attacking the defender three in from the sideline, but you also have to keep your options open if you see a different opportunity to the one you have planned for. I marvel at the ability of the great ball-players these days; I was watching the Australia–New Zealand Test match in 2007 and Darren Lockyer and Johnathan Thurston were going to the line and in a split second they'd have five options of what to do with the ball — either one had the ability to go himself; the ability to put a kick in; the ability to hit the forward running into a hole; or to find the fullback running behind or throw a long ball to the winger. Generally the players of their quality come up with the right option all the time. That is the difference between the great ball-players and the others; I don't know whether that comes through constant practice at training and on the field or if it's just the in-built instincts, but you take for granted how good some of the ball-players are.

People talk about the great players being two or three plays ahead of the others. To be honest I don't know what that means, like we're always setting for *something* in a set of six tackles. Wayne Bennett once told me that Wally Lewis would shorten the dimensions of the field in his mind and walk a rectangle inside that field. He would let his forwards go forward and he would follow inside that rectangle, then he'd identify the ruck where there was space in close or where an overlap was. Whenever Wally wanted the ball, he got it; when he was screaming for it, no one else got the ball. So he'd restrict himself to a certain part of the field and read what was taking place, just prey on the right ruck in the right position and inflict himself. Maybe that's what people mean by being two or three rucks ahead of the play. That was part of my development, hearing stories like that.

Danny Buderus would admit there was no doubt when I wanted the ball, because I would be screaming my lungs out for it. But I go back to ruck recognition — there's no need going overboard calling the ball all the time as a halfback, unless you can read when you're winning the ruck. I think teams become too obsessed with shifting the ball where there is no necessity and no advantage. If you're attacking in the quarter and there is no overlap or no fast play the ball, I don't see why teams shift the ball. You should just keep changing the angles, use the forwards up, play with patience, because if you're shifting off a slow play the ball it just gets cut down, and you lose 20 metres and have to start again. I was guilty of that early in my career; I used to shift for the sake of shifting, usually because Matthew was outside me screaming his lungs out! We would call 'two', meaning play two rucks to the middle of the field then look at the defence, or take two to the scrum-line and try to find a particular defender. If it didn't come off, you'd look to a repeat set by kicking into the in-goal and trapping their retriever, or bombing the winger and putting him under pressure.

So it is all about patience and commitment in winning NRL matches. The basics haven't changed a lot — it's about getting into rhythm early with your big boys making good yardage; getting the ball to those who need an early touch to settle down; getting the right feel with your kicking game and having a good enthusiastic chase. It's about having composure; working to the right part of the field for appropriate set plays; getting repeat possessions with a line drop-out if your scoring shots don't come off. It's about anticipation and reaction when something is suddenly 'on'; it's about communication in defence and being able to read the fatigue factor in your own team, as much as in the other side, and pushing through the tiredness when you have to keep going. Certainly it is about spotting a potential weak defender or two and working them over. It's about knowing the characteristics of your opposing player — which leg he steps off, which arm he offloads with, which is his good or bad shoulder in defence; who comes in when he shouldn't in defence; who gets lost making a decision under pressure; who is foiled easily by decoy runners; who is slow in turning to recover the ball after a kick; who tires and what he does when he does tire; who makes errors under pressure; who has good hands and bad hands and more.

But in the end it boils down to making decisions under fatigue and pressure, and the more ball you have and the better use you make out of that possession, the better chance you are of cashing in on that fatigue factor. But you have to realise that the best players can do something to defy all of that and the best teams can do something that doesn't necessarily surprise you, but they do it with such precision you can't stop it.

CHAPTER 25

THE BK BLOW-UP: WHAT REALLY HAPPENED

Let me start this chapter by saying Ben Kennedy is one of the most incredibly loyal blokes I have come across in life ... and the best signing (from another club) the Newcastle Knights have ever made. As a footballer he was awesomely inspirational and, as a mate, just a first-class bloke.

It's funny that when we first met, there had been all this speculation about how Matty had been squeezed out under the salary cap to fit in BK and he was worried it would see us get off on the wrong foot; so he grabbed me to clear the air on the first day at training. He needn't have bothered. We struck it off from the beginning.

But there was an afternoon in 2001 when we had a few too many beers and — I still don't know how it got a bit out of hand — a bit of skylarking went over the top and we stepped outside of the Beach Hotel at Merewether and took our debate across the road.

That episode somehow made the newspapers and kept cropping up in the media for 10 days — can you believe — this fictional notion that there was a massive Joey–BK rift that nearly split the club in two. It was the biggest storm in a teacup I probably came across — and there were plenty of those during my career, don't worry.

Here is the true version of what happened.

I'd been to the christening of my mate Kris and Kristy Lees' daughter Emerson, at which I was the very proud godfather, on the Easter Monday after we'd played the day before. I'd had a few drinks afterwards when I received a call from some of the Knights boys saying they were at 'The Beaches' having a great time and wanted me to join them — which I did.

There was a heap of good banter between the boys which, as it often does with footballers, turned into some lively sledging around the pool table and PubTAB and some of it went a bit far, I must admit, with me as a pretty solid contributor.

Next thing, I said something I shouldn't have to Ben and we were daring each other to go outside and settle our argument. I didn't want to fight him because I like him too much, plus I knew he would destroy me. But with our logic impaired by I don't know how many schooners, we ended up down on the beach with heaps of people gathered around. When Mark Hughes wasn't in between us like a referee trying to break up a clinch in a low grade heavyweight boxing bout,

BK would wind up a punch and stop it a centimetre from my face and say, 'Look, I could have broken your jaw, now go home,' and then Boozy would leap in, saying, 'C'mon, you are best mates, what are you doing?' It was comical if anything.

I settled down, we sat and chatted about how stupid we'd been, then later that night a few of us went and had a beer together at The Brewery and BK and I were best mates again. But, as usual, some idiot decided to take photos of our little scrap and it was all over the papers the next day. The funny thing was that while people were reading it thinking that our long friendship had been put at risk, Ben and I were having breakfast together. I apologised, we had a hug, he told me he loved me, and we were giggling away over bacon and eggs.

But the rumour, fuelled by all sorts of ill-informed theories in the press, wouldn't go away. My manager John Fordham rang me to find out what all the hullabaloo was about and I said, 'This is going to be pretty big because so many people saw us,' but he said as long as it didn't come between us, not to worry about it. BK is almost as paranoid about the media as I am and doesn't respect too many journalists, so you can imagine how he felt about it. He said to me at training later that week, 'You know how much of a non-event this is, don't you?' We couldn't believe how many legs the thing grew.

But we did gain a bit of mileage out of it. The next weekend we played the Wests Tigers and BK, Boozy and I decided if any of us scored a try we'd do a whacky try celebration, which were all the go at the time with *The Footy Show*'s encouragement. We weren't short of opportunities with Ben and Mark scoring two tries each in a 56–6 win. So when BK scored first, we pointed fingers at each other's faces and Boozy jumped in between us and pushed us apart — then we had a big laugh and hug as we walked back. It was our way of showing the fans that there was nothing serious about what happened.

It was one of the greatest travesties that Ben had to leave the Knights because of salary cap restraints; he never wanted to leave the area or the club. He and wife Emma and their three kids loved it there, but he played his last two seasons with Manly. To be chosen in their greatest-ever team is a massive testament to the influence he had on the Eagles in such a short time.

Ben is in Brisbane now after going into a fruit business with one of his good mates from Canberra, former Raiders forward Nathan Sologinkin. He is working long hours but enjoys it and is making a killing, which is not surprising because he was obviously going to put a lot of hard work into it. We keep in touch regularly by phone and I miss not having the big bald unit around.

He is just such good company and we have similar interests — horse racing, footy, family and good times over a few beers. A lot of people say we are very similar — which I think includes being moody and pig-headed. One interest we don't share is his passion for fishing; I left that to Steve Simpson and Matt Parsons to indulge with him. They were known around the Knights as Hook, Line and Sinker.

I loved playing with BK: he was talented, tough, inspirational and I've never seen a player with a greater constitution; his ability to play with pain was just out of this world. He would be in a warm-up sometimes and, in horse racing terms, he would be 'lame' — just limping awfully — and I would think, 'There is no way he can play today.' But he would get on field and get a surge of adrenalin and he'd be right as rain. There were times he played with a broken hand which was so swollen and painful it would stop any other player. But there would be no drama or attention seeking (unlike regular scenes from the person writing this book!), he'd just get out and play, and play bloody well. The injuries BK so often got were the by-product of how hard he played and trained, and in the end his body just gave in — although his mind never would.

As a team-mate he was a born leader; he would lead blokes with chit chat then lead with his actions. He was a big game player: if there were big moments in the game when we needed someone to lift us, invariably he was the one to do it — either a big hit in the line or a cover tackle when we had to scramble, or if we needed someone to cart the ball up in our own quarter when the team was under pressure, he'd take the ball up with three blokes hanging off him and make 10–15 metres and the team would lift from that.

As I said, he is unquestionably in my mind the best signing in the history of the Newcastle Knights; and I love the bloke. I just never want to fight him.

CHAPTER 26

WEEK IN THE LIFE OF
A FOOTBALLER

I am sure there are thousands of people who have the misconception that the life of an NRL player is really breezy, with all this wasted time on his hands in between training sessions and games. So I thought I'd list a normal week during the last few seasons of my career to give an insight into what it really is like.

I could often leave at seven in the morning and with training and promotional work not stop until I got home after dinner at night. And when you're attending luncheons and dinners, you don't relax and have a drink — you're talking football, giving interviews. It was a relentless workload at times.

I'll start the week with a Sunday afternoon match, after which the team would have a swim as the first part of the recovery process. If it was a home game we would then go back to Club Phoenix for the presentations for all three grades, a meal together and for most players a few quiet beers, then home to bed not too late.

I'd be up bright and early Monday morning, try to sneak a surf in if I felt up to it, have a light breakfast, then it was an 8am swim and a stretch. Straight after this I'd see the doctor to check if there were any problems or get some physiotherapy. After lunch I'd have a massage for about one and a half hours. So Monday was important to get the maximum recovery treatment because physically the game takes more out of a player as every year of his career goes by.

Tuesday morning would start with an hour-long gym session with all the squad before we'd do a review of the game, which would involve an hour video session and discussion. I'd fit in a physiotherapy session and lunch before training for about two hours in the afternoon. I would drive straight to Sydney from training and stay at Cath's Tuesday night.

Wednesday was the squad's day off but I would go and see Kay McPherson at Cronulla for treatment, which was a good 45 minutes' drive from Cath's. I'd have an hour or an hour and a half session with Kay and most probably I'd have some promotional work or other activity in Sydney, have a meeting with my management, John or Nick Fordham, maybe catch up with someone for lunch, then head back to Newcastle on Wednesday afternoon.

On Thursday morning we'd have weights for an hour, and after every gym session we'd have an ice bath treatment, which takes up to 20 minutes — that involves jumping into an ice bath for a minute, then into hot water for a minute, and repeating it. You also have to weigh in before and after a gym session — as well as matches — to see how much fluid you'd lost. (Incidentally, sometimes a player could lose 2.5 kilograms in a match and he wouldn't be allowed to leave the stadium until he'd put the weight back on, filling up on water and Gatorade. I used to lie about my weight all the time, hop on quickly when the bloke recording our weights was not watching, and say I was 91.3 kilograms when really I was 91.8 kilograms before a game.)

After Thursday's gym session I'd usually follow with some general kicking practice with a couple of our other kickers (say, Kurt Gidley and Jarrod Mullen), then some goal-kicking with Daryl Halligan who would come up from Sydney; a session with Daryl would last for about half an hour. In the afternoon the team would do a preview of the weekend's game, which could take half an hour, before we'd train in the afternoon for about two hours.

We'd generally have Friday off. It is a day when players would sometimes have a club promotion to attend or would get some extra treatment on the body — at least a massage or some physio — but the main thing is to rest and really eat up to prepare the body for the match. I generally liked to have a surf on Fridays.

In between those sessions most blokes would do their extra individual training or in small groups — say, kicking and passing for some of the backs, or the forwards would do extra defensive work or a boxing session. I might watch a personal video of my game, which can easily be packaged on the computer software every club has, or on our opposing team or individual players. When I was young I'd probably do one or two extra skills sessions a week, depending on how the body felt, but obviously later in my career when the body was getting a bit worn, my extra sessions were generally doing some boxing or a good sweat on the rowing machine or cardio machine, probably on the Wednesday. Some players would do TAFE courses most weeks as well, with a big push for player welfare in the NRL now, which is a good idea.

On Saturday morning the team would meet and train for an hour — nothing too sharp, just going through the motions with a ball in our hands. I'd do some goal-kicking which would only last 15 minutes, so all up I might be at training for around an hour. It was then mentally getting focused for the match next day if we were at home; if we were playing in Sydney we would leave about lunchtime Saturday for our hotel.

Of course, I'd also want to spend time with Samuel every week. Generally I'd have him on Friday-Saturday-Sunday when we were playing at home, and Renae and I would be flexible when I was playing away, which was good of her. But mostly, he'd stay with me for two and a half days a week.

I also had to fit in two newspaper columns (the Friday *Daily Telegraph* and *Sunday Telegraph*), which were ghosted by the *Tele*'s Newcastle-based reporter Barry Toohey — who was good to work with — so ideas for that were going through my head. As well, I'd drive down every few weeks for an appearance on *The Footy Show* or the occasional other Channel Nine work. There were times I was driving to Sydney two or three times a week which is not great on the back.

What people also don't consider is that when the Knights played in Townsville, Melbourne or Auckland, there was a lot of extra travel time, which cut into the team's preparation. There were times when it would take us eight hours or more door-to-door to get to Townsville, via a bus to Sydney, Sydney–Brisbane flight, a stop off, then Brisbane–Townsville.

I enjoyed the solitude when we played away; I'd get to the hotel, kick back on the bed and watch TV, go down for a team meeting and dinner, then back to the room and just shut it down, no distractions. It was good ... except for Bedsy walking around cleaning the room!

Now, all of the above doesn't include treatment of injuries which may have sidelined me. If a Knights player had a serious injury, a lot of times the doctors from Newcastle would send us to Sydney to get an MRI scan or CAT scan so we'd have to drive down there, which takes two hours, have the scans, see a specialist (there seems to be a different specialist for every part of the body), then come back to Newcastle and have physio. It's tougher when you're in rehab training: you have to get up at six in the morning to train with the rehab squad (players recovering from injury), then watch the other guys train. So you are at double the training sessions, with no opportunity to play at the end of the week — a great incentive to work hard and get out of rehab! It's a lonely tough time — you seem to spend endless hours training or at the physio, sometimes looking at the black lines at the bottom of a swimming pool for three to five hours a day.

I've provided an insight into the schedule 'in-season', but out of season it is probably more concentrated with training.

We'd only have five or six weeks' break from our last game to the start of pre-season training (although most players would still do at least two weights sessions a week and some fitness work in that 'break'). Then, for about the first four months, we'd only have Sundays off. In a given week we'd do probably four weight sessions, two skill-based sessions and two conditioning sessions. The hardest part of training was always the off-season; if you got through the off-season it was easy playing. I'd still go to Sydney to get treatment from Kay and fit in a really tough fitness session with Trent Langlands in Sydney first thing Wednesdays; sometimes I'd do a session with 'Chang' twice a week. I'd often also do a sharp session with Kris Lees a couple of times a week. We'd meet at Merewether ocean baths and do a 20–25 minute effort up and down the stairs — that little bit of extra work was more for mental fitness. I heard a story once about how the great tennis player Ivan Lendl, when he was on tour, used to train when all the other players were going out to dinner or having a few beers; he'd make sure some of them would see him and reckoned that gave him the mental edge over them. I can identify with that.

Of course, I have to admit there were times when Michael Hagan would give me two or three days off (yep, 'stress leave'), which was sensational. And there were times when, if we played in Sydney on a Sunday afternoon, I'd ask if I could stay down and spend the night with Cath and on Mondays get the train home — which would take two hours and 50 minutes, all stations to Broadmeadow!

I'm not complaining one bit about the footballer's lot, I'm just trying to clear the air that there is a lot of time spent on preparation, fitness, recovery and promotional work; and there is no doubt the time is much more productively spent than when full-time professionalism first came in across the game in the mid-1990s and no one knew a lot about how to handle it.

The good thing about not having to work a 'regular job' to supplement football income back then was the time it gave Matty and I to do 'extras', and we knew the value of working hard to develop our games and gain an edge over our opponents. We would train in the mornings and afternoons, and probably three times a week Matty and I would go off and do an hour or more training together: kicking, passing, footwork — all sorts of stuff, really. We used to run along the try-line and charge the goalposts, step the left upright, and then we'd run five metres and step the right upright. We'd run the different drills where we'd set five witches' hats out and step them off different feet.

Back then, the team would do all the same skills work, which was crazy — a front-rower doing the same skills as a halfback or a winger. The game has evolved to where it is horses for courses now, in both fitness and skill-based work; you never see the winger do the same as a front-rower. The fitness work for outside backs is based around repeat speed, running at high pace with little recovery time. Front-rowers obviously train a lot harder than everyone else, so they do a lot of intervals, a lot of short up-and-back stuff, getting off the ground and wrestling-type movements. The back-rowers are similar, while the halves have to be really fit so they have to do a little bit of both, doing the up and backs and the wrestles, but they also have to do speed and agility work. Everyone has their own specific weights program — it's all written down, every set.

Early in my career I used to practise my kicking for hours and hours until I got to a level where I could do it in my sleep and I could particularly do it when fatigued in a match. As I got older, all I would do was refresh my mind and my skills and that would be enough. I found if I did too much kicking during the week my groin would start to get sore, but luckily I'd done a lot of volume early in my career — ridiculous amounts really, but it was worthwhile. Sometimes I just used to go down the field and practise for an hour and a half by myself — I'd kick the ball 60 metres and chase it, and then kick it back 60 metres and chase it. Once I felt I mastered it, that was when I really started to experiment: bananas, torpedo kicks and bombs, and all these other sorts of kicks.

I first saw Ricky Stuart do some banana kicks in the mid-'90s — I think Matty picked it up first and I just started practising it. One match, I put some grubbers into the in-goal and out of the corner of my eye I could see the open-side winger was reading them and flying in to cover them up. So the next time I went to grubber I 'banana'd' it and it sort of hooked over his head and we scored in the corner. Ray Warren was calling the game for Channel Nine and went berserk and it all started from there. I used it a few times kicking for touch too; when I was a metre or so from the sideline, I'd kick it straight and the air would hit it and it would bend and I could make 40 metres, which is murder for the defending team.

I copied the torpedo bomb from Ricky Stuart too and later I did some work with Dave Aldred, the English kicking guru, and sort of mastered that one. Once you nail them they are incredibly hard to catch. Nowadays you go to training and the front-rowers can do the torpedo bomb; it's crazy how much the skills have improved across the board.

I started working hard on my goal-kicking after Michael Hagan took over as Newcastle coach in 2001. I kicked at a 65 per cent success rate in 2000 when Daryl Halligan was at 87 per cent and really didn't take that part of my game seriously enough. After practising relentlessly early in my career I had drifted away from it to focus on other parts of my game. Hages told me it was one part of my game he thought I could really improve. Daryl retired in 2000 and since then has built up a good individual coaching role. So I started doing heaps of practice in 2001 and my average went up to 81 per cent — an improvement of 16 per cent in one season. With Daryl watching me, I'd knock 20 kicks over and he would talk about the mental side of it all; of not looking at the posts but looking beyond them and just getting a nice strike on the ball. I started knocking them over from everywhere; it got to a stage where I started to really enjoy it. In the end I might only do 10 kicks in a session with Daryl but I'd make sure they were all quality. I'd really take my time and concentrate on the components Daryl had taught me, and if I hit 10 from 10 he'd say, 'That'll do, no use in keeping going.'

One aspect of his teaching is really 'managing' the ball so when you hit it nice and sweet it really spins back. I found that was a key indicator that I really got the benefit from. For a right footer, your left foot is most important; where it is placed at impact and how balanced your body is as you transfer your weight onto it. We would never practise from the sideline; we always used to practise 10 metres in, and he'd say, 'When you're out on the field, when you do get one from the sideline you'll enjoy it [because I wasn't expected to kick them and if I did it was a bonus].' I found the hardest kicks in a game were from 15 or 20 metres wide of the post, which everyone thinks you should get. But in the back of your mind you think, 'Don't miss this' or 'Don't stab it' or 'Don't hook it'.

CHAPTER 27

THE PARADOX OF BEING A ROLE MODEL

Are high-profile sports people 'sports heroes' or 'role models' to impressionable young people who idolise them? It's an important fundamental question, something I admit I have never fully been able to get my head around.

As you've gathered by now, I have massive regrets about how I've lived my life away from the field and am not proud of some of my actions on the field either, when — in the heat of battle — I have lost control of my emotions. Still, when not 'under the influence' on a manic high, I have always tried to be conscious of when I was in the public eye as a footballer and that my behaviour should set a good example.

I understand kids idolise their sports heroes and want to be like them; that's reality. And if they learn that someone they treated as some sort of a superstar has done something illegal or unacceptable away from the field, it might shatter their perceptions of that person. I must stand condemned of that, considering recent events.

But the biggest influence NRL footballers have on kids is through what they do on the field. Kids naturally want to emulate their sports heroes just as I did when I was young. That's why you see so many of them copying Benji Marshall's flamboyance or Karmichael Hunt's goose step or Mark Riddell's left arm salute when he lines up a goal-kick. It's great to know the impact players can have in making boys (and girls) want to play rugby league and be like their heroes. Players have to be conscious of how their behaviour can negatively reflect on kids who are so impressionable. And it's the same when you're in front of a microphone or camera; what you say or how you conduct yourself is devoured by league lovers.

But the term 'role model' seems to have taken on some whole new inference in modern times. Some players are comfortable with the tag, others aren't. Surely the most important role models are parents. They are the ones you should look to for guidance, not sports stars. I see myself as being a role model for my son and when I am with him, I will be the best person I can be. Of course it was devastating for me when the incident in London was made public and I have to deal with that.

Where should the responsibility start and end for a footballer as far as being a 'role model' is concerned? Where do you draw the line between when they are footballers in front of the crowds and the cameras and when they are entitled to be normal people away from the public gaze?

People are so judgemental these days — they feel there is no such thing as 'private time' any more and that footballers should just get used to the fact they will always be under the microscope and 'fair game' if they step out of line. Well, that's a very hard thing to lumber on a young bloke, and adds an enormous amount of extra pressure — pressure that was definitely not there for the previous generations of rugby league players.

Becoming 'a hero' or a 'role model' happens all too quickly these days. One minute you're hero worshipping first graders yourself, then six months later you're playing alongside them and thrust into the limelight. It's a hard thing to come to grips with. Most clubs these days have classes for young players on how to meet and greet people, how to show the right etiquette in public and how to treat the media. But what so many people overlook is that we play a very physical sport and footballers at NRL level are, to a degree, wild, tough people and that is why they are successful at rugby league. An aggressive nature is expected of them on the field, where the intensity of collision and physical impact is just awesome these days. But for the rest of the week they are supposed to be meek choirboys. Rugby league is not a sport that breeds beautiful, gentle people.

Binge drinking is a big part of our society — and I am an obvious example of how destructive that habit can be. In the NRL, with short turnarounds between games and the necessity for constant treatment of injuries, players can't let their hair down, so they save it up for one big night. The coach would even say: 'OK, we have Sunday then a Friday game and a quick turnaround after that. So three weeks from now you can go out and have a drink.' After the final game blokes would be manic — 'Oh we can have a drink, you beauty' — and they would binge; just rip in, thinking, 'We can be normal for a night or two.'

Most times they see their mates away from football working hard five days a week and then having five or six schooners on a Friday night and a big Saturday night, or having dinner parties on weekends, but NRL players can't experience that. They miss that to a degree, so they binge when they get that small window where they can 'be normal'.

If they step out of line, the consequences now can be very severe. The toughest call during my career happened to Dane Tilse in 2005 when he was sacked by the Newcastle Knights. It was the classic example of how great the expectation of players being 'role models' has become … and how easily any misdemeanour will become headline news.

Newcastle played Penrith in a pre-season game at Bathurst. The team management put a curfew on everyone after the game, in an obvious attempt to keep the boys out of any mischief. In my experience, curfews don't work; all they do is encourage everyone to go harder on the grog before the nominated deadline, and in this case that's what apparently happened. Some of the players had met some female university students earlier in the night and were told there was a party on. Someone took cartons of beer back to the hotel for a quiet drink, but then decided to ignore the curfew and go back to the party.

The boys did the wrong thing and made it worse by damaging a pushbike, letting off fire extinguishers and skylarking about. Dane admitted he went into one of the residences, jumped onto a girl's bed and tickled her on the back while she was lying face down asleep. Dane was out of line — it was stupid, unacceptable, an invasion of the woman's privacy and it would have frightened her. I don't condone what he did at all, but Dane says nothing more than that happened, and after the police investigated, no charges were ever laid.

Danny Buderus and myself weren't there, rested by the club due to Bedsy needing more of a break after going on the 2004 Kangaroo tour and me being given an extra week to return from my knee injury; so details of events were relayed to me by the players.

All 12 players involved were fined a total of $50,000 between them (plus the NRL fined the Knights $100,000, as well as another $100,000 which was suspended) and Dane Tilse had his contract ripped up — through pressure from the NRL, because there had been previous off-field incidents with players and they felt they had to make an example of someone. The fact Dane hadn't played first grade and wasn't a high-profile casualty made him expendable. I think it was a disgrace how he was sacked. If it was me or another of our representative players we would have been handed a hefty fine, publicly apologised, been stood down for a game or two ... but not been sacked.

I went into the club several times, spoke with CEO Ken Conway and said, 'You can't do this to this poor kid, you'll ruin him,' but he said the club's hands were tied; by the NRL in other words, not that anyone would admit it publicly. Tilse had just turned 20 and all the football dreams he grew up with could have been taken away from him because of that indiscretion; he was hung out to dry. He was a good young guy whose only problem was he didn't handle the grog too well while trying to keep up with others under peer group pressure. He's from around Scone where working hard and drinking hard and playing footy hard are part of the culture. Apparently there were a couple of other times where he ripped into the beer a bit too hard, but he learned a harsh lesson.

As I said, I am not condoning Dane Tilse's or the other players' behaviour — it was not acceptable. Nor am I in a position to lecture them as I've been no angel on the grog. Players do have to be more careful these days and have to be smart enough not to get caught up in those types of antics — they have the burden of carrying the image of their club and the whole game. But I don't believe what Dane did was bad enough to lose his job over. He was a victim of a spate of off-field incidents that made the news in that period and the club wasn't strong enough to stand up for itself and make its own decision. The contradiction is that the NRL have since put in a process where players caught taking recreational drugs get a warning; yet Dane didn't get a second chance for what he did. I hope he has a great career at Canberra (he joined the Raiders in 2006) and I'm happy to see that he had a good season with them in 2007.

I know that the way to avoid any scandal is not to go out drinking in public and that is what is happening more and more. Players become paranoid about going out and having a good time and tend to stay in, which is sad. The imbalance in the whole thing is that player behaviour has improved tenfold since I came into the game but the media and public scrutiny has increased 20-fold, giving the perception that the players are not improving. Generally, they are much more conscious of their public profiles but, hey, they are young men and will not always be perfect. When alcohol impairs their judgement, sometimes the wrong thing happens, but it doesn't happen nearly as regularly as a decade or two ago, from what I have heard.

The public scrutiny and the rumour mill is far more destructive than it used to be too. The internet, SMS's on mobile phones and the 'shock jock' nature of talkback radio has seen to that. The line in the sand that used to say 'this is private, this is our other life; give us some space' is not there any more. Some people these days seem to be obsessed with notoriety and fame and when they get a glimpse of anyone the least bit 'famous' out in public, they see it as an invitation to give them up.

I know you might be thinking I am being hypocritical, considering what I've done over the years that was never made public. Leaving aside my situation (and I repeat that I'm very regretful of some of the things I have done), I'm talking in general terms about when players, or any 'celebrities' for that matter, are out trying to enjoy themselves like anyone else. If a player is having fun somewhere — not harming anybody — it seems like there is always someone with a mobile phone that has a camera or video on it to capture it and send it to friends, or take it straight to a media outlet or straight onto the internet.

Word of mouth spreads like wildfire too, even though the imagination of some people is so fanciful it's beyond being funny. There have been times when I was nowhere near an event I was supposed to have been involved in, but the rumour mill and 'I have it on good authority' reports flew around the place in unbelievable fashion. The most bizarre I came across was when I was accused of being involved in a double murder in New Zealand! The sports reporter/presenter for NBN Television in Newcastle, Jim Callinan, came to me at training after we'd played in Auckland one year and told me my name had been linked to a love triangle that saw a man kill a woman and then kill himself; and what did I know about it. All that happened, it emerged, was that the woman said she was at a bar and had seen me there; next thing, I was supposed to be a third party involved in their deaths.

Steve Crowe, a former team-mate who became our media manager then football manager, could tell of some wild 'porkies' I was the subject of; including someone calling him after my second-last game, when I was KOed by Sonny Bill Williams in round one of 2007, swearing that I was involved in a big drink with the Surfest crowd the night before the game, that I was hit in the head in a fight and that's when I did the injury — and going down in the game was a cover-up. Can you believe it? I was at home with Cath the night before the game.

People spy on others, take photos, write in to the papers or call up talkback radio and tell about what everyone is allegedly doing. And too often the media relay it as fact without ever checking out the validity of what they hear. I find it so unAustralian. I also can't understand the motivation of someone to contact the media to say they saw so and so having dinner or drinking somewhere when they weren't even doing anything interesting, let alone untoward. Like Andrew Johns having lunch at Subway! So what — what is interesting about that? But people read it. The gossip columns have become the most popular part of the newspapers.

Cathrine and I were having dinner at Darlinghurst one night and there were photos in the paper a few days later; we didn't even know there was a photographer around. Another time, we were walking back to our car when a photographer jumped out of nowhere and took a shot. It is unnerving. When we decided to head up to Bedarra Island after I retired, there were photographers and journalists following us around Brisbane Airport as we changed planes. I don't know how well-known entertainers deal with it every day; I'd go wild and smash the cameras.

You wonder why it is that when players talk to the media they don't speak their minds like they used to, for fear of getting jumped on; a lot of the young players are terrified of saying something out of turn. Look at Willie Mason; I admire his courage in speaking his mind and being prepared to take the shit that goes with that sometimes. Willie is one of the best blokes to be around in camp and one of the most popular players with the fans. Often when I'd finished training in Origin or Test camp and there were kids around, the first bloke they'd go to for an autograph was Willie; they'd be hitting him and mucking around and just love being around him. My son Samuel hardly follows the football, but when he sees Willie

Mason on TV he comes alive and shouts, 'There's big Willie'; that's the impact he has because he shows character. Yet if he says something a little stupid while thinking out loud, everyone jumps on him. Anyone who knows Willie Mason loves him; he's a great fella, yet so many want to bash him up in the media.

Players are so terrified they become robotic. I use Darren Lockyer as an example; he is so conscious of what he says in public and comes across as a really conservative straight guy. Yet he would be one of the funniest and most entertaining blokes I've ever toured with, and when I tell mates that, they can't believe it; honestly, away from the spotlight, he is hilarious and just great company. But he is so worried about his persona as Brisbane, Queensland and the Australian captain, he puts the shutters up and treads on eggshells. And you couldn't blame him after one of the worst examples I can think of of how things have changed and how politically correct we're all supposed to be.

'Locky' was at a function in Brisbane when the Bulldogs were going through the Coffs Harbour sexual assault scandal (the allegations were proven unfounded). The mood was pretty lighthearted on stage when he was being interviewed with footballers from other codes and he mentioned a joke that was going around at the time, something about how St George won 11 premierships with one Johnny Raper, so the Bulldogs were hard to beat because they had x amount of 'Johnny Rapers'. He thought it was an innocent joke — we're all wiser in hindsight — but the media pounced on it so vigorously, he had to put out a public apology within hours.

One thing I'm really jealous of with players from previous eras is that they were allowed to have fun. The fun has gone out of professional rugby league now; it is so politically correct these days. And the clubs have no choice but to drum that into their players; to pass down the message that whether you think it is unfair or not, that's the world we live in.

It is pumped into the players at Newcastle at the start of every year: the code of conduct; how the club doesn't have the massive backing of its own licensed club like other teams and must rely on sponsorship and people coming through the gate, and that if one big off-field incident costs the club a large sponsorship deal, the Knights could be under threat.

It's a massive responsibility for young blokes just getting used to the big time and the profile and the adulation that comes with it; it is reasonable to expect them to stuff up just once like most young people do, but they don't get a second chance before it's plastered all through the media or becomes widespread gossip.

Players get media training from their club but it is really an education in not saying anything so it can't be taken out of context. It's like: 'Don't be your natural personality, it could be dangerous.' When the young St George Illawarra player Richie Williams came out and said Braith Anasta 'wasn't the player he was', it was dumb in the context that it fired Anasta and the Roosters up and, to me, it showed a lack of respect. But at least he said what he thought, which is refreshing in a way. I was always guarded when talking to the media because I didn't want to give anyone unnecessary ammunition.

I know there is an attitude that 'well, you're a high-profile sportsman on the big bucks, you can't have your cake and eat it too.' I don't know where people get that money argument from, or what sort of excuse that is. Not many players really are on the big bucks, and what difference does it make if they have worked hard enough and are talented enough to earn a good living out of a sport that requires them to put their bodies on the line every week of the season? I think the attitude of the public changed with the Super League war; people became infatuated with what players earn. It's none of their business. I would pay money just to see players like Darren Lockyer, Johnathan Thurston, Benji Marshall or Matt Bowen — they must pull thousands of extras through the gate themselves, so why shouldn't they get good money for their drawing power?

I was listening to a radio interview with Wendell Sailor recently and they started talking about rugby players going to Europe; honestly, every question was about money. Was it so important? It is like we are obsessed with what people earn.

Look, I'm not trying to downplay the responsibility of being a good person if you achieve some sort of profile that ensures people might recognise you when you're out in public. And I'm not suggesting that the acceptable standards of behaviour for footballers should be different to anyone else's.

What I'm trying to get across is that, away from the football field, footballers I know are as ordinary — and as human — as any young bloke and they are entitled to some privacy and to be able to be themselves sometimes. I think a lot more people should respect that.

CHAPTER 28

LOOKING LIKE A
PRIMA DONNA

Talking about being a 'role model' brings me to the latter part of the 2006 season, when I was certainly not that with my on-field blow-ups that had me in the headlines yet again and, I'm sure, had people thinking 'what an arsehole'. I'm talking about the Knights–Melbourne Storm match when I went on like a good sort with the referee over Anthony Quinn being sin-binned for having a go at a touch judge; the infamous end-of-match blow-up in our televised Friday night match against Manly when the ref and touch judge stuffed up; and the incident at Parramatta Stadium when I was accused of being a spoilt brat in not accepting a presentation from the Eels after breaking Jason Taylor's competition points-scoring record.

I'll go through them one by one.

With my 'debate' with the match officials in the match against the Storm, I still maintain the touch judge overreacted when Anthony Quinn had a heat-of-the-battle outburst; he should have been able to given Quinny a warning to settle down and let us get on with the game. But I can't deny it was ridiculous how disrespectfully I carried on.

The fact is we got a dud call — Quinny claimed he was 'grapple tackled' and appealed to a touch judge, who conveniently decided to ignore him. Quinny gave the linesman a spray, but you've got to remember that when you are out there getting absolutely pole-axed you get yourself worked up; he should have just been warned on the run to settle down. I know there has to be some sort of respect given to the referees, and I understand we influence so many kids with our behaviour, but that linesman really changed the game with that decision. We were penalised while in possession when behind 12–10 and the Storm scored in the next set to lead 18–10; they ended up winning 24–16.

I went off at Paul Simpkins, saying something like, 'It's a big game … we've worked our c*@!# out, both teams, only for you to come up with a shit decision like that … it's a game for men.' It could be heard through the referee's microphone and came through on the TV coverage, which wasn't good — for me or the game. That was the big issue: not so much what I said, but that everyone could hear it.

That wasn't as bad as my crazy behaviour in the final minute of the match against Manly in round 23 on a Friday night, covered by Channel Nine; now that was embarrassing. Again, I have no doubt the match officials blundered but there is no excuse for the way I carried on. To refresh memories, we were behind 16–14 and in possession in Manly's quarter, when their centre Steve Matai clearly played at the ball and knocked on, giving us a scrum feed and one last chance to win the game. But the referee — yep, Paul Simpkins again — ruled Matai's touch was accidental as he made a tackle. It happened right in front of touch judge Matt Cecchin's eyes but he wouldn't clarify what happened, despite some attempted 'persuasion' from me and other players. It was so clearly wrong, and cost us any chance of getting a victory.

I was livid. It was an important game with third place on the ladder at stake between the two teams, so I let fly at Cecchin and argued with Simpkins, and was reported for abusive language to match officials and hit with a grade three 'contrary conduct' charge that carried a four-match penalty.

I carried on like a maniac and even worse were my comments in my *Sunday Telegraph* column afterwards, when I said the match officials should be apologising to me and I wouldn't take anything back. When my ghost writer Barry Toohey had rung me the day after the game to discuss the column, I was at a team barbeque at Clint Newton's place and had been on the grog since the night before — the first time I'd had a few beers for a while — and was in one of my manic phases and couldn't give a shit about anyone or anything. The fact there were a few blokes around me as I was speaking on the phone probably charged me up even more. Baz didn't have to prompt me at all and I was that hyped up he wouldn't have been able to placate me even if he tried. It's another thing I just have to accept happened; I can't erase it, as much as that hurts.

After I had settled down and realised how badly I had behaved, I apologised in writing to Matt Cecchin, for my behaviour and what I said in the *Sunday Telegraph*. And while I'm sure it was seen as a token gesture to try to ensure the judiciary went softer on me (well, I was hoping it wouldn't hurt), it was genuine. As I said, I now look at the whole episode and think what a wanker I was, carrying on like I did.

What made the perception of me worse was when my manager John Fordham wrote a column for the *Daily Telegraph*, the day the judiciary hearing was scheduled, saying the game could ill afford to drive me out of the NRL, and that if I did walk away there was no shortage of 'suitors' in rugby union who would sign me, as would Warrington. Fordo went on to press the point of how the constant pressure and scrutiny had got to me, that the severity of the charge was over the top and that my playing future hinged on the result. He had the right intention but, especially when the *Tele* ran a back page screaming headline 'Joey Ready To Quit', it gave the impression I was prepared to take my bat and ball home and run off to rugby or to England. What John wrote was beyond my control (I refused to read it or anything about me at the time) and it made me look even more of a dick, to be honest; like I was trying to put myself above the game and act like a real prima donna.

As it was I was suspended for two weeks, which meant I missed the Knights' last two competition games (we had the bye in the last round) and I came back for the finals. I reckon that was a fair punishment.

The other incident in 2006 that saw my image cop a hammering was when I passed Jason Taylor's point-scoring record at Parramatta Stadium and refused to attend the presentation organised by the Eels on the field after the match. Now on this one, I'm not copping all the blame. I wasn't told about it before the game, and if I was, I would have politely declined any presentation.

All through the match Parramatta fans were really giving it to me as the Knights, and me particularly, played poorly (we were beaten 46–12) and it would have been hypocritical for them to then clap me while I got presented with the ball after the game. It was a nice gesture by the Parramatta club but if there was going to be any formal presentation to celebrate my achievement, I wanted it to be at Newcastle in front of Knights fans. From what I learned later, they did approach one of our officials before the game and while there was a brief mention in passing by our football manager Steve Crowe, the details weren't passed on to me, because they knew I wouldn't want to be in it, and Crowey thought he'd try to convince me after the match and that surely I wouldn't say no. They should have cleared the whole thing with me beforehand, not thrown it on me when I was pissed off so much afterwards. If they had, there wouldn't have been an incident and all the bad publicity.

Instead, I spat the dummy and looked like a prima donna again and copped it from the media, with one bloke in particular saying I should have been dumped as Newcastle captain and that he hoped Hazem El Masri would beat the record.

When that all went on last year, at least I was at the stage of my career where I could distinguish between Joey Johns and Andrew Johns and I'd learned to shut those sort of things out, whereas 10 years ago it would have eaten me up and destroyed me, sent me into a deep depression. I just distinguished that it wasn't the 'real' me, it was that other personality on the field. But unfortunately I can't go back and change time and it hangs on my 'record'.

CHAPTER 29

THAT'S MY GAME

I've often been asked to give my opinion on different aspects of rugby league, on and off the field, but while I was playing I was conscious of how much I should say, my responsibility to the game, and not upsetting anyone. Often I wouldn't have a strong opinion on subjects that were put to me anyway; so I was happy to keep out of the politics and controversy. But for the purpose of this book, I have recorded some thoughts on issues of the game I do have strong opinions on. Here they are, in no particular order.

One thing I feel very strongly about is the excessive demands put on players these days from a season that is too long. Most teams start training somewhere between the start of October and the start of November, depending on when their team finished the previous season. If you make it through to the last couple of weeks of the finals (late

September-early October), that's 11 months of torture. And that's not including end of season internationals which put added pressure on our most elite players.

A season of 26 rounds plus semi-finals is too much. I think there should be an agreement between clubs to scrap trials, then for a 20-round competition to be played, which would involve all 16 teams playing each other once, then some system where the five extra games are allocated with some equality based on the previous year's competition table. I'd include split rounds (a round played over two weekends) to coincide with each of the three State of Origin games. Then we would have 23 weeks for preliminary rounds and four for the finals, for 27 weeks all up — two less than now — but with each team getting three weekends off during the duration of the season. If we take out trials, that's four to five weeks less of playing games.

The other thing I'd change is from a top-eight finals series to a top six. Having half the teams making the finals is too low a benchmark; I'd like to see the top five or six sides rewarded more for their consistency. Currently a team can come seventh or eighth and still win the competition, yet under the McIntyre System, the team coming first can have one bad game and be forced into sudden-death on virtual level pegging with the other teams that survive the first week of the finals.

I would also cut back on Kangaroo tours; they have become less special, which has led to players passing up opportunities to play for their country because they happen too frequently. We should tour Great Britain every four years like it used to be and the Poms come here every four years, so we would have an Ashes series every two years. To make that work, the International Federation should make the touring country finish its season four weeks before the end of the other country's so that the touring team could come over while the finals are being played and get some good lead-up games against club sides.

So if we were touring Britain, we'd finish our season, say, the second-last Sunday in September (remember we'd have two less weeks in our season than we have now) and the Poms go until mid-October, which they do now anyway. We could have three or four lead-up games over three weeks against their clubs as they drop out of the finals — giving the Test side a couple of hit-outs and the 'Emus', the emerging Australian players sent over for experience and as back-up to the Test side, good experience just like it used to be when we had fair dinkum Kangaroo tours. We could even drop into France on the way and play a one-off Test against them.

When it was the Poms' turn to come here we could start our season later, or they could start theirs earlier, so that they could come here and play lead-up games against our club teams. I'm not sure how it could be organised so the Kiwis could tour England in other years or how we try to fit in a three Test series against the Kiwis some years, but I'm sure some sort of system could be worked out — especially if the domestic seasons are cut down; the Poms play far too many club games too. For those who say we can't bring our season forward, well it worked OK in 2000 when we finished a month early to avoid clashing with the Olympics.

Australia toured England every year bar one between 2000 and 2005, before contesting five games in the Tri Nations played here and New Zealand in 2006. I know players who exaggerated injuries to get out of a Kangaroo tour, because they were too worn out, which is such a great shame. I could have toured England in 2005 one last time after playing in the first Tri Nations game against New Zealand but I elected to have surgery on my knee, when I easily could have played. I was simply burnt out and needed a rest, after playing in Warrington — and my knee was crook. I remember one year Danny Buderus played 35 games and that is just too demanding; if you used the analogy of a racehorse, the RSPCA would intervene for doing that.

Now another thing, while I'm talking about match scheduling, is that I'd love to see the grand final brought back to a daylight kickoff. I have no doubt 99 per cent of players would say they'd prefer to play it in the day; from a ball-playing point of view it is so much harder to play at night when the ball is dewy and slippery and that is too big an evener between teams. It's hard to play an attacking style, it's hard to move the ball laterally, and I don't think that should affect a grand final. Most fans I speak to want a day grand final too, so they can go back to the tradition of holding barbeques and everyone comes around; and the kids can watch without staying up late.

Generally, I always loved most playing on Sunday afternoons, and I reckon a lot of the fans like it too. And I maintain that generally the quality of the football is better in the afternoons compared to nights. But I know we have to abide by the wishes of the television stations that are pumping big money into the sport and that's why we have so many night games now.

The fact is that the football we use hasn't changed for the past decade and I think we should challenge Steeden to produce a different ball to suit different conditions. The ball they produce now is sensational for the day — when it is pouring rain the grip is unbelievable — but on a steamy night when there is dew on the ground, it is like a cake of soap. If they could come up with a ball that is great for handling, even if it was ordinary for kicking, so be it. Kicking is 10 per cent of the game — no one goes to a match to watch people kick goals.

Now, State of Origin ... and the money it generates.

Willie Mason copped a lot of flak for his outspoken views on this early in 2006 but I believe he had a very valid point, which most players agreed with. Origin is the jewel in rugby league's crown and even though I'm like most players and would have played Origin for nothing early in my career, I don't think the players are genuinely rewarded enough.

Few people would be aware that when Danny Nutley played his only game for Queensland in the final match of the 2005 series, he apparently owed the Queensland Rugby League money because he'd spent more than his match fees getting tickets and signed jerseys for his family and friends. That's wrong. Did you know that when you make Origin you only get four free tickets — that's your parents and your partner, plus one more. You have to pay for any extras — at well over $100 a pop, which quickly eats into the match payments. Most players are affiliated with a charity or two and if we want signed jerseys to raise money for them, the charities have to pay for them too.

For the entertainment and the profile for rugby league that State of Origin players bring, not to mention the income from merchandising and TV rights, they get paid bugger all. I know they get looked after like kings and their performances can increase their market value when it comes to negotiating their next club contract, but the direct payment for being the ones who millions want to see at Origin level is not proportionate with their value. And people don't realise the effort they put in, which often flattens them physically for the rest of the season.

Put it this way: if you go to a U2 concert and there are 80,000 people there paying over $200 a head, the band gets the net gate takings (I assume). The fans don't care if they're getting millions of dollars out of it, nor probably even think about how much they are getting. In State of Origin, when there are also 80,000 there (in Sydney; or 52,000 in Brisbane) and probably three million watching on TV (enough for Origin games to be listed in the top 10 highest rating programs each year), footballers aren't getting anywhere near the pay-scale of entertainers. Origin players now get $12,500 a game ($5000 of which goes into a retirement fund), which has increased quite a bit over the past few years.

I think the players should get something like 50 per cent of the net gate takings; I don't know how much that would add up to, but it would be significantly more than they currently get. Now that sort of reward would make a lot of established players think twice about going to England to play in Super League or to rugby union, or retiring early from representative football.

I know the counter argument is that the income from Origin must fund the game outside of the NRL — all the development and promotion. Well, if the game wanted to be more efficient with where the money goes, the first step should be to cut all the unnecessary levels of administration. Why the hell do we still have a National Rugby League, Australian Rugby League, New South Wales and Queensland Rugby Leagues, the Country Rugby League and I don't know how many other tiers of administration? Why isn't it all run by the one body under the one board? I can only guess at how much duplication and wasted costs there are.

A subject I feel strongly about in rugby league is something most fans would not be aware of — the over-coaching of junior players. Too often I see teenagers at 14 or 15 being coached the same ways the first graders are — with too much emphasis on success. There is too much onus on winning premierships and playing with the structures NRL teams use, rather than concentrating on the kids enjoying the game, developing their skills and just being allowed to go out and play footy.

I speak to Phil Gould about it a bit, and he says how he sees 14 year olds playing exactly the same as the first graders: the back-rowers get wide and run and don't look to offload; the halfbacks get so much room; every play is structured; they're not trying things and not making errors; they're not playing off their vision and instincts. I think that has led to the demise of the genuine halfback and five-eighth with natural instincts — they're told too much how to play, rather than seeing it for themselves. Coaches should give them the ball and let them play.

The result is that we are breeding too many athletes and not enough footballers; and too many players come into grade with too many manufactured things in their heads, as if every play had to be programmed. I saw it when Danny Buderus came into grade. He was talking about all these lines he was supposed to run and I had no idea what he was talking about. I was like, 'Mate, what is that?' When young players came to first grade, it was like we had to reteach them how to play.

I was lucky in a way. When I came through the juniors I was never really taught any structure until I was 17 or 18; until then I was just sort of out there playing it as I saw it. It was enjoyable. I question whether too many kids at 14 and 15 are enjoying the game — they might be winning, but how much do they enjoy their own roles? Gus talks about starting an academy to teach halfbacks how to play and what to try to see on the field; it's not a bad idea.

Now to the salary cap, that old chestnut in rugby league that polarises plenty of opinions. Look, the game must have a salary cap, otherwise the rich and powerful clubs will attract all the best players and the other clubs will be left to struggle. The NRL competition is a lot more even across the board than 10 or 20 years ago and just about all the games are a lot closer, so from the fans' perspective the cap has been a winner.

The downside is that I don't think we will ever see the great teams any more, like Canberra of the late-1980s/early-'90s and Brisbane of the 1990s. There will never be another great dynasty, with a team winning even three successive competitions. And I think that is sad. Because what a salary cap does is bring the top teams back to the level of other clubs, rather than making the other clubs aspire to match the heights of the champion teams. I had a discussion with Matty not long ago about it, and we admitted that we wouldn't have become the players we were if we hadn't played against the dominant Canberra and Brisbane teams; they were so good that they made us push ourselves to perform at as close to their levels we could reach. Look at Tiger Woods in golf: he became so good, other players had to push their games to new levels to compete against him. It's the same in tennis with the opponents of Roger Federer.

If we are going to have a salary cap, we have to include more concessions for long-serving and loyal players. It is a joke that a player has to have 10 years with a club before part of his contract can be salary cap exempt, and then the limit is $100,000 per season per club for all 10-year players. The benchmark should be eight years in the grade system (from Jersey Flegg upwards), and once they reach that level 50 per cent of contracts of all qualifying players should be cap exempt.

I think it's very important that the fans can see a young player come through from the juniors, see him play Jersey Flegg, then go through Premier League and into first grade (or from national under-20s into first grade under the new system to be introduced in 2008), and then have every confidence the club is going to be able to keep him. The club should have a bigger advantage in stopping that player from being grabbed by another club as a reward for the time and effort put into developing the kid. Under the present cap rules, the better you do as a team, the less likely you are of keeping a bunch of good youngsters.

When you have a premiership-winning club it is not the top players who are let go. No, the eyes get picked out of the middle of the road players or the young blokes coming through. They might be earning $120,000 to $130,000, but because they have played in a grand final team, they then get offered $250,000 by other clubs and you can't knock them for going.

Another thing in the game that has made a big impression on me is the capacity of some of the game's younger players to 'get up' mentally each week for the hard slogs which are part and parcel of the NRL competition. It is amazing how, at such a young age, so many can play three games in a week or so — backing up from rep matches — and still be the best player in the team. But I fear that that pressure they have to perform so consistently is going to burn too many of our best players out. Something has to give with the scheduling of games.

I'd like to see the Players' Association being more active in decisions in the game that affect them and the players far less apathetic towards an association; they should have a strong voice, like they do in the Australian Football League. Tony Butterfield made giant strides when he was boss of the association, but it seems to have lapsed in strength since he left.

The players should unite in a more formal way and have a say in things like the manufacturing of the footballs; State of Origin payments; match scheduling; post-football education, which is an area in which the game is making inroads; retirement plans and the like. It's just a pity that too many players are so preoccupied with their own careers, rather than the overall player situation.

The overkill in the use of the video ref is something that is killing the game. It has become a lottery and the more the video refs replay incidents in a futile search for perfection, the more boring and frustrating it becomes for the players and the fans. And the decisions they come up with are still a lottery. The video ref should have one look at a try situation at full speed, one in slow motion, get another angle if it isn't clear, then make a decision — not look at it five times on slow mo, then three more on super slow mo. I believe too often the video ref is looking for reasons not to give a try rather than to give a try. It is so frustrating on the field: I don't know how many times when I was out there, players from both sides would be screaming, 'Just make a %&*$%# decision!'

There has to be some agreement between the NRL and the TV networks to get on with the game and not harp so much on decisions; and the quicker the game gets underway forcing the broadcaster to keep up with the next play, the quicker the decision would naturally be forgotten anyway. I do feel sorry for the video refs. They must shit themselves every time they have to come up with a decision, because of the scrutiny they know they will be under in all the post-mortems in the media, but they have to learn to cop that.

The worst thing I've seen in years, as far as interpretations go, was the overpolicing of obstructions in 2007. Surely there has to be a clear-cut obstruction to award a penalty, but that was thrown out the window until the coaches and refs' bosses had a pow-wow and everyone saw sense. Every team runs decoys, and it is all based around the third-last defender (in from the touchline) where a forward goes through in attack and if he draws in the third-last defender, the player going around the back creates a three-on-two around the edge; so the obstruction rule is only an issue if it causes interference with the third-last defender. The fact that we were seeing anyone penalised if they ran behind a decoy runner was ridiculous, and showed the penchant for overpolicing the game; we seem to harp on decisions too much and that has put extra pressure on the match officials.

And there is too much coaching of the referee by the video ref. Whenever I was next to the ref I couldn't believe the dialogue going into his earpiece; it must be so distracting. The touch judge has become too involved too. He should be in charge of the ball or bodies going over the sideline, keeping the defending team back 10 and keeping an eye on back-play: that's it. One thing they shouldn't be involved in is ruling on forward passes because too often they get them wrong and they don't understand natural inertia. If you are running forward, naturally the ball is going to go forward, but if it comes backwards out of your hands, it's not a forward pass.

Having said all of the above, I think we have it pretty right with most things in the game. The 'product' on the field is outstanding; the judiciary system is fine; the presentation of the game is excellent; the coaching is first class; the quality of players is as high as it has ever been; the crowds are fantastic. It's a great game.

CHAPTER 30

'BOOZY', 'BEDSY', 'HOYO' AND 'LEESY'

I feel fortunate that I have had some great mates during my football career and here I'd like to talk about four of them; two are football mates and two are knockabouts who add balance to my life away from football. They are Knights teammates Mark 'Boozy' Hughes and Danny 'Bedsy' Buderus, plus surfing 'identity' Matt 'Hoyo' Hoy and horse trainer extraordinaire Kris Lees.

Of course, when I talk about mates the two greatest I have had in life are my brother Matthew and fiancée Cathrine. But I've mentioned them prominently in this book already, as I have Ben Kennedy. I've been fortunate too to have forged some other great friendships through football, like with Clint Newton (and his whole family, really) and Kurt Gidley.

Boozy and Bedsy became my official taxi-drivers when Matty left after the 2000 season, but to the rest of the Knights they were better known as the 'Odd Couple', when they took on a de facto relationship as house-mates for a couple of years. Fair dinkum, they were like husband and wife, not wild-boy bachelors. They'd be arguing at training about what they were going to have for dinner that night and who was going to do the dishes. We'd be stretching after training and one would say to the other, 'I left those pork chops out to thaw — can you put them on when you get in?'

I could not have asked for two better mates in the world — they are two champion blokes and rate with Matthew Gidley and Billy Peden as the nicest guys I came across during my career; and there were plenty of other great blokes I could name.

Boozy, incidentally, went to the same high school as me (St Peter's at Maitland), although he was two years below me. When we met in later life he was a classic club man and an underrated player. He would always be the one organising social events; and the one to sort out any drama between players. In those player profiles every club and every sport seems to troop out for websites or magazine insights, 90 per cent of Newcastle Knights players would have listed Mark Hughes as their funniest team-mate. He had such a dry wit and often you'd laugh at him rather than with him — like when he would try to gee someone up by pretending to be Malcolm Reilly on the phone; we'd be laughing at him because his accent was more like Chinese than Yorkshire, but he would think that we thought he was hilariously clever.

I'll let you in on a secret that will make Boozy cringe when he reads this. Mark Hughes has this peculiar physical characteristic — his toenails are as big as dinner plates! He lets them grow far too long and I used to say to him, 'Booz, you have to do something about them, they are a lethal weapon and you are going to hurt someone.' He went to France to play for Les Catalans in the English Super League in 2006 and when a birthday card arrived from Perpignan, I thought, 'Gee, this is nice of you, Boozy.' When I opened up the envelope there was no writing included, just his massive toenails taped onto the card.

Young blokes used to come into first grade and tease Boozy about his lack of 'styling'; at the time these young guys would trim their pubic hair and have all the right toiletries and blow wave their hair and gel it. Boozy was a boy from the coalfields and would refuse to play ball with the new-age grooming trends, which used to disgust the young blokes.

Mark Hughes played 161 first grade games over nine seasons, played in two grand final winning teams and played all three State of Origin games for New South Wales in 2001, which is a career to be extremely proud of. But while the Origin opportunity was his on-field highlight, it turned out to be, typically for Boozy, his biggest off-field regret.

If anyone was made for Origin camps it was Boozy Hughes; he loves a good time and a drink and is the best bloke to have around if you want to bond a team together. Can you believe the first night in camp after he was chosen to play fullback for the Blues in '01, he had a massage and his neck kinked and immediately caused shooting pain up his back? He was in bed for four days — meaning he missed all the early-camp bonding sessions — and was in doubt to play right up to the last minute.

When he went into camp for the second game, he was able to get in one night of bonding before he picked up a stomach bug and was in bed for days again. For the third game he was able to remain intact but with the series thrown into a decider, traditionally the pre-game socialising is kept to a minimum. So he never got to leave his mark (excuse the pun) on Origin bonding — although he did leave an impression, albeit a bad one, on his room-mate Trent Barrett. The movie *Notting Hill* had been showing at the cinemas not long before. You might remember the scene where Julia Roberts stayed at Hugh Grant's place and was trying to escape the paparazzi, when his mate 'Spike' came to the door to greet a swarm of camera flashes, dressed only in his undies, with his pencil-thin body striking a very unattractive pose. Noticing the similarities after watching Boozy constantly walk around the hotel room in his undies with his hair sticking out everywhere — always unshaven and with the same hollow legs — Trent soon nicknamed him 'Spike'.

He might have been lean and possessed a baby face any mother would cherish in their son, but he was tougher than he was given credit for, old Boozy. In one game he came in at half-time and said to Michael Hagan that his ankle was buggered; but we were short on troops so he had to go out with about 12 painkilling injections and play out the game. The next day, x-rays confirmed he had fractured his ankle.

Danny Buderus helped fill the void when Matthew left for the UK by becoming a close mate and transport provider. I'll avoid driving every chance I can, even if it is a few kilometres to training. Bedsy is one of the genuine nicest blokes you could meet — which was obvious the first time I met him when he was 17; although I'm sure he wouldn't have said the same thing about me at the time.

He'd made the Australia Schoolboys side in 1995 and, seeing I'd just dislocated my collarbone and was out for a few weeks, I was asked to go up to his home town of Taree to help out with a fund-raising event for him. He was playing halfback in the Knights' SG Ball side at the time and boarding at Francis Xavier College in Newcastle. So this fresh-faced really well-mannered kid drove up to my old house in Lambton, in his beat-up little car, to take me to Taree for a lunch. As he pulled up I was sitting on the front porch with a long-neck stubby in my hand; he must have thought, 'What's going on here? This bloke is playing State of Origin and is my hero.' He drove me to Taree and we went to his house to meet his parents, Gus and Chris, I had the traditional greeting beer with his old man before we went to the function and everyone was feeding me more drinks. I was such a mess, they decided not to get me up for a speech! But they still raised a heap of money which was good. Later that year Danny came up and played a few games in our under-21s and hurt his ankle really bad in one match. I went into the doctor's room to see him and his parents were really distressed, as they thought he was going to miss the Schoolboys tour; and Danny looked devastated. As it turned out he recovered in time to tour England with a Schoolboys squad that included future Knights team-mates

Owen Craigie and Matthew Gidley, as well as Trent Barrett and Nathan Cayless.

Most people know the story about how Danny received his nickname when a hotel staffer called out 'Beds-Are-Us', rather than Buderus, when we were checking in as a team once, so it was shortened to Bedsy and has stuck ever since. But he has several other nicknames too; the one he dislikes most is 'Blubber'. Danny has this hidden switch that gets turned on when he's had a few drinks: his teeth grow, his body and face seem to shrink and his voice goes really high. It's hilarious. Someone will say, 'Look over there, Blubber is starting to appear.' You'd take a glance and he'd have this big cheesy grin and someone would comment, 'His teeth are starting to grow, it's happening.' He gets really defensive about it, especially if someone calls out, 'Hey, Blubber.' He stiffens right up and fires back, 'What are you talking about?' and you know his favourite saying is not far away — 'whatever then'.

Every off-season for three years Boozy, Bedsy and I would go to Darwin and enjoy ourselves for a week. That's where Bedsy met his wife Kris; I still can't remember where or how they met, because I was too preoccupied with having a good time. But I still maintain it must have been Blubber she fell for before she met Bedsy, because he was in a scratchy state a good deal of the time.

Bedsy has an incredible pain threshold too and capacity to keep going throughout our long season. He played almost a full season with arthritis in his toe in 2005 which was really painful. He's had a heap of injuries over the years that he would shrug off for weeks or months, yet keep playing to his incredible high level. When the rep games came around he'd top the tackle count, be the first man scrambling to stop tries, he'd be running out of dummy half even though he must have been just about out on his feet because of the workload and the injuries he'd be carrying. He is the ultimate professional and he doesn't know how to play any other way. Bedsy turns 30 in February 2008 and has played 205 first grade games for the club, so there's a good chance he'll break my record of 249 games for the Knights, and I couldn't think of anyone more deserving of that honour. To think he has averaged 20.5 games a season for the Knights since becoming first choice hooker in 1999 (and he'd be unavailable for two games most years through State of Origin duties) is amazing, considering the injuries and pain I know he has had to endure and the fact he is responsible for the highest work-rate of anyone on the field most weeks. And he's been able to put his 91-kilogram frame through 15 Origin matches and 24 Tests since 2001 as well. Those stats just show what a whole-hearted, genuine team man he is, an outstanding talent, and how hard he has worked on his game.

I met Kris Lees in the mid-1990s through my interest in horse racing, which has been strong since my early teens; I love studying the form and going to the races. I knew him as the son of Max Lees, who was the leading Newcastle trainer at the time, and found that he also played rugby league for Souths Newcastle as a hard-tackling lower grade hooker who had a promising future until he broke his leg badly (well, that's what he tells me). We formed a strong friendship and I used to love going to the races in Sydney with him most

Wednesdays when that was my day off from training — up until before Samuel was born, anyway. Very occasionally I might get up early enough to go to dawn training trackwork sessions at Broadmeadow but, to be honest, if I'm out of bed at first break of light I'd rather be on a surfboard than smelling horse manure.

'Leesy' is another genuine, champion bloke; and a very fit person too. We used to meet at my place and run up a circuit we'd mapped out. We'd hit the sloped hill in a park area overlooking the beach, sprint back and try to do it in three minutes, which is pretty good going. We'd push ourselves to do it five times. Then we'd do the stairs at Merewether and some boxing together. Leesy still runs 40–50 kilometres a week and always goes in the City to Surf, which is why he's always complaining about a sore back, I tell him. We still try to get to the gym together three times a week and have lunch when we can. With him working at the track early in the morning and having plenty of time during the day, it works in well with each other.

His father Max was a great bloke too and it was tragic how he died so young, and so suddenly, in August 2003. We were at lunch one day and Kris said his dad had to go into hospital. They thought he had diabetes — he'd been losing weight and feeling crook. The next day Kris rang me to say Max had cancer ... and he was dead five or six weeks later. For Kris to handle the responsibility of taking over the management of the stable, to keep all the owners and train 50 or 60 horses was a phenomenal effort. It isn't until you go over there and you see how much management skill it takes to train a large amount of horses that you appreciate how good horse trainers in the larger stables are. Leesy is up at 4.30am every day: he works seven days a week, with no days off except Christmas Day. That takes a lot of devotion and discipline.

It's great to have a mate who I don't need to talk footy with; I bore him because all I want to talk about is horse racing when he probably wants to talk about football. He's become a good mate with other Knights players and a few now have ownership of a few of Kris' horses. I love the culture of horse training and I'm always fascinated about how they can pull out all the excuses in the world when a horse doesn't go well: the track wasn't right, the jockey slaughtered it, it missed its work early in the week, it had a bit of a virus. They never say the horse is a dud and to get rid of it. I'll ask Kris after a race, 'What happened to that horse?' He'll put his trainer persona on and I say, 'Mate, you're talking to me now, c'mon,' but, no, he'll come up with the same routine of excuses. But he must be alright at his job when you consider he recently had an owner who paid $1.5 million for a yearling he wanted Kris to train; that's a big responsibility. I've been to the sales with Leesy a few times; it really is fascinating. While I'd never consider spending $1.5 million even if I had 10 people in a syndicate, I've got four horses under his care — I'm in one with Clint Newton, another with Danny Buderus and a couple with Col Keane from Eagles Plumbing Plus, who is a good mate who loves the Knights and the gee-gees.

That brings me to Matt Hoy, my mad surfing mate. I met Hoyo through my brother Matt's wife Trish, who is a good friend of Hoyo's wife Leanne, a lovely person who has the patience of a saint (and needs to have). We started surfing together from the mid-'90s, not that I am anywhere near his class — he won three tournaments on the world circuit before he retired in 2000, including the Bells Beach classic. Hoyo is like me in that he loves getting away from things on the board or having a few beers and letting his hair down, but he also loves time with the family, especially his three children, Tex, Axle and Ginger, who absolutely idolises Danny Buderus.

I don't know what Hoyo does with his time when he's not out in the surf; he supposedly has a gig with Quiksilver's Research and Development team. I'm not sure how much it involves but it must pay OK, because he just built a new place at Merewether. He also does a bit of commentating at different events and makes surfing DVDs. As with Leesy, Hoyo has time to get together during the day, so when there are waves we'll surf all day. We've been overseas on boat trips, surfed the Maldives, plus all over the east coast of Australia. Now this guy is a pleasure to room with. His bed is never messed up because he rarely ever comes home to sleep in it ... which is a blessing, because he's got 'Kurt Gidley syndrome' and can snore the house down.

Hoyo is always the life of the party and is the sort of bloke who no one has a bad word for. He loves a good time, would give anyone the time of the day and, being a tragic surfer, nothing worries him too much. He gets me boards from Pacific Dreams for free, gear from Quiksilver and Electric Sunglasses, so he can't be too bad a bloke. He's a cult figure in the surf industry. Sponsors stuck with him for years after he retired because of his personality and the following he maintains.

Even though my footy days are now behind me, I know the friendship of these four guys will remain strong for many years, and I am very thankful for that. We can get in some good-natured strife together, and we know we'll always be there for each other.

CHAPTER 31

TWENTY20 VISION

I have been lucky that my rugby league profile has enabled me to compete in other sports at 'first class' level and to meet top-level sports people from other fields. The most publicised was definitely the 'infamous' Twenty20 cricket games I played for New South Wales in January 2007.

The Twenty20 cricket appearances were a result of a long lunch between my manager John Fordham and NSW Cricket boss David Gilbert. The idea was thrown up while they were discussing how the condensed form of cricket should be kept as an entertainment vehicle only, and never promoted to rival one-day or Test cricket. Having me play for NSW was certainly one way of showing it isn't too serious!

Actually I'm not the first international rugby league player to be a NSW cricket 'ring-in'. Fordo tells how Reg Gasnier played for NSW against a touring Fiji side in 1960, in a team that included Richie Benaud, Keith Miller, Neil Harvey and Norm O'Neill.

I jumped at the opportunity. It was a chance for me to have a novel experience and also to help raise money for the charity I support, Ronald McDonald House in the Hunter; every dollar of profit from the game in Newcastle went to them. It's funny how earlier, when I got back from England one year, I told Channel Nine's head of sport Steve Crawley, 'Mate, you've got to get this Twenty20 going in Australia, it's booming in England. They have live bands there, the fans love it, it's a real young crowd they're trying to attract. It would be sensational out here.' Never did I think I'd be involved with it as a player.

As usual, there were some narks out there who saw the negative side of me playing at that level, and there was a bit of an uproar over it; former Test bowler Geoff Lawson was one who gave it to me. But what they overlooked was that it is all about sports entertainment, nothing else. And that showed on the day; they had a near sell-out crowd of 10,600 at the No. 1 Sports Ground in Newcastle when the Blues took on South Australia. I was told afterwards that it was the biggest crowd to ever attend a cricket match in Newcastle and that includes when the West Indies and England played there.

The downside for me was that the day before, I attended Danny Buderus' wedding, and I had the hangover from hell, which was probably a good thing in one way because I went out there with no fear and a very relaxed attitude. We fielded first and I could hardly see the ball, let alone stop it, and the cricket pants they gave me being about two sizes too small didn't help. I was terribly conscious of these bloody tight pants; especially after I put them on, thinking, 'Shit, these are tight,' and I looked around the room and they were all pissing themselves laughing. The pants were just hugging on my arse and I said, 'Tell me how big my barge-arse looks,' and they were all saying that I wouldn't be able to put a thigh pad on inside them — and I couldn't when I had to bat.

But I can't rap the players enough in how they welcomed me, from captain Simon Katich down to the young blokes in the team. And it gave me a whole new appreciation of how talented you must be to play cricket at that level.

My previous senior cricket experience was a couple of seasons with Merewether fifth grade. There was one tactical problem I had there — if we batted first I was OK, and could get a fair score as a hard-hitting, cross-bat slogger; but if we fielded first we'd take a few stubbies out on the field and my reaction time would be impaired somewhat by the time I was due to go to the crease. Luckily, we played on cement (with synthetic grass) and the boundaries would only be 30 or 40 metres from the bat so it suited my bottom-hand style.

I had a couple of training sessions leading up to the first Twenty20 game in Newcastle and to face some of the bowlers in the nets was terrifying. Australia's World Cup left-armer Nathan Bracken was bowling at about 125 kilometres an hour at my ribs — I was thinking, 'Are you right, mate?' Then I thought, 'Imagine facing Brett Lee or Shaun Tait at 150 kilometres an hour or whatever they bowl at.'

We batted second in Newcastle, after I received about a thousand 'barge-arse' remarks from the crowd in the field —

it was an effort to stay on my feet, thanks to the combination of a hangover and Billy Elliott tights. I bowled one over for the tidy figures of none-for-nine during South Australia's innings of 150. I had a catch dropped off my second delivery in the deep by Daniel Christian — who's normally a safe catcher, they told me. Somebody wrote in the *Sydney Morning Herald* that the ball deserved to be hit onto the sand at Merewether Beach, which was about two kilometres away.

When it was our turn to bat, I was last man in and I survived one ball from Dan Cullen. We needed 13 runs in the last over from the Croweaters' opening bowler Ryan Harris, who had fire in his eyes as he banged them down to Simon Katich. Simon decided not to run and expose me to the strike, which I wasn't arguing with, and we only got four runs from the last over and lost by eight. He got booed by the crowd and carpeted by the media, the critics saying he gave up any chance of us winning and robbed those in the crowd who had come to see me play, I mean, make a fool of myself. He was only trying to protect me, which wasn't a bad idea considering how I was feeling, and I think everyone took the whole thing too seriously.

In the second game, we played Tasmania at Telstra Stadium in Sydney and I got to face Ben Hilfenhaus who has played one-day internationals for Australia. He was apparently bowling at 130 kilometres an hour. Now that's lightning quick for a bloke who struggled in Merewether's fifth grade, and watching it from side on it seemed quicker. I was thinking, 'If I get in there and bat against this bloke, I will dead-set shit my pants.' The plan was to keep me out of the action until I could face the spinners and not get hit, but unfortunately we kept losing wickets chasing Tasmania's 202 and I had to go out in the middle, batting at number nine. Now I wasn't nervous, oh no; when they called my name I didn't have my gloves on or my box in and I couldn't put my helmet on properly! When I got out there, I thought Hilfenhaus was going to throw me a soft long-hop but he ripped one into me and I missed. 'What's going on here?' I thought to myself.

I was able to 'block' the next ball and got a single to get off strike. The next ball I had to face he kept it up for me, I half drove it to mid-on for a single and the crowd (over 18,000) went crazy. As I got to the bowler's end I said, 'Sorry about that, mate,' and he said, 'You are taking the piss.' He stared at me and then announced, 'I'm going to bounce you next ball'; dead-set my backside was dragging on the ground in fear. He was true to his word too. I was able to get four runs from off-spinner David Marsh in the next over, but when I was back on strike to Hilfenhaus he ripped in a short one. I leaned back on it and put it down to third man, and I'm sure for a moment Hilfenhaus thought I was his Tasmanian hero Ricky Ponting, such style did I show; I thought it was going to go for four but I only got a single.

I ended up getting nine runs, giving me a Twenty20 average of nine from two innings (one not out), which is not too bad to tell the grandkids one day. Oh, we were all out for 165 — so we copped a thrashing. But the main thing was I helped raise much-needed money for Ronald McDonald House and I got to meet some great guys. I even took back a couple of their warm-up drills to the Knights for the outside backs. We'd bomb a football and throw a cricket ball along the ground; it is good cross training.

I enjoyed the Telstra Stadium game best. I wasn't hungover, for one, and the crowd wasn't sledging me, and I just felt better after the one-game experience. I even made a couple of diving saves in the field ... made easier because I had bigger cricket pants! After the game, Ben Hilfenhaus brought a beer into our dressing room so I sat and had a chat with him. They were all good blokes and that's probably something missing in rugby league, having a beer with the opposition after the match.

Simon Katich got up in front of everyone in the dressing room after the game and thanked me for coming down. He said the guys really enjoyed me playing and I responded by saying, 'Thanks for the opportunity, although I'm a bit disappointed with what you did to me in Newcastle — I think I could have got the extra five runs we needed to win,' which gave everyone a giggle.

I've kept all the gear, including my blue shirt with number seven on the back. We had our annual Newcastle Knights cricket challenge a few weeks later and I had to wear the whole NSW gear, of course. When I went out to bat, Danny Buderus came on to bowl and I did a Gary Sobers on him — hit him for six sixes in the over! He reckoned I'd been in intense training and he was restricted to a two-pace run-up, which is nonsense.

The other novel experience I had against top-level performers in another sport was during Surfest three months later, when organisers put on a special tribute to Mark Richards, Newcastle's surfing legend.

On the last day they got Mark, Luke Egan, Simon Law, Matt Hoy — all the top local surfers — to do a surf-off and invited me to take part. I thought, 'What a great experience,' and it worked out well that it was the day after we played St George Illawarra in Wollongong (we beat them by 54–6).

A three to four metre swell was predicted for later in the week but it was just my luck that it came a few days early. When I got up on Sunday morning and saw these big waves pumping in, I decided there was no way in the world I was going to surf in such dangerous sort of conditions. Anyway, 20 minutes before the event, Hoyo realised I hadn't lobbed and hopped on the phone. 'Where are you, mate?' 'I'm at home watching the beach getting churned up and I'm not going anywhere near that surf today, mate.' He said, 'You've got to come and surf — people are asking where are you, they are on the PA announcing you're going to be here, there are thousands on the beach. The waves are only four foot down here [at Newcastle's main beach] and there'll be a jet-ski to take you out the back.' So I agreed to turn up.

When I got there, all I saw was this massive set coming in, all of 10 feet, and I was standing there with Hoyo and Luke, saying, 'I am not going out. I could get killed out there.' A couple of Merewether local boys grabbed me, including Billy Anderson who is a local legend, and he said in a fatherly voice, 'Andrew, you could die out there,' and I said, 'Mate, don't worry, I'm not going out there anyway.' Next thing there were about 20 locals egging me on to get out in the water and the guy running the jet-ski grabbed me and told me once I was out the back I'd be fine. So I decided to go, although I was literally shaking in fear. When I was dropped out the back, Mark Richards looked at me all stunned, and said, 'What are you doing out here?' and started giggling to himself.

Next moment this big set came in. I was looking at the beach and there were like 10,000 people there and I thought, 'I've got to go now.' So I put the head down and paddled as fast as I could ... and I got on this eight to 10 footer. Whoa! That night it was on the local television news and there was this great shot of me on the wave, and Hoyo paddling over it, on the front page of the *Newcastle Herald* next day.

I caught three waves without killing or injuring myself and couldn't get back to the sand quick enough after that. I only had a small board which was made for much smaller waves and if the jet-ski wasn't there, there was no way I could have paddled out in those conditions. I made sure every time I got a wave I waved to my jet-ski driver, so that if I fell off he'd be able to grab me before the next wave arrived, because it was pounding down. If I got caught on the inside there, I would have got hammered.

When I got back to the beach, I think everyone was stunned that I actually caught three waves. It was such a buzz as it turned out, despite all the apprehension I had. I was on such a big high Cath pretty much locked me in the house and I missed Surfest Sunday down at The Burwood; she knew I wouldn't have come home for days!

I haven't got as happy a story from another time I surfed 'competitively' — in the annual single-fin competition at Burleigh Heads on Queensland's Gold Coast, which always coincides with the big Magic Millions horse-racing carnival.

I've been up there a few times for the single-fin festival — it's a great event that raises money for charity — but this one time I ended up in hospital. Here's the story …

You have to enter from the rocks from the point where there's a famous break. I was carrying my board into the surf and getting ready to jump into the water from these big round boulders, which are so slippery Kelly Slater fell off once and injured himself, so at least I'm in good company. Just as you get to the water's edge there are all these barnacles on the rocks. So as I was getting my footing right to jump off, someone behind me did a big wolf whistle and I turned around to see who it was; only to over-balance and fall on the barnacles, knees first. I scraped my knees pretty badly and the swell washed me out before a three-foot wave hit me and started pushing me back in. I'd borrowed a board and the last thing Hoyo said to me before I went out was 'don't you dare ding this bloke's board', so I was more worried about the board than my own body. I was trying to push the board away from the rocks and hit my knees on the barnacles again.

When I finally got to safety I was digging massive barnacles out of my knees and there was blood pissing out everywhere. I was out the back by then, so I thought I may as well surf my heat, and when I reached the beach, everyone was shaking their heads at the blood, so I was taken to hospital to get stitched up. I'd planned to be up there for another three days, so I went to the races, had a few beers and enjoyed myself despite my lack of mobility. When I flew home I could hardly walk, my legs were so badly infected and swollen. I was put straight into hospital and kept on a drip for four days.

The right knee was the worst. I had eight stitches underneath the top point of my shin where it protrudes just below the knee cap, and that part was too wide to get stitched, so when I went back to training it kept opening up. I still have a scar the size of a 10 cent piece as a memento from that fateful trip to Burleigh Heads.

Another offbeat experience I was fortunate to have was appearing on the iconic BBC television program *A Question of Sport* in England. The show has been running since 1970 and has an unbelievable following — not that I knew any of this when I arrived to play for Warrington in 2005 and was asked to go on the show. Originally I said 'no thanks' — I didn't want to be out of my league on a quiz show. Then Cath told me how she loved the show when she was growing up and it was one of the biggest things on TV.

For those who aren't familiar with it, there are two teams, each captained by a resident skipper who has two guest sportsmen or women as team-mates. You are asked sports trivia and then there might be a film clip where you have to guess what happened next and that sort of thing; it's a lot of fun. It's hosted by England tennis legend Sue Barker and captain of my team was the ex-Rangers player and Scotland soccer legend Ally McCoist, while England rugby halfback Matt Dawson was the other captain. It was so funny because I couldn't for the life of me understand a word Ally was saying

ABOVE: Surfing in Mentawai Islands in Indonesia, 2007 — I'm in absolute paradise.

BELOW: With one of my best mates, horse trainer Kris Lees. This shot was taken after his first Group 1 win with County Tyrone.

ABOVE: The infamous tea party in full swing, England 2001.

BELOW: With my prized Golden Boot in England in 2002. 'Booze' was awarded his Golden Boot of Kurri Kurri.

RIGHT: I had another great catch on Lord Howe other than Cathrine (who accepted my marriage proposal) — one big kingfish.

BELOW: Do you think my bum looks big in this? Skinny-dipping in Lord Howe.

ABOVE: My breakdown in Dublin in 2000. Check out the eyes — someone has been bawling! That's my 'minder' Matt 'Gids' surveying the damage.

BELOW: A 130kph thunderbolt from Ben Hilfenhaus aimed at my head during the Twenty20 match against Tasmania. All arse, this shot.

ABOVE: Bedsy's wedding — a great day. No, we're not the Beach Boys!

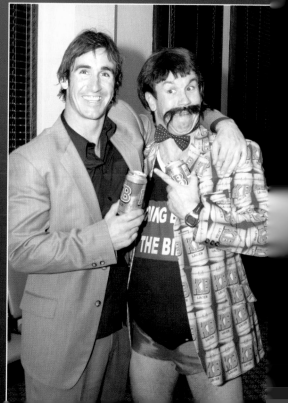

RIGHT: At Reg's DVD launch — my hero!

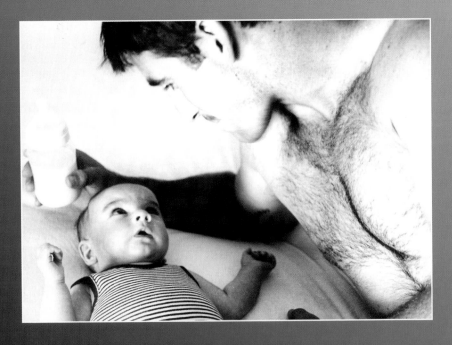

ABOVE: The best thing I have ever done in my life ... having Samuel.
BELOW: Samuel and me at Daydream Island the week after I retired
from footy. I felt like it was the start of a new life.

ABOVE: Me and my beautiful girl Cathrine.
BELOW: At Lord Howe Island — I had just popped the question an hour before.

ABOVE: At sister Kate and Pat Curry's wedding. A lovely day.
Back from left: Trish, Matthew, Pat, Kate, Mum, Dad and me.
Front: Samuel, Cooper, Fletcher and Jack. By the way, Cooper and
Jack are Matthew and Trish's boys; Fletch is Kate's first child (she has
since had a daughter, Emerson).

in his thick Scottish accent; I was just staring at him when he spoke and he was pissing himself laughing. But somehow we won on the night.

The other player on my team was the famous striker Kevin Phillips, who holds the record for the most post-war goals for Sunderland and the other team had the cricketer Phil Tufnell and a bloke called Peter Reid, who is an ex-English soccer international who was then the manager (coach) of Sunderland. Before I went on the show I asked who the other guests were and rang Cathrine's dad Peter, who is a real Sunderland nut, all excited to tell him that his team's manager was on with me, so I'd get him an autograph. Sunderland were relegated after Peter Reid's last season as manager, so naturally Cath's dad wasn't over-enthusiastic about my news. I found him a really good bloke, so friendly, when we were backstage. I obviously thought no one over there in soccer would know anything about Australian rugby league, but he told me he loved watching me play on Sky TV, which was a big surprise. I got his autograph anyway, which Cath's dad did appreciate — although he wishes I'd got Kevin Phillips', as he reckoned he was Sunderland's best player of all time.

CHAPTER 32

MY SOUL MATE AND MY BOY

OK, what can I say about one Cathrine Mahoney (that's 'Ma-hone-ee', as in the *Police Academy* movies, not 'Mar-ney')? Well, I love her with all my heart; she is my soul mate, my best mate, and the best thing that has happened to me in my crazy life.

I'll try to paint a picture of what a great woman she is. She is the sort of person who walks into a room and lights it up — people are just drawn towards her. She is bubbly, positive and intelligent, and her people skills are phenomenal. I always joke with her about how she 'works' a room when we go to a party or a function; I sit in the corner and she goes and talks to different people and has so many great relationships. I am very proud of how good she is at her job too. Samuel loves her, which is really important, and it is great to see how well they get on.

Cath understands me — as she says, I'm 'a bit of a loonie' but she is prepared to love me, warts and all. I have told her most of the things I have done, the crazy life I have lived, but she doesn't judge me. She doesn't judge anyone and she gives everyone the time of day, whether it is one of the most important people in the media in Australia or one of the drinkers down at The Burwood Inn. The blokes down there say, 'Gee that girl's nice. Of all the girls who come here, she is the only one who says hello to us.'

Cath has made me realise there is more to life than myself. In this fake world I live in, it is too often all about me and all I used to focus on was my football or living it up. Cath has emphasised to me that there are other people in my life and there has to be compromise — and there are other things to look forward to. I had never done that before in a relationship — it is not just about my career and my life, but hers too.

We met a couple of months after Renae and I separated when Cathrine was assigned to do the publicity for the DVD on my career which was released by Sony BMG. I wasn't looking for a girlfriend at all, but in hindsight it was important to me to meet someone who wasn't interested in rugby league and hardly knew who I was, so they could get to know Andrew Johns the person and not Joey Johns the perceived persona. Cathrine was born in the north of England and was raised in Porthcawl, Wales, about 20 minutes out of Cardiff. Although she'd been in Australia for three years, she knew very little about rugby league or who I was, until she had to do the DVD publicity.

I felt so comfortable around her from the start. I'd always struggled to talk with people and keep eye contact with them but I had no trouble with Cathrine — I could talk and look her in the eye (well eventually; if you ask her it took a while). She was also a good type and I was doing my best with the old Joey charm. I probably wouldn't have turned up to all the promotional events if she wasn't there — but she said we had to be professional while working together and nothing was going to happen. So I had to show some patience, which was against my nature, especially when Cath had to leave Australia and reapply for a visa. When she got back we started a relationship and I was a different person. One of the staff at the Knights office even said to me that it was good to see me smile, that she hadn't seen that for years.

Ours hasn't been the normal relationship other than for the 18 months or so Cath moved in with me at Merewether in 2005–06. The other times Cath has been living and working in Sydney and I've been in Newcastle and we see each other a couple of days during the week and on the weekend, but it's worked out well.

I almost lost her just after the 2006 season finished when I was out of control again and she'd understandably had enough. I didn't appreciate enough what Cath had given up to live with me — leaving her job, lifestyle and friends in Sydney to work for herself from home and rely on my circle of friends. She loves being with and talking to people, but she would get up at my place and go downstairs to the office all day and have no face-to-face contact with people other than my friends. Moving to Newcastle would have been a big enough culture shock in itself after going to university in Manchester, living in London and then inner Sydney.

Cath went back to Sydney in October 2006 with the message I'll never forget: 'Andrew, you've got to find balance in your life. Until you can find some balance, I'm not going to be here.' Her leaving made me pull my head in; I felt so empty without her, so I knew she was the one for me. We went to the races at Randwick on Melbourne Cup Day — and I asked for a second chance. She then went overseas to catch up with old friends after landing a job at Channel Nine and all the time we kept in contact. We gradually started seeing each other again and over Christmas we went down along the Great Ocean Road in Victoria. It was just like we had met each other all over again.

I am so fortunate Cathrine loves me truly for who I am and not what I have done as a footballer. I want a partner who is also my best friend. And that is what Cathrine Mahoney is to me.

She is a big part of why I think I'm so relaxed now. My footy career and the pressure it brought is now finished. I'm in a great relationship, I am really excited about our future together, I have a great relationship with my son, and Cath has a great relationship with Samuel too. I know it should be a traumatic time for me, and Cath has long worried about how I was going to handle the transition, but she's been a great support; she is the rock alongside me.

She has a wise head: she just seems to put things into perspective and she's a straight shooter, telling me sometimes when I'm being a dickhead or being too self-centred. There have been times when I was injured and stressed and I'd think the world was coming down on me and Cath would tell me how life really is, and I'd realise how lucky I am. And she encourages me to do different things — to go and study and do courses and this sort of thing. She says I train so hard and physically have so much discipline, but I'm not training my brain. I'd love to learn another language and am about to start a basic computer course.

Cath realises that the fact I am bipolar means I'm not going to be the 'normal' partner (whatever normal is?) and she recognises the tell-tale signs when the mania starts to build inside me. She just sends me out in the surf or tells me to go train for an hour; and she's right, if I release some energy I'm OK. Then she'll grab me in a headlock and wrestle me and get us to go out and have a drink or a meal together.

I can't wait until we start a family together; and travel and do what I regard as the normal things other couples do — to be able to even have friends over for dinner in football season and not have to worry about the weekend game. I want to be a good husband to her, a good father and a good mate, because she deserves that and more.

And then there is Samuel, who is a treasure in my life. I love spending time with him, I love talking to him on the phone when we can't be together, and I love taking him to places, whether for the day or when we get away on holidays.

He was born on the ninth of the ninth, 1999, and I was bawling my eyes out when he came into the world; hysterical is probably the right word to use. It was a long labour and the obstetrician came in to join the nurses and I was watching the heart rate ... then his head came out and it was blue and they were freaking out a bit. I was screaming — it was the most heart-wrenching thing in my life as I didn't know what was going on. I'd been awake all night and the emotion of it all got to me. Renae was in so much pain and obviously there were complications; I started howling and the doctor ordered me out of the room! Renae was screaming at me to 'get out and get your shit together — go on, get out', so I had to go outside and get some composure back. When I went back in, I saw we'd had a boy and I started screaming with joy this time, 'It's a boy, it's a boy' — they could hear me in the next ward.

Winning a grand final is not as special as having children. I used to dote on Samuel so much. I used to get up in the night and feed him all the time; the 5am session was the start of my day and I loved it.

He's eight now and can be a handful like any young boy. He is very active and demanding at times, but he brings out the good in me and we have such a strong bond. I know I am going to love watching him grow up and being there for him.

I know how fortunate I am to have a wonderful partner, such a lovable son, such a close brother and good parents, sister and great mates. The right people make your life so much more satisfying and I'll never take that for granted.

CHAPTER 33

WHY I LOVE ANDREW

By Cathrine Mahoney

When I was told that the next project I was to do publicity for at Sony Music was a DVD on Andrew Johns, the first thing I did was Google him. I can put my hand on my heart and say I had never heard of Andrew up until that point. Looking back this was a real plus — it meant I fell in love with Andrew Johns, not Joey the footy player.

Growing up in the UK, 'footy' was a game played with a round ball — in fact, during my first three years living in Oz my only league experience consisted of one State of Origin match watched on Channel Nine with the sound on mute, listening to Roy and HG's hilarious commentary on Triple J. I watched the DVD two days before I met Andrew and, although my league knowledge was zero, I was blown away by what he had achieved.

Andrew and I met in September 2002, the day the DVD was launched. I was only slated to have one day of publicity with Andrew, and one day when there was to be an in-store signing appearance. But fate stepped in, or Luke Bailey's knees to be precise. Andrew and I often thank Luke for bringing us together. Two days before the launch, Andrew's season was cut short during the Dragons clash when Bailey's knees accidentally collided with Andrew's back. His season being over meant that our two days together turned into a few months — enough time to fall for each other. Although, as I always like to stress, there was no 'hanky panky' until our work together was finished!

Not long after our time as work colleagues ended, so did my Australian visa — seeing me return to the UK while Sony Music arranged a new visa for me. Andrew and I were apart for almost two months and he called me twice a day the whole time. We were lucky in a way that the distance — coupled with time when we worked together — meant that we had got to know each other really well mentally, as opposed to physically. So when I finally made it back to Oz it felt as if we had been a couple for a long time.

It is hard to put into words why you love someone, as describing feelings isn't always easy. I love Andrew for many different reasons: he is my best friend, he is kind and thoughtful, makes me feel like a million dollars, and has me laughing out loud with his one-liners.

What sealed the deal for me was when I saw that the movie *Dirty Dancing* was on the TV one evening, he immediately said, 'Nobody puts Baby in the corner!' (a line from the film) and I knew he was the one for me!

What else? Well, Andrew is very handy in the kitchen, cries at movies, loves art and reads a couple of books a week. He knows all the words to tragic pop songs (including the verses), and has a wealth of bad dance moves in his repertoire. Oh, I should also say that he is a handsome sod too or he might get put out reading this!

Our life together is very normal — an ideal night for us is just spent hanging out with his son Samuel, or having friends over for a meal. We do love a good takeaway and *Super Saturday* on Fox Sports or *Friday Night Footy* on Channel Nine! I am thrilled to have found Andrew — many people have told me I have been good for him, but in turn he has been just as great for me. He is amazing company, inspiring (never more so than watching him strive to get back on the paddock after a season-ending injury — and there have been a few), and so devoted.

Andrew is a fantastic father to Samuel; I love seeing them together and the bond they have. Samuel had just turned three when Andrew and I got together, and I have loved seeing him turn into a beautiful little man.

I can't wait to have children with Andrew and it seems the three of us are ready for a baby — Samuel has already put his order in for a little brother. I'm lucky that Andrew's time with Samuel often falls on a weekend as it means we all get to hang out together. The only downside is the constant battle with the TV remote — depending on who gets it first, you'll see TVN, Nickelodeon or UKTV on the screen!

Family is really important to both Andrew and myself. It is always daunting as a partner meeting the 'in-laws' (especially for Andrew as my dad is 6 foot 5), but we all get on really well. Gary and Gayle welcomed me into the Johns family with open arms and were great surrogate parents until my own folks Anne and Peter arrived in Australia last year from Wales.

Andrew is a real romantic too, although when he has a surprise for me he often gets too excited and blurts it out before he gives it to me. (He really struggles with secrets too — so never tell him anything you don't want the Hunter knowing about.) My favourite thing that he'd do was, when he ran on the field to play footy, to let me know that he was thinking of me he'd rub his chest with his two hands. One away game when the Knights played the Warriors, he almost rubbed the sponsor's logo off! See, it's not all mouthguard throwing and expletives.

One aspect of Andrew's personality that may surprise many is that he is painfully shy and very humble. Walking into a room full of strangers fills him with dread — he almost has a panic attack at the thought of it. And although he may come across as cocksure about his ability on the field, nothing could be further from the truth. One night that really highlighted Andrew's modesty came in 2003 when *Big League* magazine compiled 'The Greatest Kangaroos' — an all-time-great Australian team that featured legends such as Wally Lewis, Dally Messenger, John Raper, Clive Churchill, Arthur Beetson, Ron Coote and Peter Sterling. The 28-man Kangaroo squad only included two current players: Darren Lockyer and Andrew. The event was held in Darling Harbour with all the living members of the squad present. Andrew spent the entire cab ride home telling me how he felt like a fraud and didn't deserve a spot in a team made up of such greats.

No, Andrew is not perfect, but who is? And there have been some hard times. I'm glad he has revealed his bipolar condition but, as he says, living with it is not all negative. When he is 'up', life is so wonderful with him, his love and sense of fun are so intense and being with him is fantastic.

Neil Halpin said to me once as a warning about how rocky our road could be that 'living with Andrew will be difficult at the best of times, and at the worst it will be a nightmare'. I totally understand what Neil meant, but I don't see it like that. The best of times are the greatest of times; and the 'bad' times have become far less frequent.

I did find it too difficult towards the end of 2006, after having lived in Newcastle for 18 months, and went back to Sydney to be my own person and restart my own life. This was after — as Andrew has admitted in these pages — he went off the rails for a few weeks when the season ended. I returned to Sydney and then went on holiday overseas. We kept in touch and I told Andrew I'd always love him and be there for him and to call me any time he felt depressed, but I needed time to look at my own life.

But I am so glad we decided to give it another shot. We'd put too much into our relationship over four years: we'd been through his injuries, the bipolar, living with the public scrutiny and me moving to Newcastle. The time since we've been back together has been amazing. Of course, the incident in London created difficulties, but again we made it through together.

How did I feel when I got the call from Andrew in the UK when he was arrested? Well, of course I felt a mixture of emotions — anger and disappointment, as well as concern for the man I love. I must say the airport welcome wasn't quite how we'd planned it over the weeks leading up to his arrival back in Australia. Seeing him push his luggage trolley towards me he looked like a broken man, and when I got close he started to cry, which meant we were both in tears.

Andrew was back for a whole day before the story broke, long enough to get lulled into a false sense of relief that the incident had gone unnoticed — although we should have known a story like that involving someone in the public eye wouldn't stay a secret for long.

I woke on the Thursday morning to John Fordham's text, letting us know the media knew — and soon after the text messages started to come in thick and fast from friends watching the story unfold on breakfast TV, the radio and newspapers. I felt sick to my stomach and my main concern was how Andrew would handle the situation. One thing I know we both regret is not telling our parents when he first arrived home, as both Andrew's and my folks heard it from the media that morning.

I stayed with a friend that day instead of going to work — working at Channel Nine I couldn't have faced the office. It felt like one of the longest days of my life. That Thursday culminated in Andrew's full confession on national television on *The Footy Show*. I stood in the dressing room watching the monitor and felt like I was watching a movie. I was astounded at how brave Andrew was and how honest too — I was so proud of him.

Before the interview it had been decided that although Andrew would mention depression and medication, he wouldn't mention the word 'bipolar'. This was for several reasons: firstly, Andrew was keen to not look like he was making excuses for his behaviour; and secondly, as it was a big revelation in his upcoming book, the publishers wanted to tone this aspect down. Those closest to Andrew wanted the bipolar to come out that night and in hindsight I wish it had.

Of course, the media frenzy worsened after the confessions of drug taking. Although the depression was referred to, it was almost in passing, as opposed to being the main reason behind Andrew's behaviour. I guess drug-taking stories in sport sell papers and are better for TV and radio ratings than mental health problems. The onslaught of negativity focusing on Andrew after this revelation wasn't good, though. In fact, on Friday and Saturday after the *Footy Show* interview, I, along with Andrew's family, was well aware of how suicidal he had become. His condition simply had to be made public.

I tried to put Andrew on a media-watching ban — but when every TV channel, radio station and newspaper was leading with his story, it was difficult. And to a man in a manic state of depression, hearing people say, 'He is an appalling role model', 'I paid to watch him play — Johns has let me and the whole Hunter region down', 'Joey has brought disgrace on the game of rugby league', 'I wouldn't let my kids near him', was all he needed to believe he was worthless and shouldn't be here any more. I hope most people don't have to experience camera crews and photographers outside their home, or their parents' home, or their partner's home and workplace — and I can say first hand that being chased down a busy street by the media is a hideous experience.

Once we gave Professor Gordon Parker permission to

speak on Andrew's behalf and the bipolar was finally out there, I believe that public opinion swayed. To anyone who understands the condition that Andrew suffers — along with two per cent of the Australian population — his erratic behaviour both on and off the field is more easily explained. One in two people with bipolar will find themselves at the mercy of alcohol and drugs at some point in their lives.

Some people will always focus on the drugs and only see Andrew for that — but I believe unless you understand mental illness or have been touched by it, you shouldn't judge such situations. I get really angry at the people who look down their noses and stare at Andrew, or the ones who drive by our house so slowly, as if they are looking at the home of a murderer; but then, as Andrew says to me, we should only care about the people close to us.

Our family are definitely closer now, having got through this tough time together, and we have all been blown away with the amount of support we have received. We all made sure Andrew saw every card/text/email and heard every story that was passed on. I know this made him stronger, and I think we all took comfort from what we heard.

The irony is that, since retiring, Andrew had been in such a great place: calm, relaxed and loving life. While what happened was initially awful, it could turn into the best thing for him — already he feels like a massive weight has been lifted off his shoulders.

Andrew is such a wonderful person deep down and, although recent events have been really challenging for him, he is now learning how to live without the extremes that have been so much a part of his life.

CHAPTER 34

NOT SUCH A TRAGIC ENDING

The moment I bounced off Adam Woolnough during a drill at training on Thursday, 7 April 2007, I knew that something was seriously wrong with my neck — and that my career might have just ended. I'll be honest ... when Professor John Yeo and Neil Halpin told me, four and a half days later, that I'd be putting my health at unreasonable risk if I didn't retire, I felt relief more than anything.

I'd decided 2007 was going to be my final year despite having a further season to run on my contract. I still had the desire to play, but I was quickly realising my time in rugby league was just about up.

I saw it in the little things that don't lie. For the first time in my life I was taking short cuts at training. In the gym, rather than do sets of eight I was doing six, and I would never ever do that. I remember thinking, 'This is not in your nature.' I would do some training by myself and write down beforehand what I needed to do; I'd put down 20 sets of 100 metres, but only do 14. It was the sign to me that I was losing the killer, the drive to succeed.

And my body was starting to shut down — that was obvious. I carried a hamstring injury for six weeks leading into the competition and couldn't do much training; I had never suffered a hamstring injury in my life and don't even know how I did it. I had too many signs that my body was getting back at me for what I'd done to it over the years. The indication that my neck wasn't 100 per cent had been there for a few weeks too but, as I had probably done too often during my career, I shrugged off the soreness and kept going. I'd surf, then go to training and do some weights, and wake up the next day feeling like there was a big kink in my neck. I haven't exactly treated my body like a temple; I trained hard, played even harder, then partied hard on top of that. The body was telling me it had had enough and, to be perfectly honest, so too had the mind.

I'd had a bonus two seasons anyway after the run of injuries I had from 2002 to 2004. It could have easily been over a lot earlier for me. I know I was incredibly blasé about playing with the neck injury since 2003 and how lucky I'd been by playing with certain injuries and getting away with it. There is a fine line between being brave and reckless and I know that too many times I was extremely reckless.

Neil Halpin knew my body had had enough. He said that when I was knocked out in the tackle by Sonny Bill Williams against the Bulldogs in the opening game of '07, he was thinking of saying to me then that I'd had too many knocks and should walk away. Both my parents were in tears when they visited me in hospital.

I was resigned to the fact I was going to retire when I saw Professor Yeo at his house on Good Friday, and that was a wonderful gesture by him to see me on a public holiday at his own home. I could see the concern in his and Neil's mannerisms that it could be serious, but they didn't let on too much, saying they wanted to wait until the results of the scans came back. I knew the media speculation over the long weekend would do my head in, so I tried to play the seriousness down.

On Tuesday morning my manager John Fordham picked me up at home and we went to collect the results of the scans at Cardiff. I know I wasn't supposed to, but I opened up the envelope and read the report. I couldn't understand most of the medical terms but I could interpret enough to know the news didn't look good. So by the time we reached Neil's office in the Knights building and saw him and John Yeo, I was resigned to the inevitable. The professor's exact words were, 'I can't let you go back,' but with a sort of question mark on it, as if he expected I might argue or ask if he was sure. He said, 'Is there anything you'd like to say?' and I just said, 'Yes, I want to retire.' I could see the relief in both their eyes. John said he hadn't seen a disc that had protruded as much as mine and that he'd seen people with far less disc protrusion who'd gone back and ended up in a wheelchair. He also told me that when he showed other doctors the scans the first time I'd hurt the neck in '03, they couldn't believe he hadn't operated. He also admitted that every time he saw me get hit, he was a little worried. That put the wind up me a bit, I tell you, but he assured me that he considered the disc had settled down well enough from the rest back in '03.

So that was that. There was absolutely no question about the risk I would take if I ever went back onto a rugby league field. Right at that moment I didn't feel any great sadness rush over me like I thought I should have; a part of me was disappointed it was all over, but a bigger part of me was relieved.

I walked out of Neil's rooms and I spoke first with Cathrine and my family; my parents were so happy it was over. I broke down and started crying when I spoke with Matty and I still can't explain why — the emotion just spilled out of me. Maybe it was because the finality that the combined Johns era was over hit me hard, I just don't know.

There were probably 40 media outside the club's offices. I asked if I could have a day to take it all in and come back Thursday and do a press conference, but there was no way we could keep it under wraps; I was only kidding myself. The club wanted to do a press conference straight away, but I insisted that I had a chance to tell the players first. Then I went home to gather my thoughts and wrote some notes about what I was going to tell them.

Channel Nine provided a helicopter to bring Cath up to Newcastle, which was great of them, so she was there for support when I had to tell the world. Facing the players that afternoon was one of the toughest and most emotional things

I've had to do. The squad of top 25 players were in the gym at Club Phoenix and they all stopped what they were doing. When I spoke to them I had a big lump in my throat, my voice was crackling and I was pretty upset. It was tough getting the words out as I told them that the greatest thing I got out of playing the game was their friendship and those friendships were going to be for life. I told them I wished I could have been out there for the rest of the year, but I'd be supporting them in whichever way I could and thanked them for their contribution to my career and the memories they'd helped me create.

I looked up and a couple of blokes were crying; everyone looked stunned. It was a real tough, emotional moment. They all shook my hand and, really, little was said. I had to go over to the ground soon after to face the media — and I could tell by the TV broadcast vans and cars in the car park there was going to be a high attendance rate for this one. As we walked over from the club's office, which is in the old squash centre building on the edge of the stadium's car park, I had a strange feeling — I was upset, I was disappointed, but such a big part of me was relieved in that I was facing a press conference for the last time.

It was tough holding myself together during the 35-minute conference and I was determined I wasn't going to shed a tear in front of the cameras; but I was happy how I got through it. And it was really a nice touch when all the media stood and clapped me at the end — that was something I really appreciated.

When I walked outside I felt like a different person, the anxiety and weight lifted from my shoulders instantly. It just seemed symbolic — it was as if I'd left Joey Johns the footballer in that room and Andrew Johns was now walking to the car.

It was really weird. Instead of slumping on the steering wheel and breaking down in distress, I sort of wanted to punch the air in relief. It's crazy, I know, but it was as if some overpowering voice inside me was saying, 'You knew your time was up, you couldn't have done any more with your career ... now you're free to get on with the rest of your life.'

CHAPTER 35

A MEDICAL INSIGHT

By Neil Halpin, Newcastle Knights Doctor

In 458 BC, after a series of defeats by neighbouring tribes, the very existence of Rome was threatened. The Senate resolved that the one man who could save the state was a retired former consul, L. Quinctius Cincinnatus. According to legend, the senators travelled to his farm where they found him ploughing the fields and asked him to become dictator and supreme commander. Cincinnatus did save Rome and then resigned his offices and went once again into retirement.

The comparison of Cincinnatus with Andrew Johns is, of course, fanciful, but there are interesting parallels with his performance in the second State of Origin game in 2005. According to many commentators and Andrew himself, this was the high watermark of his football career. Prior to this, he had played only eight games in the preceding 22 months and none at this elite level. He had had a series of severe long-term and career-threatening injuries and had just resumed playing three months earlier after an anterior cruciate ligament reconstruction, only to have then broken his jaw. Most people would have considered Andrew's career at the elite level to be finished and that he would fade out of football entirely in the near future; some thought that he wouldn't be up to the task and risked humiliating himself. In passing over seemingly safer alternatives, the selectors, like the Roman senators in the case of Cincinnatus, certainly took a chance in picking him; but clearly they also knew their man, and Andrew succeeded in putting on a virtuoso performance in the key halfback role.

To my mind, however, his single most impressive performance was the 1997 grand final against Manly. Three weeks beforehand, Andrew had fractured three ribs on his left side. He played in the preliminary final a fortnight later with an injection to relieve the pain, but during the game his lung collapsed after being punctured. That evening, an intercostal drain was inserted between his ribs into the pleural space (between his lung and chest wall) to reinflate his lung and he spent the next two days in hospital. Speculation about his possibly playing the grand final — and the danger involved — led to a series of articles and headlines, even suggesting that he could die if he played.

On grand final day he still had a good deal of pain from his broken ribs and his lung was still not fully inflated, but after being cleared by a cardiothoracic surgeon he played the whole game, including the memorable last minute.

Each of these episodes shows an amazing degree of physical toughness, but even more so a truly extraordinary ability to detach himself mentally from pain, doubts, fear of injury and fear of failure. On both a physical and a mental level, his playing in the 1997 grand final would have to be the most remarkable feat I have witnessed in my 25 years as a club doctor.

Andrew has had a large number of serious injuries throughout his career, but most notably in recent years he has had: groin surgery on both sides in 1999; torn medial ligament in his left knee in 2001; multiple transverse process fractures (back) in 2002; disk injury to his cervical spine (neck) in 2003; anterior cruciate ligament tear in his right knee in 2004; pulmonary embolus (blood clot lodged in his lung) in 2004; fractured mandible (jaw) in 2005; right elbow surgery in 2006; and a further injury to his cervical spine in 2007.

In his last six years of football, four of these were season-ending injuries (2002, 2003, 2004 and 2007). These would have forced most players into retirement, but he has also suffered a large number of less severe injuries and over the years has had many operations and other procedures. The result has been that he has constantly had to contend with injury, pain, surgery and long periods of treatment and rehabilitation, and has also had to fight against the psychological effects of these injuries, with long periods off the field and doubts about his ability to resume playing. His physical and mental resilience has been truly remarkable.

It has often been suggested that Andrew should have retired sooner. Although he did suffer a large number of quite serious injuries, each of these until 2007 was in a different region of his body, without any pattern of recurrence in any one area. Furthermore, none — with the possible exception of his neck in 2003 — was life-threatening or likely to cause severe long-term disability. Andrew was well aware of the risks of playing on and the long-term consequences of injury, and I believe that in each instance he made well-informed decisions about continuing to play. He did understand, however, that if he were to develop a pattern of recurrent injury, especially to his neck or head, this would be a different situation and that he would have to retire.

Andrew was finally forced to retire from football with a neck injury on 10 April 2007. His neck had initially become a problem in July 2003 when he developed a disk protrusion at the C4/5 level with severe pain extending into his left arm. He was examined by Professor John Yeo, an eminent and respected authority on neck injuries. It was decided to treat him without surgery and although he was unable to play the rest of that season, his disk did 'shrink back' and he was able to resume football at the beginning of 2004. Although he subsequently had several minor episodes of pain in his neck, it was felt that these were muscular and not of any real concern.

Andrew developed severe pain in his neck once again during the week preceding his retirement. He had been injured in the game against Canberra the previous weekend and again at training two days later. I was unaware of either of these until I called in at training on the Thursday evening and found that he had just injured his neck a third time.

It was obvious that the situation was very serious. He had severe pain on pressing over the facet joints on the left side of his neck, but alarmingly this pressure also caused a feeling of 'gooseflesh' in his left thigh. He was examined the following day, Good Friday, by Professor Yeo and further investigations were arranged. Scans of his neck the following week showed that the previous disk lesion at C4,5 had essentially healed but that he had developed another disk lesion, this time at C5,6 and this was causing pressure on his spinal cord and exiting nerve roots.

From a medical point of view it was clear that he had no other option but to retire. Quite simply, he risked catastrophic spinal injury if he were to play on. Given his age and the degenerative changes present at other levels of his spine, surgery was not a realistic option.

In retrospect it seems that he had actually been quite lucky not to have suffered a spinal cord injury. The protruded part of the disk was calcified, suggesting that it had developed a considerable time, perhaps even many months, beforehand.

In some ways an enforced retirement came as something of a relief to Andrew and certainly to those close to him. His rate of injury was escalating and it was clear that his time in football was nearly over anyway. In his last few years he was confronted with the problem that many sports people face towards the end of a career. It is not only the major injuries which become a problem, but frequently the minor ones are even more troublesome. With age they become more numerous and slower to heal, causing the player to be constantly carrying nagging complaints, with chronic pain, reduced performance, interference with fitness and training and the need for constant treatment and rehabilitation. Every player, and perhaps great players even more so, need to know when to retire. Some are able to do this at the time of their choosing, others have it forced upon them. Many a footballer has played on a 'season too many'. Although his retirement was not necessarily at the time of his choosing, his neck injury made the decision to do so a simple matter. His time had come.

But Andrew's greatest problem over the years has not been with injury, nor has it been on the field. He was formally diagnosed as suffering from a bipolar mood disorder in 2000. This condition, also known as manic depression, causes mood swings varying from severe depression on one hand to an excited, agitated and euphoric state on the other. It is generally regarded as being a metabolic disorder although affected by psychodynamic and environmental factors.

In Andrew's case each of these mood states has been severe and while the depression has been the more distressing, the manic phases have been the more destructive and disruptive. In retrospect, it is clear that he had been suffering from this for years prior to diagnosis, which is unfortunately a common situation. The indications are that there are many people in the community with undiagnosed bipolar disorder and that there is frequently a long lag between the onset of the illness and diagnosis. This delay can be catastrophic. Some patients with depression commit suicide, sometimes without any real indication that they would do so. Others during a manic phase may behave in a severely self-destructive, anti-social or even criminal manner.

It is often said that this condition is common in intelligent and highly achieving people. Andrew's greatness as a player obviously is the result of many factors, but it may well be that his sudden and unexpected flashes of brilliance, his impulsiveness, his almost reckless indifference to danger and his 'cocky' self-confidence on the field are at least partly attributable to this condition.

On the other hand, Andrew has suffered from periods of severe depression. He has also had episodes of manic-type behaviour, including some which he regrets and of which he is certainly not proud. It is not my place to elaborate on this, but each of these extremes has been profoundly disruptive to his life in general and his relationships and football in particular.

His bipolar disorder is so fundamental to his personality and behaviour that it is not possible to understand him without an appreciation of it, and this is one of the principal reasons for his making this public. He has not done so to unburden himself nor is he on any 'mission', but he does hope that in making the public aware of his illness, he will help others with the same condition, including those with high public profiles, who would otherwise be unaware of their problem or not seek treatment. Footballers are usually seen as role models and it may well be that he will also be able to be a role model for people with bipolar disease as well as other emotional disorders, and help them avoid much of the pain which he has suffered.

Like all people, Andrew has his flaws and limitations and he has come to accept these. Doing so is part of the 'healing process' and is essential to successful treatment. He does not wish to excuse his behaviour in the past or to minimise it by 'medicalising' it into an illness. He accepts and takes full responsibility for his actions. Like most people with a bipolar disorder, or for that matter most emotional disorders, he has only slowly gained understanding of and insight into his condition. It took him a long time to acknowledge it but much longer to 'own' his problem, accepting it fully on an emotional level and complying with treatment.

His decision to make his bipolar disorder public is an act of great courage. Some people in going public about their private lives and emotional problems may be simply self-indulgent or publicity seeking. In some the need to do so may actually reflect the severity of their disease. But Andrew made his decision publicly to acknowledge his bipolar disease some time ago and certainly it is not some sudden impulse. He no longer feels any fear of being found out or stigmatised. Many of his friends and colleagues have said that they were not at all surprised to find out that he has a bipolar disorder, although they could not have put a label on what was wrong with him. Almost everyone closely associated with him basically knew that he was suffering from some sort of emotional disorder.

Bipolar disorder is not curable and treatment, although effective, is not perfect. It involves not only medication but also supportive therapy and other strategies. Andrew has done well so far and has been well supported by his fiancée Cathrine, as well as his family and friends. At the age of 33 he is still a young man. His playing career may be over but he is really only entering another phase of his life with many possible avenues ahead of him.

In the classic 1950 movie *All About Eve* there is a memorable scene where Bette Davis coolly surveys a crowd at a party from a staircase and says caustically, 'Fasten your seatbelts. It's going to be a bumpy night.' This is often slightly misquoted as 'it's going to be a bumpy ride'. Andrew has certainly had quite a few bumpy rides, and bumpy nights, but seems to have at last gained a large measure of peace and stability in his life.

CHAPTER 36

THE LOWEST POINT
IN MY LIFE

This is the chapter I wish did not have to be added to this book — after it had been virtually completed and I'd already exposed my life. It's about a stupid decision I made when I was in London on the last day of a six-week overseas holiday and how it plummeted me to my lowest-ever point, coming the closest I ever have to taking my own life.

Words can't adequately describe the shame, the humiliation and the regret I feel about what that episode did, not just to me, but also people close to me.

I'd imagine most readers would be aware of the screaming headlines about my drug use after I was arrested in a London tube station with one ecstasy tablet in my pocket on 26 August 2007. It led to me 'fessing up' about my lifestyle on television in an interview with my old Origin coach Phil Gould, and that sparked days of headlines that dragged me, my family and the game of rugby league through the dirt. On one hand that weighs very heavily on me; on the other hand — now that I have got through those first few dark days — I feel that maybe it was the jolt I needed to seriously confront how I'd lived my life, and it might end up a positive.

It is 12 days after that London incident that I'm sitting here now recording this. It's tough reliving it, but I'm conscious that for the sake of this book being a true and complete account of my life, I have to. So here is the whole story.

I'd agreed to go on a surfing holiday on a boat in the Mentawai Islands in Indonesia for two weeks with Matt Hoy and a few guys from Electric Sunglasses, a popular surfwear brand who sponsor Hoyo and me. I thought, 'I'm going halfway to England, so I may as well go over and catch up with friends and travel around Europe.' It was sort of the bridge between my footy career and the next stage of my life, a break I felt I desperately needed.

I surfed three or four times a day and had a great time in Indonesia and when I got to England I did some coaching here and there, caught up with Warrington boys for five or six days and saw my Newcastle Knights mate Matt Gidley, who was playing with St Helens. I then went to Rome by myself for four days, then to the south of France to a place called Hossegor, which is regarded as the surf capital of Europe. I planned to stay for a couple of days with a friend of some friends from Newcastle, Reid Pinder and his family, but ended up staying for a week they looked after me so well; I can't describe what a great week it was.

Until that time, sure, I was having an enjoyable time, having a few beers and catching up with people, but I was certainly under control and doing a lot of looking around at the sights and felt great.

I headed back from France to Manchester a week before the Challenge Cup final was to be played, and stayed with Warrington owner Simon Moran. When I got off the plane I found my two bags had gone missing. In one were all my clothes, toiletries and my medication for bipolar disorder, and in the other one were six pairs of shoes. It was just such an inconvenience; I had to go out and buy some clothes and borrow others from Simon. I was told by British Airways that my bags would be there the next day, then the next day again and eventually it was a week before I saw them again.

I went with Simon to a gig called the V Festival in Chelmsford, that his company promoted, and was supposed to go to Munich for a couple of days but canned that because I had no clothes. By the time I got back from the V Festival on the Monday, I'd gone three days without medication and was highly agitated; I'd been constantly ringing British Airways and they kept telling me my bags would definitely be there soon. That's why I didn't go out and get some replacement medication, I always thought I'd have my bags back the next day. As it was, the bag with my clothes and medication arrived in Manchester the following Saturday morning and Simon, who was going to London on a club coach to watch the Cup final, brought it down to his hotel. So it wasn't until after the match on Saturday that I picked it up from him. The other bag arrived in London on the Thursday.

I took the train down to London, did all the touristy things for a couple of days, carried out some coaching with the Harlequins rugby union club which was organised through my good mate Billy Peden — the strength and conditioning coach at their rugby league club — and then I went to the Challenge Cup final at the new Wembley, attending a corporate function with Simon.

I got a bit pissed at the footy but was under control because I wanted to enjoy the match. But I could feel the coil unwinding inside me and went for a big night at a London pub on Saturday night; I was manic by this stage, wound up and ready to let rip. By then I hadn't had medication for over a week. I dropped my bag off at my hotel, got changed and rushed out. In hindsight I should have taken some medication then.

After a big night, I got about four or five hours' sleep before I was ready to go again. So we went straight to The Church nightclub, a place where heaps of expat Aussies and Kiwis hang out, which is legendary for its Sunday afternoon party atmosphere.

I could feel myself getting wound up even more and I flogged myself that Sunday on the grog, and yes I'll admit I took ecstasy before I left The Church. Some people don't realise how others will come up and just give the tablets to you, maybe because you are recognised as some sort of celebrity. I had been at it hard for close to five hours, and my mate Dean and I were going to go to a nearby pub when some girls he knew said everyone goes to this other place, but it meant going on the tube. Just as I left some bloke put an ecstasy tablet in my pocket. I was too pissed to remember exactly how it happened but I knew what he was doing.

One of the girls had some sort of swipe pass to get through the barriers at the train station and I went through with her. When we got out at Kings Cross, about 4pm, there was a mass of people. I'll admit I was off my head from the combination of heavy drinking and taking ecstasy.

When we got to the gates at Kings Cross there were a few police there. I thought nothing of it and went to go through with this girl but, for some unexplained reason, I went to a policeman and asked where I could buy a ticket. He pointed in the right direction, and as I went to go there he called me back and asked to search me. Whether my eyes or how I was walking gave me away, I really don't know, but just then I thought, 'Shit, I've got that thing in my pocket!' I panicked and slipped it onto the ground, thinking no-one would notice in the crowd. The policeman picked it up and asked if it was mine and I said I didn't know whose it was. They obviously didn't believe me and handcuffed me in front of everyone, and I stood there, my arms bound, for 20 minutes. They searched all the other people who were with us and then put me in a Tarago-type van, took me to Central London police station and put me in a cell.

I can only describe that experience as frightening. I was in a cell on my own, about three metres by four metres, with a toilet and a tiny gymnastic mat on the floor and I stayed there for five hours, because apparently there was some sort of blitz on with the Notting Hill carnival taking place over the long weekend and the police were flat out. These big mad African guys were in the cell next to me and they were throwing themselves against the walls and banging on them screaming out in English and then in their native tongue. The whole thing was terrifying, and degrading. I was photographed and had to take my clothes off and be strip searched; they took the shoelaces out of my shoes; I felt like a criminal. I will make sure I never feel like that again.

I couldn't see any light other than under the door. I'd hear footsteps up the corridor and whoever it was would stop near the door then keep walking. I couldn't think straight, it was mental torture. The feeling of helplessness, of not knowing what was going on, of coming off the manic high into a deep depression: people talk about hitting rock bottom in their lives, well I was there right then. I could see my whole life flashing in front of my eyes and I'd stuffed it up by living so recklessly. I was thinking about the embarrassment, the humiliation I felt, the shame. I felt sure what happened would get out, and I was thinking about what I would do when I got back to Australia, how all my prospects of employment would be lost; I was thinking of Samuel and Cathrine and my family, and how I would explain to them. I was on the verge of being suicidal. It was definitely going through my mind, that's how low I felt.

When I was in the lock-up someone asked me if I had any medical conditions. I told him I had bipolar disorder and how I'd lost my bags that contained my medication, so I was taken to a doctor who gave me my medication, Epilim 500.

One of the cops ended up entering my cell and said, 'Are you the famous rugby player?' I replied, 'Why's that?' and he said they had a rule in the UK that if you haven't been in trouble there before, and you're caught with one ecstasy tablet, you'd be let off with a caution. He asked if I would admit the tablet was mine and I said in that case I would.

I went into the interview room with two policemen, we sat down at a big table and the tape recorder was turned on; just like on the telly. I said the tablet was mine, I was going to take it and I wasn't going to sell it. One of the two coppers told me I was a silly bastard and to get my act in order, and said something like, 'You seem like a good fella — just don't go down this road in life.' Then they said I would be given a caution and could go.

It was well after 9pm by this time. I asked if what had happened was going to get out and they said they wouldn't tell the media. I still don't know how it snuck out — I can only assume someone at the police station blabbed. One of the interviewing police actually asked for my autograph; when I was signing I felt so ashamed.

I want to make it clear here that I'm not blaming my predicament on British Airways for my medication going missing. I am not blaming bipolar, or the bloke who slipped me the ecstasy tablet or the freakish coincidence that I happened to be on the tube the same time there was a police blitz. I blame me, no one or anything else. I put myself in that position. And I have to face the consequences. I had an ecstasy tablet, just as I'd had in the past, and I was going to take it.

I walked out of the police station in such a bad state — I was waiting for camera flashes to go off. I got a taxi back to my hotel and took a couple of sleeping tablets to help me sleep. I had never been so scared in my life. Beforehand I rang John Fordham to tell him the story and how paranoid I was about it getting out. I also rang Cathrine and apparently called Kris Lees too. Matthew rang me — Dean had contacted Brian Carney, Matt's good mate and my ex-Knights teammate who Dean and I had caught up with the previous week, and Brian had called Matty. I really can't remember who I spoke to or what was said; it's a blur. I do vaguely recall Matty being quite emotional and saying he thought I might have been dead.

My flight was at midday but I got up at 6am and left the hotel, got to the airport at seven, checked in and hung around the terminal counting the minutes until I could get out of the country. I was in such a state, thinking the media would be at Singapore when I stopped over there. I thought they'd grab me at the airport and lock me back up. My mind was racing.

On the plane trip home I was having panic attacks; I had to reach for the vomit bag and was trying to control my breathing. I had the sweats really bad and couldn't sleep even after taking sedatives. I was picturing in my mind getting off in Sydney and journalists would be haranguing me and I could see Cathrine in the corner shaking her head, saying, 'I always told you this was going to happen.' I was so ashamed, so low.

I got off at Singapore and just walked and walked around in a daze until we reboarded. John Fordham texted to update me that nothing had come out in the media, which was some relief. When the plane touched down in Sydney about 6pm I was paranoid about whether the customs people at Sydney Airport had a record that I'd been locked up or whether they'd search me. When I got safely through customs and it got to going around the corner to where everyone meets passengers, I froze. I couldn't walk around the corner. I got myself together and thought, 'This is crazy,' so I hurried out and saw Cathrine. We walked straight to the car park with hardly a word said and hopped into the car. She instantly gave me a big spray: 'I always told you something like this was going to happen and, you know what, I'm glad it has happened — maybe finally you're going to learn a big lesson from this.' I sat in silence.

I stayed at Cath's that night and was able to sleep OK, but woke up at five and just lay there, waiting for the phone to ring. I survived the Wednesday with Fordo in contact, confirming nothing had leaked out. But at 3am next morning, Thursday, I got a text message from Billy Peden in London, saying there was 'weird shit about you on internet over here, are you OK, you better check'. Then Fordo texted me and said he was getting phone calls from the media. I went to the toilet and I was sick. I felt like a walking shell — I felt that bad I was near collapse.

First thing in the morning I spoke to Fordo and he worked out a statement confirming what happened and saying that someone had put the tablet in my pocket — which was true, but it seems as if that statement came out as a token excuse.

I had Samuel in the house and had to get him ready for school; but first I had to sit him down and tell him what I'd done, which was heartbreaking. He knew about drugs and he said they were bad — he asked me questions about them. I will never forget that conversation.

Then the circus began. There were media out the front of my house, some were ringing the doorbell on the front wall. I was on my own, pacing the house, going up and down the stairs, looking out the curtains ... a prisoner in my own home with journalists and TV cameras parked on the footpath outside.

That's when I became close to being suicidal. I consciously thought of taking my own life. I was in a massive state of depression, thinking, 'What have you done to your family and those closest to you? What have you done with your life?' This was all while the media were outside my house sweating on a big story. How ironic that was.

I'm not disclosing this to dramatise events or get any sympathy for myself or to make the media feel guilty. It's not easy admitting a tough big-shot footballer was on the verge of suicide because he'd got some bad headlines. But it's fact, part of my story. And maybe it might bring home just how bipolar can affect someone; the fact that 15 per cent of people who suffer the condition commit suicide is a scary statistic. I'm sure as hell glad something stopped me taking that way out of my dilemma that day.

I appreciate that the media have a job to do and how competitive the industry is when it comes to not letting the opposing paper or TV station get a 'scoop'. But what happened that day shows that sometimes they don't really understand or consider how events are more to those involved than just a headline or a TV news grab, and how unnerving it can be when they stake out someone's home for two days; to those involved it's real life and it can be devastating. Apparently, the media even staked out my parents' place in Cessnock and Cathrine's in Sydney over the next few days too.

I felt I had to get out and go for a swim, hoping it would help me clear my head. So I yelled out to the lady behind me and asked if I could jump the back fence. She said, 'No worries, Andrew, away you go.' I found a place on the beach where no one goes, jumped in the ocean and paddled around for a while. I went home via the back fence so no one would see me.

Late morning, Fordo rang and said he and Steve Crawley, the boss of Channel Nine sport, were coming up in the chopper. When they got there I couldn't talk to them. I hopped in the hire car to the airport; I had my sunglasses on and they could see I was shook up. People had been ringing me all day and were obviously worried what state I was in, but I didn't answer most of the calls.

We got down to Channel Nine, and my brother was there, saying, 'Mate, that half-hearted statement you put out was bullshit — you have to tell the truth.' Matthew and Phil Gould spoke to me about doing an interview on *The Footy Show* but I said I couldn't go on live TV. I would break down, I couldn't do it. We talked more and then suddenly I thought, 'Stuff it, I'll go on, ask me anything you want to — I'm coming clean. I'm sick of living a lie, being deceitful, skimming around the truth of my life and carrying the burden, worrying whether people knew and whether it was going to come out.' I then went back to Cathrine's and slept for a couple of hours and went through in my head what I was going to say. There was no rehearsal — Gus could just ask me what he thought.

I was dry-retching during the interview, but once I started it I just wanted to get it out. I wasn't supposed to mention the bipolar, because I didn't want to make any excuses and we wanted it to come out in the right context in this book. But the way the interview went I referred to depression without expanding on it.

When I came out of the studio, I just wanted to get out of the place. There were news cameras following me, which was unnerving; a security guard grabbed Cathrine and me and ushered us to her car about 100 metres away. We went back to her place and I was a mess as the whole consequence of what just happened hit me. But, strangely, the major feeling was of relief. I felt this was a springboard to move on and clean my life up.

I didn't read any of the newspapers and tried to avoid the TV news; if I had read a paper over those days I think it would have sent me right over the edge. But people told me a bit of what was being said — I knew I was getting hammered. Cath and my family were concerned for me and felt my bipolar should be revealed in the media.

From what I understand, Neil Halpin too was unfairly being smashed by the media for supposedly letting my lifestyle of alcohol and drug taking continue unabated, which is absolute bullshit. As I've described earlier in the book, Neil couldn't have done more to help me, but I wasn't always ready to listen to him.

On the Saturday morning Professor Gordon Parker called and said he thought it was imperative that the bipolar disorder be made public. So it was arranged for Professor Parker to make a statement to the media, with my approval, which I'm glad happened although, again, I don't want it to be an excuse — more an explanation of my state of mind.

The most disappointing thing about the initial media reaction was how it was apparently portrayed that my drug taking was frequent, as if I was some sort of hopeless addict. I know I used the words 'Russian roulette' and 'dodging bullets' in regard to avoiding testing positive to drugs, but I thought I'd made it clear in the TV interview that I took drugs only occasionally during the season, but more often in the off-season. Sometimes I'd go a whole season and not take any drugs but hit the alcohol so hard it was ridiculous, and self-damaging. When I did take drugs it was mostly ecstasy, because it gave me that out of control feeling that I craved when manic. I sometimes took cocaine. Never anything else. It was never an every day or every week thing. Sometimes I would take it on a Friday or Saturday — only when I was out, never at home — then not take it for weeks or months. I'd never go and buy ecstasy and go out; I'd always have a few drinks and then decide whether to get some. It is readily available at nightclubs.

My reference to playing Russian roulette apparently created quite a response about how I could constantly avoid drug testing over all the years of my career. As I have tried to point out, I wasn't a frequent user in-season and I can't say how many times I was tested at a time that I had taken drugs. But it wasn't a good feeling being at training on a Monday and constantly looking at the tunnel waiting for the drug testers to appear. I'd constantly be drinking water and wanting to piss, and taking saunas, hoping the drugs would get out of my system. It seems ridiculous and shameful now that I put myself through that trauma.

I did say in the *Footy Show* interview with Phil Gould that I assumed people within the Knights would have known about my drug taking. Look, I'm really not sure of that and I don't want to go there — I don't think it will achieve anything. I do believe all clubs will take a more vigilant view of potential illicit drug taking in the future, with harder attitudes already evident. A lot of people tried to responsibly help me with my behaviour, and I selfishly didn't listen for a long while.

The other thing I want to clarify is that people might have confused my appearance when I was out on a 'session', thinking that I was on drugs when the fact was I was just blind drunk and on a massive manic high. I'd be talking at 100 miles an hour and doing crazy uninhibited things. I wouldn't sleep when I was like that; after an hour or two's shuteye, I'd be up and saying, 'What are we up to now, let's go again.'

Drugs were sometimes part of my life but alcohol was a much bigger problem, the major contributor towards my reckless and irresponsible behaviour, and that has been skimmed over. My issue is with alcohol — I've known that for a long time.

Like Neil Halpin, Mick Hagan could not have done more for me over my career without standing there and physically stopping me putting a beer to my mouth. I am so disappointed and regretful at the criticism levelled at them when this all came out. I was so stubborn and so selfish for such a long time; I don't know what would have stopped me — probably only the sort of public humiliation I went through in late August/early September 2007.

One of the hardest things through all this was telling my parents what I had done. Dad was working not far from my place, and the day after I returned from the UK I went around to tell him but didn't have the guts to do it. When it broke overnight I had to ring Mum and Dad at 5.30am and Dad had already listened to it on the radio. That was tough — he was naturally devastated, as was Mum. He didn't go to work for a couple of days. I felt terrible for putting them in that state. They're at least glad now that we can talk about my depression. They were like Matthew; they feared one day they were going to get a phone call saying I was dead.

I was beside myself for a couple of days after the *Footy Show* disclosures. I virtually locked myself inside the house, although Cath and my family made sure there was always someone with me, thank God. The following Sunday was Father's Day and I spent it with Samuel, and Kris and Kristy Lees came around for lunch with their kids, which helped me. I picked up day by day after that, to the stage where I could accept what had happened and could face the world again. I went for a walk — I think on the Tuesday — past a group of schoolchildren and their teacher. I put my head down and was really self-conscious about what they'd think about me, and whether I'd shattered some of their illusions of me. They all cheered me and wanted to give me high-fives. They would never know what that meant to me; it was breaking the ice after days of bad depression.

The well-wishers and the phone calls got me through those few days, along with my close friends and family; I was blown away by their support. I know out of this absolute chaos I have to take some positives, there are so many lessons that have to be learned. The whole family realised we should have confronted this earlier but we always skimmed around it. The one major positive of what happened was that it forced me and my family to stop sweeping my condition under the carpet, and for the first time we spoke openly about it, whereas in the past the word 'bipolar' would make me scurry out of the room.

Cath has been an absolute rock beside me through all this, even though the London episode naturally put a massive strain on our relationship. I can't thank her enough. She was very disappointed with what I did: she won't ever bullshit to me, and I need someone being straight with me like that — not too many people are. Her parents are living in the Newcastle area now too and her father has to go to work and answer all the questions that people obviously ask. Her sister works in Scotland Yard, so you can imagine the embarrassment there. Cath has said this was the kick in the arse I needed and I should never touch alcohol or drugs again. That's my big challenge — that's what I am determined to do. I have been like a broken record over the years, doing something stupid that could have put me on the front pages and then swearing that I'd stop. I'd be good for two or three weeks but then get back to my old ways. But I mean it this time.

Cath says she can genuinely see something different in me now. It will take more than willpower; I need to have specialised help and I am prepared to do that. A few high-profile people who have been down the wrong path with alcohol have contacted Matthew and I'll talk to them and see what they say.

I'd like to say that I know I will never take drugs again. Of course, I can't guarantee it when I suffer bipolar disorder and may at some stage get out of control on a manic high. A reformed alcoholic can't be absolutely sure he or she will never have another drink. But from the bottom of my soul I have no intention of ever touching another illicit substance. I don't want my life to be a circus; any time I'm out now having a good time there are going to be mobile phone cameras aimed at me or newspaper photographers just waiting to pounce. That's part of the territory with where my life is at now. I don't want to be a George Best, seen as a pathetic drunk and fallen has-been; but to be honest, that's where my life was heading. The strong part of me is going to be staying on the straight and narrow.

The real pity is that I was feeling great before I went overseas. Even when we spent two weeks on the boat surfing in Indonesia, Matt Hoy said to me that he couldn't believe how much I was surfing and not partying so hard. Sure, there were times away when I let my hair down, but I was fairly under control.

Where to now? Well, the next big challenge is developing something for myself in life after football. I don't know how the recent revelation will impact on work opportunities in the future; only time will tell.

I hope players who have watched how much public humiliation, embarrassment and shame I have brought on myself by living such a lifestyle and getting caught, found it to be a big deterrent; I hope it has changed some players' attitudes.

That might be my calling. I don't know if I could go around and speak to 50 players at each of the 16 clubs, sitting down and lecturing them about why they shouldn't take drugs and binge so heavily on alcohol, and what they should and shouldn't do with their lives. But every club would have a few guys who are reckless and susceptible to following the path I did — that's just the way it is — and I'd like to be able to talk to them one on one and explain what I have gone through and hope it helps them sort out their lives.

I don't think the NRL stepping up their drug testing is going to be the massive deterrent it is being made out. I wouldn't think most players would take drugs during the season; it would be more during the off-season when they tend to let their hair down. I think it is more identifying the people who are most prone to these things and trying to educate them. I'm happy to play a role there, as I've said. The drug testing of social or illicit drugs has to be done by the clubs and dealt with in-house. I don't think it is the NRL's responsibility as much as the clubs. The NRL should certainly be vigilant on performance-enhancing drugs — steroids and growth hormones — which I still think are in the game but in a very small way now compared to 10 years ago.

One good thing to come of this awful mess has been how it has increased the awareness about bipolar. I had said earlier in this book, before we belatedly added this chapter, about how rewarding it would be if my 'coming out' helped someone who has been suffering like I have, especially a teenager. Well, some people have come up to me in recent days and told me about people in their family who suffer from it and that my story has opened up dialogue between family and friends. And two NRL players have contacted me confessing they suffer bipolar disorder. Gordon Parker had already told me he sees first-grade footballers all the time. They are out there; I can often see who suffers from it in their behaviour.

There are so many people I want to apologise to for my actions. It really plays on my mind what some of the older footballers in the game might think of me. I have to see some of those guys and look them in the eyes and say, 'I'm sorry for how I have dragged the game through the dirt'; that will be part of the healing process.

During the aftermath of the London incident, the story was dragged out about how Mal Meninga and Kevin Walters ripped into me at the casino in Sydney one night over my shocking behaviour. I was out injured at the time and was off my face and deserved what they forked out to me.

I have spoken to Kevvie on the phone since then and buried the hatchet but I haven't with Mal. The sad thing was that he was in the same function room as me at the Challenge Cup final at Wembley and I was going to go up and say hello but

I couldn't even do that because of our history. It just weighs heavily on my mind that here is a guy I have so much respect for but I couldn't even go up and shake his hand; I should have taken the opportunity then to tell him how ashamed I was of the things I'd done but I didn't have the guts to do it. That's just one of the many fences I have to mend.

CHAPTER 37

POSTSCRIPT

I'm searching for the positives in my life. I feel relieved that the 'dark side' of me is now out. I have a whole new chapter in front of me — life after football. It's something I thought a lot about for the first time during the 2006–2007 off-season, and Cathrine and I spoke at length about it after we got back together. We had to really get down to what our lives were going to be like without the major thing I had devoted most of my time and my thoughts to all my adult life. Cath was certainly concerned about what I'd be like if I became a little aimless in occupying my time or if I felt I had no great cause in life. Part of me was certainly worried about what I would be like without the routine and discipline needed to play rugby league.

Now is the time to put the plan into action. OK, we have had a setback, but before that I was feeling incredibly relaxed within myself, and I know I will be again. I was naturally missing playing football a lot, but not the attention that came with it. There is so much stability in my life in Cathrine and Samuel and I'm fortunate to have a few options in what I can do. And a big positive is that I'm not getting those crazy highs when I manage my life correctly. Only now can I contemplate just how much my bipolar behaviour was caused by my lifestyle of having to get myself up so much mentally for football, and then feeling like I had to try to cushion myself from the inevitable massive fall by getting myself in a state that I was somewhere else or someone else during my binges on the grog. I don't feel the need to do that any more. After the massive jolt I received in August, I'm more determined now and I hope I am strong enough to *never* go back to where I was, even briefly. I am genuinely looking forward to the next stage of my life and generally I feel so content — and I could rarely have said that before.

I was sick of all the exposure and being constantly in the spotlight while I was playing. I needed to get away from it, although only time will tell to what extent that will realistically happen. I think it will be an enjoyable transformation. I don't know if my future is in the media, or doing coaching, or whether I should get away from the game altogether. I will make the call that will make me happy, not anyone else, and it won't have anything to do with living up to other people's expectations of me.

People said to me that I'd go through this great level of grief or trauma, but I genuinely haven't felt that, purely because I knew my time was up and I'd done all I wanted to do in the game.

Sure, I miss the adrenalin rush of going into a game and I miss the physical contact of getting hit and hitting blokes in defence. But I am so much more relaxed not having to get myself wound up to play, or to train, and busting my gut at training. I am still training every day, but doing it at 80 per cent instead of 110 per cent. My body feels different; I've dropped four kilograms from not doing the intense weight training and eating so much because the body needed it.

I know I have to leave Newcastle for a while. Everything is too comfortable for me there. I know I could probably get a job because I'm Joey Johns the footballer, but I feel I need to go somewhere and find how Andrew Johns the person can survive and prosper without being Joey Johns. I want to challenge myself and do something different. There is no way I could coach 20 to 25 footballers, because coaching first grade would be so full of extreme highs and lows and if you mix that with my volatile personality, it is a recipe for disaster. Some sort of specialised coaching appeals but sometimes I feel I'd actually love to get away to Western Australia for a couple of years, although I have media contracts with Channel Nine and News Limited, and I have an involvement in a pub as an investment. It appeals to me to have a break from the game and for people to have a break from me; I have been in the media so frequently for so many years, I'm sure people get sick of it.

Why WA? When I had a great time there in 2006 it felt like I wasn't even in Australia — it was that far away and no one knew who I was. I'd be out surfing with 30 or 40 blokes and not one of them knew who I was — it was tremendous. (I ran into Danny Green while over there, actually, and went surfing with him a couple of times. He was a great fella.) The Margaret River area — the coast, the vineyards — is one of the most beautiful places I have seen. I love travelling and I'd like to make a list of all the places in the world I want to see and I want to be able to — at the drop of a hat — say, 'The waves are going to be great in Fiji, let's go for a week.' I couldn't do that if I was coaching.

I'm sorry there has been a touch of doom and gloom in this book, but I couldn't pretend it wasn't part of my life. But I hope you walk away after reading this knowing that I feel absolutely blessed with what I've been able to achieve as a rugby league player. I could not have chosen a better sport, or a better situation than playing in the NRL with the Newcastle Knights and running out so often in front of the most parochial and loyal fans in the game. I can't describe what a great positive rugby league has been for me and how much I owe it, and I appreciate that even more now that it is all over.

It's been a hell of a journey, as you have just read. I turned 33 in May 2007 and I've fitted an incredible amount of living into those years; good living and hard living. I have enough memories to fill three lifetimes, yet I know I have so much more life to live.

RIP 'Joey'; Andrew is now ready to be his own man. That feels good. *Finally.*

OUR TAKE ON JOEY

PETER SHARP, *Andrew's former coach, now coach of Hull in the English Super League*

I still vividly remember my first formal meeting with Andrew Johns. It was early in 1992 and he had been dropped back from the Knights' President's Cup because his attitude wasn't good enough, and he was to play with my Jersey Flegg side. I picked him up at the International Sports Centre [now EnergyAustralia Stadium] to go to Dudley for training.

He asked me if I had a bet [on the races] that day — I said if I didn't bet Saturdays, why would I bet on a Monday? I thought to myself, 'Gee, I've got my hands full here. If this kid bets on a Monday, he must be in the TAB every day.'

But we struck a good relationship from the start. I was tough on him, I had to teach him discipline, and he could be prickly; but we learned to trust and understand each other. Before too long, he was staying over at our house baby-sitting, often with his girlfriend of the time Brittany, most Friday nights.

I'll naturally never forget that Easter Friday training session that Joey has no doubt written about. I knew I was in trouble when not one player was there for the 9am start and they came in dribs and drabs until Joey arrived last with his best gear and these moccasin-style shoes on. So I told them all that whoever didn't train wouldn't play next day. Joey trained in his going-out gear and I remember thinking, 'He's better than all these guys even in his moccasins.'

It was a quiet trip to Sydney next morning ... but I knew Joey would play well because he was up against Wes Patten, who was Balmain's gun halfback of the time. The only thing I ever had to say to him if I thought he was off the pace a bit was something like, 'Gee, that Wes Patten is a good player,' and Joey would say, 'Do you think so?' I knew I had planted the seed and he would make a point of having a blinder that weekend.

What has set Andrew Johns apart from all other players is his competitiveness; every week he was motivated to play well and you could count on one hand the poor games he has played over 15 years. And people too often overlook that he is a great defender, not just a genius with the ball in his hands.

He was born with a real gift, but I tell you I haven't seen a footballer work harder to improve even more. When I was coaching the senior grades at Newcastle I'd always get to training at least 40 minutes before start time and I never once beat the Johns brothers onto the field; they would be there practising kicking and other skills. They had a passion for football few could match.

We have remained good mates and if I ever want a tip on a young player, he's the first person I call. He would spot kids in the lower grades and predict they were going to be good players and inevitably he would be right on the money.

He's the best footballer I have ever seen — that's an understatement. As a bloke, he takes a bit to get to know because he is shy and doesn't let a lot of people in. But he is a tremendously genuine and humble person and that's the result of growing up in Cessnock with a good family in a real working-class environment.

MARK SARGENT, *Knights first international, team-mate of Andrew's and later his football manager*

I relive this tale with the blessing of Joey as it typifies his football career and his character. During the round 25 match against Penrith in September 2002, Joey was placed on report for a high tackle on Joel Clinton. The next day he was handed a 'grade 3 careless high tackle' charge, and seeing Joey had just returned from a suspension, the potential penalty had been 'loaded' and he was facing a long stint on the sidelines.

A close examination of the video revealed that, while the shot was high, Clinton had parried it off with his forearm — Joey hadn't actually made contact with his head: we had a defence! I rang Joey to let him know we should defend the charge. He was hardly overwhelmed by the news — indifferent might best describe his reaction.

The hearing was set for Wednesday evening, and by that morning we had a good defence and Alan Sullivan, QC, was set to represent Joey. There was only one ingredient missing:

Joey. Media manager Steve Crowe and I began calling everyone we could think of to try and locate him. With the hearing set for 6pm in Sydney, we finally established at 2pm that Joey was at his house. I drove over to pick him up but he wasn't there. Crowey called again to say he had finally tracked him down at The Burwood Inn in Merewether.

When I opened the door to the pub, the publican Baz was leaning over the bar shaking his head ... sitting in the corner, on the floor, was Joey, a schooner in each hand. He was drunk. Three-days-on-the-drink drunk. He was wearing an undone business shirt and undies. The rest of his suit was thrown on the floor in the corner. He couldn't have looked worse and my patience and Joey's sobriety were about on par.

And so it began ... he wasn't going ... he didn't give a rat's ... for all he cared they could suspend him for a year ... I was a prick ... on it went. His mate Matt Hoy had been accompanying Andrew on his adventures and finally convinced him that it might be an idea for him to get up, get ready and get going.

We got him partially dressed, but again he refused to leave — without two long necks for the road. So finally he tumbled into the car, barefoot, beer and all. It was 2.30pm. We had a meeting with one of Sydney's most prominent silks scheduled for 4.15pm.

I rang John Fordham, Joey's manager, from the car and asked him to meet me at 4.30pm at Alan Sullivan's chambers with a razor, shaving cream, toothbrush, toothpaste, deodorant, brush, towel and tie.

After having been so wound up and dirty on Andrew for most of the day, his antics had me laughing all the way to

Sydney. He had a priceless 45-minute phone conversation with his brother Matty, which I wish I could have taped. It was bloody hilarious.

Andrew finished his second bottle of beer as I parked the car in Sydney. Fordham met us outside the chambers in Phillip Street. As we tried to get Joey upstairs, he was more interested in talking to a couple of fans who bailed him up on the footpath. Andrew finally shambled into the lift and upstairs, and as he tried to charm everyone in the chambers, Fordham dragged him into the men's room to tidy him up.

I went in to see Alan. My jaw nearly hit the floor; he'd had his wife bring the kids in to meet the great player. White as a sheet, I told Alan I'd go and get him. I went out and told Fordham, who was beside himself.

I went back into Alan's office, and a few minutes later, in strode Andrew, looking a million bucks, perfectly well behaved, talking to Alan's kids about school and sport and signing autographs. I was absolutely stunned.

On the way to the NRL's offices at Fox Studios for the hearing, Joey fell asleep in the car and when we got there and I thought, 'Here we go.' Again, he just switched on. He obeyed our instructions and kept pretty quiet in the hearing, but what he had to say was fine. The media were there in droves and had no idea of our 'adventure' or his true condition. An hour and a half later, we were sitting in Ziggolini's restaurant in Woollahra, with Joey exonerated and free to play the following weekend. He had a couple of celebratory beers, but you could see he'd decided it was time to straighten out ... it was back to business.

It was an extraordinary performance from an extraordinary bloke. Joey could test your patience to the limit, but just when you felt like belting him, he'd win you back over with a bear hug, or a joke or something. He is a bloke who obviously commands respect, but in return he is fiercely loyal to those who have earned his respect.

He could be hard to handle; there were reasons for that. But what a player! From the day he came into the team on a permanent basis in round one of 1994, he immediately changed the destiny of the Newcastle Knights. I was in the back end of my career by then, but a team including Andrew, Matty and Adam Muir, among others, convinced me to go around again. This team would do something with these blokes on board, I thought, which they duly did.

I've often said that if you sat down to design the perfect footballer, you'd end up with something that looked very much like Andrew Johns. He is without question the best player I've ever seen and I can't imagine I'll ever see one better. And despite all his faults, Joey remains one of the most endearing characters I've ever met.

EDDIE JONES, *former Australian (Wallabies) rugby union coach*

Andrew Johns is one of the best rugby players in league or union I have seen. I have always admired his toughness, his ability to play at the line to create opportunities, his all-round kicking game and his strong defence.

I had the pleasure of meeting Andrew on a number of occasions in 2004; 'player Y', as John Fordham called him. I was very keen to get him across to rugby, as I thought he would be an outstanding player in our game, and take the Wallabies from being number two in the world to number one. Any player who dominates rugby league will do extremely well in rugby. Andrew is in this category.

He impressed me by his enthusiasm and his knowledge of rugby. Like all the really top sportspeople, Andrew watched all sports and had already formed some views on how he would handle the transition.

To me it was a 'no-brainer'; however, the ARU felt differently, their reasons being that Andrew was 30 and injury prone. Any player that consistently takes the ball to the line like Andrew, like Steve Larkham, suffers some contact injuries.

It was rugby's great loss — a once in a lifetime chance for an all-time league great to be an all-time union great. Needless to say, the major decision makers at the ARU at that time are no longer in rugby. I wonder why?

DAVID GALLOP, *chief executive officer of the National Rugby League*

It was one of the great moments in my time as CEO of the National Rugby League to be out on the field when Andrew Johns walked around the ground to farewell the Newcastle Knights fans before the clash with Brisbane in April 2007. The passion and tribalism of our game isn't captured anywhere better than in Newcastle. We don't need a draft in our game — it would take away the local kid becoming a local hero and Joey is the best example of that I can think of.

In 1997 when the game was split between two competitions and was not travelling so well, the players kept delivering something special to keep rugby league's head above water. Then when Joey threw that pass to Darren Albert to win Newcastle the grand final, I can clearly remember thinking, 'How good is that — the game has done it again!' That was his special ability: to do things others couldn't, when others wouldn't even dare.

I admired how much players wanted to play with him too. Seeing him in dressing rooms and at representative team camps, he was a special player and other players knew it. There is no greater respect than that of your peers.

I sometimes got an insight into the scrutiny that he was under over the years. I particularly remember going surfing together with my son, Bryan Fletcher, Robbie Kearns and Craig Wing before State of Origin one year and the press were there taking photos, all because Joey was there — talk about living in a fishbowl. The constancy of that must have been difficult for him.

MARK HUGHES, *long-time Knights team-mate and NSW State of Origin representative*

My association with Andrew first took place back in our high-school days at St Peter's High School, Maitland. Joey was in Year 9 and I was in Year 7 but our relationship went to new levels the day I moved down to Newcastle from Kurri Kurri.

I'll never forget when Danny Buderus and I picked up Joey for a game against the Canberra Raiders in 2001, when Bedsy and I were both injured. Joey slumped into the back seat and he told us he wasn't feeling himself and wished he wasn't playing that day. Concerned, I watched him closely for the rest of the day and it was like one smell of the liniment in the sheds was all he needed to click himself into gear. He scored a club record of 34 points from four tries and nine goals that afternoon. This was just one of his championship qualities; once he hit the playing field, whether training or playing, he would showcase all of his brilliant skills and competitiveness.

When I first started playing first grade and was a junior development officer at the Knights, I thought I was doing pretty well. When I conducted clinics, my most-asked question from the kids (who I thought were my adoring fans) was: 'Do you know Andrew Johns?' When I indicated that I did, they would then chase my signature.

Another thing I have witnessed over the years is what a wonderful father he is to his son Samuel. Joey is the type of bloke that gets along with absolutely all walks of life; he is quite smart, knowledgeable and good at all sorts of trivia. I have seen him foot it toe-to-toe with politicians, holding his own on all sorts of topics, and equally at home sitting on a stool at his local, The Burwood Inn, chatting with all of the regulars about all sorts of topics; quite often in the late evening, the language spoken there can sound like fluent Chinese.

He has an amazing ability to light up and liven up any room he walks into. He would turn pre-game dressing rooms into a fun and happy place to be. He would be walking around throwing fists in the air, yahooing and high-fiving his team-mates. By the time you took the field, you felt 10 foot tall and knew you had an alley cat in the '7' jersey that would do absolutely anything for his team-mates; he just made the game so much fun.

Like every player who has played for the Knights in the last 13 years, through Joey's help and encouragement, he improved my personal game no end; I certainly owe him a lot for everything I got out of my career. We enjoyed many great times on the field together, and boy-oh-boy have we enjoyed some good times off the field as well. I always know that whenever I am in his company, there will be lots of laughs and good times — there is never a dull moment. (Like his brother, he has a unique and extremely funny sense of humour.)

Joey is a man who always has a great story. Often people gather around, hanging off his every word, as he is holding court. He has many a great story and often he'd dress his stories right up for the younger players coming through the ranks only to be given a nudge by some of us older blokes who are aware of his legendary exaggerations. I find it funny because Andrew Johns should be one bloke in the world that doesn't need to exaggerate his life experiences. I wonder if he has kept this book all fact or dressed up a few stories here and there?

Amongst all of the wonderful things he has done in the game, he has remained the same bloke that grew up in the coalfields. He is a great family man and, like the champion he is, has handled retirement very well and I have no doubt he has lots of great things in life to look forward to.

This lovable larrikin has achieved absolutely everything there is to achieve in the game, although one award he missed out on was the Knights Clubman of the Year award. Seeing as though I have four of these in my rather bare trophy cabinet, I suppose I will do the right thing and give him one of mine, and I will just swap him for a Dally M or a Golden Boot. After all, that's what friends are for.

Andrew Johns: a brilliant footballer ... an even better mate.

MICHAEL HAGAN, *Newcastle Knights coach 2001–2006*

Andrew Johns has left a legacy on the Newcastle Knights that may never be able to be fully measured. He and his brother Matthew changed the way the Knights played the game when they came together in 1994 and suddenly the team could blow teams off the park with an expansive style.

The enormous period of success the club has had since — being semi-finalists in nine of the 12 seasons from 1995–2006, and premiers twice — would not have been possible without Andrew's astonishing dominance. A great number of people came to watch him as they would have Michael Jordan in American basketball — and the value he brought to the Knights in gate receipts, sponsorship, merchandise sales, plus the media profile that grew infinitely because of his greatness as a player, are all absolutely enormous. He was the heart and soul of the Newcastle Knights. Even people in the Hunter who didn't usually support rugby league would come and see him play.

It's fair to say we wouldn't have won the 2001 premiership without him; he was responsible for so many victories that season and completely dominated so many matches. As his coach for six seasons, I regard it as an absolute honour to have worked with him and watched him play — some of the performances I witnessed were far beyond what the next player in the game could have achieved. I cite the 2001 match when we beat Brisbane 40–0, when we beat North Queensland 60–24 in 2003 (we led 60–4 when he was rested because of a knee injury), and as late as when he terrorised the Dragons in Wollongong the night we beat them 54–6 in 2006; they will forever stick in my memory.

Joey made so many other players so much better and that is the best compliment he could be given. Some became State of Origin representatives mainly because of him when they probably were not entitled to, and Mark Hughes would volunteer himself as the greatest example of that.

All the while he remained charismatic, a likeable rogue with a great sense of humour and always well liked by team-mates, opponents and fans, who voted him their favourite player in the NRL five seasons in a row; he was Don Bradman with a larrikin touch.

I'll never forget the day he scored four tries in a match against Canberra in 2001, running no more than 10 metres each time, and on three occasions he went past their front-rower Luke Davico who, when he joined the Knights in 2006, said he still couldn't believe how it happened or Joey's ruthlessness that day. The goal he kicked with a reverse banana kick from 10 metres out from the try-line and on the touch-line against the Warriors in 2001 is something no other player would dare attempt, let alone pull off. He won more games for the Knights in the last three or four minutes of a game than anyone else could possibly have done.

The greatest testament to his talent and willpower, though, is how he could shrug off pain, personal issues, marriage problems or his sometimes wayward lifestyle, yet always produce an amazing standard of performance on the field. There were several times when I thought to myself, 'There's no way he could possibly play at anywhere near his best this week,' only for him to stagger me with some amazing touches on the field. It was as if he never felt fully comfortable and happy unless he was on the big stage with a football in his hand.

Andrew Johns was a once-in-a-lifetime player and we'll be sitting back in our rocking chairs one day talking about how privileged we were to see him in the flesh. That's certainly how I feel.

DANNY BUDERUS, *Australian Test hooker and current Newcastle and New South Wales captain*

The first time I had to speak to Andrew Johns was when I was 17 and the club asked him to go to my home town of Taree to attend a fund-raising lunch after I'd made the Australian Schoolboys. Trying to be as respectful as I could, I think I called him Mr Johns in the phone call.

Back then all I wanted to do was be a professional footballer with the Newcastle Knights. To go through the steps of becoming Joey's mate, then a team-mate, then play with him for New South Wales and Australia and then become one of his closest mates and share some of his great and also tough life experiences, is something I could never have dreamed of.

He is greatly responsible for how I've developed as a competitive footballer. He taught me how to compete and to follow his attitude that no matter what issues were in your life, once you stepped over the white stripe the only issues were the ball and who you were playing.

I have seen him face more personal troubles or injuries than any human being could tolerate, yet once he crossed the sideline his ability to put any drama aside and perform to an incredible standard was just phenomenal. The emotional roller coaster I saw him ride at times, and the public expectation and pressure he was under, was just incredible, but it never once affected how he was able to play.

He was as competitive at training as he was on the field. He'd scream if he threw a bad pass and he'd scream if he kicked into touch on the full; he created an intense atmosphere at training and no one was in any doubt about the effort he expected from them — the same as he was putting in. If I couldn't put a ball on his chest 10 times out of 10, I thought I was letting myself and him down. But straight afterwards, the likeable larrikin would emerge in him.

On the field he could tear strips off you if you didn't meet his tough standards, to the extent that you knew it was inevitable you'd get a spray. But that was left on the field as soon as the siren went. Then again, he could be so intense and brilliant he could take a whole team along with him and lift us all to a new standard. For me, his voice was like a homing device; if he wanted the ball I had to give it to him as cleanly as possible.

It's hard to put into words the extent of the legacy Joey has left the Newcastle Knights, but it is one that I feel compelled to try and continue. He was as local as you could get, being the son of a coal miner, and he has left the path to success that every country boy like me, or local boy, wants to emulate.

His greatest legacy was showing us all the mental toughness that is required to be successful, and that is something that rubbed off on me and made me an infinitely better player. I intend trying to pass that down to younger players before I retire and I hope it carries along the line for generations.

RICKY STUART, *current Australian Test match coach*

Andrew Johns was one very special footballer. As a one-time opponent and later his coach in two Origin games and one Test match, I admired his high range of skills and the positive influence he had on his team-mates.

Only two other players in my time — Laurie Daley and Brad Fittler — influenced a team as much. 'Joey' had that unique ability to transfer what he did at training — and the game plan — to match day.

A player who thought deeply about the game, he had greater influence on the end result than anyone else. His peripheral vision, coupled with the magnitude of his skills, lifted those around him and made them much better players. Through his influence, club players became Origin players and Origin players became Test players.

Joey was always the major playmaker whose contribution to the team's performance was extraordinary. He was able to withstand pressure to tire his opponents out. He always had to maintain a huge effort in defence and then have enough gas left in the tank to keep attacking and challenging the opposition right down to the final siren.

Put all together, Andrew Johns was the complete package. The finest rugby league player of his era.

DAN CARTER, *champion All Blacks fly-half and goal-kicker*

Even though Andrew Johns plays a different code, he has been a great influence on me and other rugby union players; I think he'd be surprised how widely he is respected and recognised in our game.

No player in either code could change the fortunes of a team like Joey could and that was a tribute to how he played the game and the array of skills he had — kicking, passing, defence and his ability to position others in attack. He was a very special player.

I've liked watching NRL games since I was at high school and he was the guy who always stood out when playing for Newcastle. I was still watching him closely right up to this year and tried to shape some of my game on the way he did things. In fact, most of the All Blacks keep an eye on the league scene and we would talk about one of his awesome passes that put a team-mate in for a try and would take pointers from the subtle things he'd do.

I'd often talk to my coach about what I could add to my game based on Andrew Johns' play — like 'selling' your decoys with how he positioned his hands, how he could hide his options from the defence and create space for second phase runners.

To have had the opportunity to go to Newcastle and meet him and do some kicking with him and find what a great bloke he is as well as a champion footballer was pretty awesome, and it's great we have kept in touch since. He's a legend, even in rugby union.

DARREN LOCKYER, *current Australian, Queensland and Brisbane captain*

The thing I'll remember most about Joey Johns is the effect he had on other people in the team. By far his greatest trait was the ability to breed confidence in the guys around him. Before a game he was very upbeat and he took that onto the field, which seemed to lift people.

In 2001 I saw him at his peak. It was the year Newcastle won the grand final when they completely destroyed Parramatta in the first half.

I went on the tour to England with Joey and even before we went over he was teaching blokes things at training. He was unstoppable, bringing an amazing feeling to the players around him. Only certain guys have it — they can sit in a dressing room and just being there they make you feel comfortable and confident. Joey was the ultimate at that.

Let's take when he came back to Origin in 2005. He was probably struggling with confidence himself — he'd come back from a long lay-off with a leg injury, and everyone was saying he wasn't right. The funny thing was, he was spending a lot of time in Brisbane doing his rehabilitation, so we talked quite a bit on the phone around that time. By the end of that series he had come back and he ended up being the nemesis of the whole state of Queensland — and we helped him get right to do it!

Although he had a fiercely competitive streak in him on the field, he made good friendships off it. I enjoyed the Joey I knew off the paddock. I went away on a few tours with him and he was a real larrikin.

Don't get me wrong, he was ultra professional at training and during the game — but off the field he loved a laugh. The best way to describe him was he was a personality, and I don't think the general public always got to see that personality. He was entertaining to have around. He used to love getting music out in the hotel hallway before games — things like Powderfinger and Silverchair.

The best way to sum up that side of him was that he was a skilful and professional player but he was always a real bloke's bloke.

Rating players of different eras is impossible to do, and I'm sure there are plenty of guys whose achievements and statistics will measure up to Joey's. But there are few who can stand with him in the area of natural talent. The best thing I could say is there is no player I've played with or against who was more complete in skill level. There just wasn't anything he couldn't do.

BRAD FITTLER, *former Australian rugby league Test captain*

Andrew Johns was the most complete player I've seen. The influence he had on those around him on a football field speaks for itself when you look at his results with Newcastle, New South Wales or Australia.

There are some games Joey played in that I'll never forget. One was a semi-final against my Roosters team in 2001 when late in the game he took me on close to the line and scored. I prided myself on my defence but there was nothing I could do to stop him. Joey was KO'd early in the game but stayed on the paddock and led the Knights to a 40–6 win. It showed that when he lifted for a challenge, whether it was against an individual player or as a team, he could be unstoppable.

The other was the second Test in England in 2001. We were beaten 20–12 in the first Test but Joey was just really determined to show the way in the second game and scored two tries and was outstanding in a 40–12 win. He just decided that day he was going to lead the way.

But while he took the game and the preparation for a game seriously, he allowed himself to enjoy life and lived by that motto, which I admire. He's always remained a good, laid-back Aussie bloke who is always great company to be with.

MALCOLM REILLY, *former Great Britain player and coach of the Newcastle Knights premiership-winning team of 1997*

What hasn't been said about the greatness of Andrew Johns as a footballer? He was such a naturally gifted player, but perhaps what not everyone appreciated was how much effort he put into acquiring the skills he showed on the field.

Andrew's biggest quality was that he made the game fun. His confidence came from sheer commitment; he loved competing. Everything seemed to be a personal challenge.

Preparation was the key to his success and he and his brother Matthew worked tirelessly to develop a special combination, which enabled the Newcastle team I had the privilege of coaching do a great deal. Both were excellent students of rugby league who always looked for fresh ideas, whether it was attacking plays or offensive kicks. It was a privilege to coach them, and the whole Knights team from 1995 to 1998.

It's no secret, however, that Andrew and I were not always on the same wavelength. He could be high maintenance and was a wild boy off the field then. I used peer-group pressure when I could — with Matthew, Paul Harragon, Tony Butterfield, Marc Glanville and others — to keep him in check. I had to make exceptions for him at times, but it was always to the benefit of the team because he was such an integral part of our ability to succeed.

But no matter what happened around his football he had a great desire to succeed, and he enjoyed playing so much that that enthusiasm was infectious for the players around him. Personally I just loved watching him play because he was just a nightmare for defenders to try to read; he always had time with the ball at hand and that is the obvious quality of the very special players.

For him to deny his brother Matthew one last shot of glory in the 1997 grand final and instead evaluate the Manly defence on the short side and create the winning try for Darren Albert was one of the most incredible judgements I have seen on a football field; you can't coach that. In fact, his coach was expecting him to do what the thousands of Knights fans, and the Manly team it would appear, expected him to do — to send a crisp pass to Matthew for one last field goal attempt. And to think he played that game with broken ribs and a punctured lung! I know what it's like to play injured and Andrew was one of the bravest players in carrying injury that I have been associated with.

I'll never forget the last game in which I ever coached Andrew — the semi-final against Canterbury in September 1998. Our team was running on empty with so many injuries that should have sidelined several players, but we led 16–0 against the Bulldogs in one of the gutsiest efforts I witnessed while at Newcastle. His performance that day was exceptional — he almost carried a team that was out on its feet to victory (we were beaten 28–16) in one of the finest individual games I have seen.

The game of rugby league is so much richer for Andrew Johns having been part of its great history. He will be missed but never forgotten, certainly not by me.

SIMON MORAN, *major shareholder, Warrington Wolves*

The reaction to Andrew's signing with Warrington in 2005 was huge throughout the rugby league world in the UK, with the town of Warrington absolutely buzzing.

The first game against Leeds was up there with Warrington v Australia in 1978 and Warrington's 1990 Wembley appearance in terms of excitement for me. The ground was packed to capacity (13,500), and live on Sky. The first minute was unbelievable. Andrew kicked off very high and spinning, which Rob Burrow dropped. From the scrum, with the crowd noise deafening, Andrew threw a bullet pass to Martin Gleeson who moved it on to Henry Faafi'ili to score in the corner, which Andrew converted. What a start to a game!

Andrew went on to a man-of-the-match performance, setting up a great try for Logan Swann.

Sport doesn't get better than that night, and I remember celebrating with Andrew in the town's bars, along with half of Warrington. The next match was away at Hull where another victory was achieved, if not in quite the same flamboyant style. Unfortunately, the third and final game at Warrington saw a defeat to Hull in the first play-off match, where Warrington and Andrew weren't at their best. So the dream of a grand final appearance ended.

However, the three weeks Andrew was at Warrington brought such a sense of excitement it was a privilege to be involved. I would have obviously liked to have seen Andrew wear the primrose and blue of Warrington again, and was trying to persuade him to come over for the '08 season, which wasn't to be.

As well as being a great player, in my short space of time in knowing Andrew, he's a top fella, as well as having a good taste in music (Oasis and Wolfmother).

JOHN FORDHAM, *Andrew's long-time manager*

It's Joey's professional approach to playing the game that's a standout in my books. He is as astute off the field as he is on it. He reads situations off the field as well as he does on it.

As a player, he is the complete package. His skills go beyond other players. I'm fortunate to have managed two great halfbacks — Andrew Johns and Ricky Stuart. Ricky reshaped how the game was played in the early 1990s. Joey did his own reshaping when he arrived on the scene in the mid-1990s.

When they came together in 2004 for New South Wales and 2005 for Australia, I just knew that something magical would happen. Stuart, the complete coach; Johns, the complete footballer. Both men have great passion, determination and commitment. They delivered accordingly.

CAREER OVERVIEW
Compiled by David Middleton

CLUB CAREER	Games	Tries	Goals	F/G	Pts
Newcastle Knights *1993–2007*					
Premiership matches *1993–2007*	249	80	917	22	2,176
World Club Challenge *2002*	1	2	3	–	14
Warrington *2005*	3	1	12	1	29
TOTAL	253	83	932	23	2,219

REPRESENTATIVE CAREER

CITY-COUNTRY

	Games	Tries	Goals	F/G	Pts
Country Origin *1995–1996, 2003*	3	1	7	–	18

NEW SOUTH WALES

	Games	Tries	Goals	F/G	Pts
State of Origin *1995–2000, 2002–2003, 2005*	23	4	37	4	94

AUSTRALIA

	Games	Tries	Goals	F/G	Pts
Tests *1995–2003, 2005–2006*	21	9	89	–	214
World Cup *2000*	5	3	–	–	12
Other matches *2000*	1	–	1	–	2
Total	27	12	90	–	228

GRAND TOTAL

	Games	Tries	Goals	F/G	Pts
All senior matches	306	100	1,066	27	2,559

NEWCASTLE KNIGHTS RECORDS

Most points in a match — 34 (v Canberra, July 29, 2001)
Most tries in a match — 4 (equal) v Canberra, July 29, 2001)
Most goals in a match — 11 (v Canberra, March 19, 2006)
Most points in a season — 279 (14 tries, 110 goals, 3 field goals, 2001)
Most first grade appearances — 249
Most points for the club — 2,176

AUSTRALIAN PREMIERSHIP RECORD

Most points in premiership history — 2,176 (80 tries, 917 goals, 22 field goals)

INTERNATIONAL RECORD

Debut scoring record — 30 points v South Africa in the 1995 World Cup, which at the time also equalled the world record for points in a Test held by Australia's Michael O'Connor
Record points haul in a Test with 32 points (two tries, 12 goals) in the one-off Test against the National Rugby League of Fiji in 1996. His 12 goals equalled the world record set by New Zealander Des White in 1952
Most Valuable Player in 1995 World Cup final at Wembley Stadium

INDIVIDUAL AWARDS

Dally M Gold Medal (best player in NRL competition) 1998, 1999 and 2002
Provan-Summons Medal (fans' favourite player) 1998, 1999, 2000, 2001, 2002
Golden Boot (best player in the world) 1999 and 2001
Clive Churchill Medal (best on field in grand final) 2001

GENERAL

Captained Australia twice and New South Wales in six State of Origin matches
State of Origin man of the match in Game 2, 1996; Game 1, 2002; Game 2, 2003 and Game 2, 2005

WIN-LOSS RECORDS

Newcastle Knights

	Games	Wins	Losses	Draws	Win %
Premiership Career	249	154	90	5	61.8
Finals Football	17	10	7	–	58.8
Captaincy	103	67	35	1	65.0

New South Wales	Games	Wins	Losses	Draws	Win %
State of Origin	23	13	8	2	56.5
Captain	6	3	2	1	50.0
Australia					
Tests	21	18	3	–	85.7
Captain	2	2	–	–	100.0
All matches	306	194	105	7	63.4

GOALKICKING	Goals	Attempts	%
Newcastle Knights	917	1,236	74.2
Warrington	12	14	85.7
Country Origin	7	10	70.0
New South Wales	37	57	64.9
Australia			
Tests	89	115	77.4
Other	1	1	100.0
All matches	1,066	1,438	74.1

ACKNOWLEDGMENTS

From Andrew Johns — My biggest thanks go to Cath for encouraging me to open up so much of myself in this book and being such a great support — and good proofreader — during the process. To 'Caddo' (Neil Cadigan), thanks for putting the nuts and bolts of the book into structure and for knowing the right words to use when I couldn't quite come up with them. Thanks to those at HarperCollins who have been so encouraging and enthusiastic about the book. Over my career, I was naturally grateful for the support of team-mates, coaches, club officials, the Knights fans, my management and sponsors, and my family and friends — rugby league is not a sport where you can be successful by yourself. I have tried to portray my appreciation in this book.

From Neil Cadigan — There are many people who played an important role in ensuring this book is what it is, and need to be thanked: Alison Urquhart and Shona Martyn at HarperCollins for your enthusiasm and faith in the book;

Patrick Mangan for a great editing job and being so good to work with; John and Nick Fordham for help with research and recall of events and general support; Mel Cain for a wonderful job with the promotion; Janette Doolan for a sterling job in turning around subscriptions of Andrew's tapes — we wouldn't have made such a tough deadline without you; Cath Mahoney for being a great supporter and confidante to both of us during the compiling of the book, and for inspiring the book's title; Matthew, Gary and Gayle Johns for some terrific insights and memories I was able to prompt Andrew with; David Middleton whose *Rugby League Annual* is the essential reference tool for any league journalist; Newspix and the News Limited photographers whose many shots in the book provide such a comprehensive pictorial record of Andrew's journey; to those who provided their tributes to Andrew which appear in the final pages; and to my dear wife Chris who allowed me to live a life of a hermit in our tiny study while I juggled this project with too many others and while she was left to carry out house renovations.

My biggest thanks go to 'Joe'. From our first session together he was nothing but extremely candid and committed in his attitude towards making this book a very real account of his life. It was obvious, as we sat there with the tape recorder running, how difficult that was for him at times; on other occasions he had me in stitches at his legendary yarns. I was fortunate to watch Andrew Johns' entire senior career, and that in itself was a great pleasure. But I regard co-writing the autobiography of the greatest footballer I saw as the gold medal assignment in my journalistic career. Thanks for the privilege, mate.

INDEX

Index

Index

Index

Index